SPATIAL POLITICS IN THE
POSTCOLONIAL NOVEL

To the memory of my Grandfather, Reginald Fredrick Ling:
for his love,
and for believing in me.

Spatial Politics in the Postcolonial Novel

SARA UPSTONE
Kingston University, UK

ASHGATE

Published by
Ashgate Publishing Limited
Wey Court East
Union Road
Farnham
Surrey, GU9 7PT
England

Ashgate Publishing Company
Suite 420
101 Cherry Street
Burlington
VT 05401-4405
USA

www.ashgate.com

British Library Cataloguing in Publication Data
Upstone, Sara
  Spatial politics in the postcolonial novel
  1. Harris, Wilson – Criticism and interpretation 2. Morrison, Toni –– Criticism and interpretation 3. Rushdie, Salman – Criticism and interpretation 4. English fiction – 20th century – History and criticism 5. Postcolonialism in literature
  I. Title
  823.9'14093582825

Library of Congress Cataloging-in-Publication Data
Upstone, Sara.
  Spatial politics in the postcolonial novel / by Sara Upstone.
    p. cm.
  Includes bibliographical references and index.
  ISBN 978-0-7546-6552-6 (alk. paper) –– ISBN 978-0-7546-9312-3 (e-book) 1. Space in literature. 2. Postcolonialism in literature. 3. Personal space in literature. 4. Self in literature. 5. Geography in literature. I. Title.

  PN56.S667U67 2009
  809.3'93581––dc22

2008044369

ISBN: 978-0-7546-6552-6

Mixed Sources
Product group from well-managed forests and other controlled sources
www.fsc.org Cert no. SGS-COC-2482
© 1996 Forest Stewardship Council
FSC

Printed and bound in Great Britain by
TJ International Ltd, Padstow, Cornwall

Contents

Acknowledgments

This book would have been impossible without the assistance of a large number of people and organisations. Financially, the project would have been impossible without the support of the AHRC, who supported the postgraduate research which made both this project and my academic career possible.

Early ideas were fostered by the staff of Birkbeck College – first through Steve Connor, and then by both Jo McDonagh and Mpalive Msiska, who supervised the subsequent doctoral research. The latter must be thanked not only for his academic support, but also his continued friendship. I also owe a debt of gratitude to Paula Burnett, whose inspirational teaching at Brunel University first introduced me to the writing of Wilson Harris, and who first encouraged me to pursue an academic career.

More recently, I would like to thank my colleagues at Kingston University; in particular, Avril Horner and Sarah Sceats for their good advice and generous support, and Erica Longfellow for the same, but also for her friendship, and for dairy-free cakes! I have also been lucky to have been able to try out these ideas on a number of my students, discussions with whom have proven invaluable. I would also like to thank all those, too numerous to note, who have provided comments on this work at the numerous conferences I have attended over the last five years. I am extremely fortunate to have had such a supportive editor in Ann O'Donahue at Ashgate, who has received my numerous queries with incredible good spirit. I am also particularly grateful to the anonymous reader, whose comments on the manuscript were both challenging and insightful.

Finally, I would like to thank my family and friends for their good humour, unfailing interest, and unwavering enthusiasm. In particular, this project would have been impossible without Philip Upstone and my mother, Christine Dailey, who have between them read so many drafts of this work that I fear they may know it as well as I do. Philip, you have kept me sane in moments of crisis, and the magic and joy you bring to our lives made the continued development of this project possible. Mum, the sacrifices you have made for me are unfathomable, and too vast to ever account for; without them, I would never be in the position to be able to realise the vision presented here.

Earlier versions of some of the discussions here exist in the following publications, material from which is reprinted with kind permission. The discussion of spatial politics in the introduction and of Ben Okri in chapter three first appeared in 'Writing the Post-Colonial Space: Ben Okri's Magical City and the Subversion of Imperialism', *Partial Answers* 2.2 (June 2004). Discussion of Rushdie's journeys initially appeared in 'The Fulcrum of Instability: Salman Rushdie's *The Ground Beneath Her Feet* and the Postcolonial Traveller', *Wasafiri* 21.1 (2006).

Discussion of domesticity in Rushdie's novels first appeared in 'Domesticity in Magical-Realist Postcolonial Fiction: Reversals of Representation in Salman Rushdie's *Midnight's Children'*, *Frontiers*: *A Journal of Women's Studies* 28.1/2 (2007), and is reprinted by kind permission of University of Nebraska Press. Quotations from Salman Rushdie's *The Satanic Verses* and *Midnight's Children* are reproduced by kind permission of Random House Publishing; quotations from the works of Wilson Harris are reproduced by kind permission of Faber. Finally, the beautiful cover image is the work of Kerry McLennan, and is reproduced here with her permission.

Introduction:
The Politics of Post-Space

> The acquisition of land in the name of a writing requires the establishment of borders and ensuing subdivision. This in turn leads to an ever increasing segmentation and fragmentation of space on almost every level ... And this fragmentation brings with it the necessity of crossing, a constant violation of the boundaries it has created. The colony must, however, present itself as a unity, not only for the purposes of ideology, but also (and perhaps this is a more important consideration), for the purpose of communication – its very ability to function as a colony.
>
> (Noyes 162)

For the ancient Greeks, the notion of the political – as encapsulated in the *polis* – was a broad definition encompassing the aesthetic and the cultural, as well as the governmental. Yet in contemporary society, the political is often perceived as a narrow term referring predominantly to the large-scale: those acts that change national policy or legislation. In terms of space, such definition has meant that it is often the nation – that imaginary space of government authority – that seems to be the subject of political action. In terms of postcolonial space, this has raised the problematic spectre of political negotiation being confined to a territory that is often a product of exactly the system – colonial or neo-colonial – that is being protested against. This book offers a reading of the postcolonial novel that is centred upon an alternative concept of spatial politics: one that is rooted not solely in a politics of the nation, but instead reflects the diverse spaces that construct the postcolonial experience.

History/Space

The shift from a diverse, multi-faceted notion of political space to one centred around concepts of the nation reflects a more dramatic shift in the attention given to space by key thinkers of the modern period. What I present in this book as a postcolonial spatiality emerges, therefore, in the wake of a lack of attention to spatial matters in contemporary debates and, indeed, a neglect of the full possibilities of studying a variety of spatial locations. The rise of the spatial as a factor for critical consideration, what Doreen Massey refers to as the 'inherent spatiality of the world' (7), has been a comparatively recent phenomenon; while Immanuel Kant may have privileged space in his *Critique of Pure Reason* (1781) and Gotthold Lessing may have explored the relationship between the arts, time and space as early as 1766, the period between Kant's work and the mid twentieth century has been one in which space has frequently been subsumed by time and an affiliated concept of a linear, narrative history. As Edward Soja emphasises, 'putting phenomena in a temporal sequence … somehow came to be seen as more significant and critically revealing than putting them beside or next to each other in a spatial configuration' (*Thirdspace* 168).

In the second half of the twentieth century, however, study of the spatial has increasingly found a renaissance. As early as 1945 Joseph Frank was highlighting specifically the spatiality of modern writing. Yet it is the focus of dominant philosophical thinkers on the spatial that has perhaps had the most tangible impact. Most notably, it is Michel Foucault's comment, only translated into English and published posthumously in 1986, that 'the present epoch will perhaps be above all else the epoch of space' ('Of Other Spaces' 22), that appears to have opened the way for greater consideration of space as an important context for considering issues such as power relationships and negotiations of identity. For geographers such as Edward Soja, Foucault's work marks an explicit turning-point, but also an undercurrent of spatial concern that can be traced all the way back to the events in Paris in 1968, and to poststructuralism. This has been emphasised in an entire collection concerned with Foucault's spatial concerns: Jeremy W. Crampton and Stuart Elden's *Space, Knowledge and Power: Foucault and Geography.* For the writers in this collection, Foucault's concerns with mapping are central to his deconstruction of dominant power structures, with connotations that are directly relevant to postcolonial concerns.[1]

This spatial turn, however, raises for me more questions than it answers in terms of clearly defining a postcolonial response. Rather than a straightforward alternative to a historiography which, in the context of postmodern and new historicist theories, is increasingly involved in self-reflexively defining its own nature rather than acting as a tool for the definition of outside elements, space, too, is riven by such debates. Theorists seem to find little consensus when it comes to defining what is meant by 'space', let alone reasoning what spaces should be focused upon. While Kant references space as a medium within which geometrical propositions are 'apodeictic' (80) and spatial dimensions and measurements can be relied upon, this conception is likely to be challenged, for example, by the postmodern geographer, for whom space is instead shifting and indeterminate. The locations chosen for focus are also widely divergent, ranging from the very physical space of the nation, to the conceptual status of the text itself as a spatial entity. In these terms, there is no clear direction which a postcolonial spatial politics should follow. Indeed, my understanding of postcolonial spatiality here is that, as part of such a complex reassertion, it necessarily draws upon a diverse definition of what might constitute space.

---

[1]   See Crampton, and Legg.

It is also my understanding that to consider postcolonial spatiality is not to reject postcolonial history. Awareness of the traditional privileging of time, and the study of history, over space and the study of geography does not result in the need for an alternative hierarchy. Instead, the opening up of history to the spatial offers the opportunity for a powerful critical fusion. Such conjunction would follow texts such as Roger Friedland and Deirdre Boden's *NowHere* (1994) that calls for a definition of Modernity that '*is* precisely the transmutation of time and space' (xi). It would acknowledge that a key part of Derrida's 'Being-spatial' (*Margins* 42) is also a concern for the temporality of this experience, where 'time is the truth of space' (*Margins* 42), and where the two terms are ultimately inseparable. It would reflect Einstein's notion of space-time that foreshadows Derrida, and, echoing both these theorists, Soja's 'trialectics of being' that reprivileges space only as part of an experience that includes both 'historicality' and 'sociality' (*Thirdspace* 71). Ultimately, it would address the fact that what is required is spatio-historical analysis or – perhaps to reverse the hierarchy this terminology appears to often imply – historico-spatial analysis.

To reassert spatiality is therefore to privilege it as a context that must be read alongside temporality as a factor of equal significance. At the centre of this shift is a movement towards space rather than place, towards a philosophical concept rather than a study of location, where texts such as Steve Pile and Nigel Thrift's *Mapping the Subject* (1995), Marcus Doel's *Poststructuralist Geographies* (1999), Soja's *Postmetropolis* (2000), and David Harvey's *Spaces of Hope* (2000) predominate. These are not geographical studies in the conventional sense as they use a sense of space rather than place to interrogate society, philosophy, literature, politics and the academy itself. Thus while the study of place is not wholly disassociated from this book's concerns, I present it as just one manifestation of space: its representation in intensely physical forms which create sites of identification. The notion of space is wider than this definition. It encapsulates not only physical location, but also abstract conceptual space. A key part of this book is therefore aimed at calling into question simple oppositions between space and place, such as those advocated by Kate Darian-Smith, Liz Gunner and Sarah Nuttall, for whom it is place that holds meaning, while space is simply – echoing the Enlightenment tradition – a container (3). Rather than rejecting space for its abstractions, it is precisely because of this openness that I claim it here. This usage reflects Massey's definition where space is 'predicated upon the existence of plurality. Multiplicity and space as co-constitutive' (9), and, equally, Bill Ashcroft's argument that it is place which signifies colonial control, space which offers a more fluid and open form that the imperial attempts to obscure ('Newness' 95, 97).

Without space, any negotiation of place is incomplete. For when the meaning attached to place is so often an imposition of signification, it may be that to claim the abstraction of space is to subvert totalising definitions of what a particular location signifies. This is not to repeat the hierarchy and reject the importance of place; indeed, throughout this study I draw on both place and space. Rather, choosing 'space' is a conscious attempt to draw attention to the fact that making space from place – reinstilling the undefined – may be as subversive as the more common focus on the action of redefining that place through territorial reclamation.

Space/Power

This book suggests that it is no coincidence that the time in which history comes to overshadow space – the nineteenth century – is also the height of empire and spatial violence. There is no greater example of spatial upheaval than the imperial projects that ushered in the twentieth century. As the zenith of several hundred years of military seizures of territory by economic trading groups, and appropriations of land and culture by religious missions under the approving gaze of their governments and sovereigns, these projects have been defined as 'geographical violence' (Said, *Culture* 225).[2] As a result of this, colonial analysis has seen the spatial as inherent to the questions of identity, power and resistance it often raises, seen in the highlighting of geography in seminal texts such as Edward Said's *Orientalism*, in the considerable attention given to issues of space in major anthologies such as *The Post-Colonial Studies Reader* (1994), and in the growing awareness of the significance of colonialism within the academic discipline of geography.[3] Colonialism as a claiming of territory in the name of religious evangelism, economic development or *lebensraum* sees the appropriation of space for empire – often via a correlative appropriation of the hearts and minds of the indigenous population – as the very purpose of its efforts. The colonial achievement was often judged in terms of the magnitude of space acquired, and, as secondary concerns, the subsequent productivity and political stability of this space. The territory's status as a mapped and finite locale is integral to the definition of a colony: as the *Oxford English Dictionary* notes this colony is not only a community of settlers, but also 'the territory' occupied by that community.[4]

What this means is that any imperial population exists within a highly specific spatialised locale. Space appears to be fixed, territorial boundaries unquestionable. The colonialists' right to territory is enshrined in the authority they give to their spatial divisions. This authority is explored by Benedict Anderson in his revised edition of *Imagined Communities* (1991), discussing how the census and the map – the devices of geography – actively reproduce from space the colonial territory. On the surface, space is given the appearance of being fixed, absolute and controlled. The territory is presented as natural, as all that it is built upon is obscured by the pervasiveness of the colonial concept. In terms of specific geographies, such ideas are also foregrounded by Paul Carter, who in *The Road to Botany Bay* (1987)

---

[2]   This position has been echoed more recently by Mbembe, 'Necropolitics', 25.

[3]   For the latter point, a seminal text is Godlewska and Smith's *Geography and Empire* (1994). See, in particular, Crush's contribution.

[4]   Throughout the book, references to the *Oxford English Dictionary* are noted by the abbreviation *OED*, referring to entries in Simpson and Weiner's second edition of 1986.

locates colonisation of Australian space against an imaginary grid; by Robert Marzec, who in *An Ecological and Postcolonial Study of Literature* (2007) locates spatial ordering in the British colony as a mirror of land enclosure policy at home, 'the setting up of boundaries to stop the flow of transgressive multitudes' (119); and for J.K. Noyes, for whom, in *Colonial Space: Spatiality in the Discourse of German South West Africa 1884–1915* (1992), the colonial attitude towards South West Africa is one of the assumption of a Euclidean space of points, lines and linearity (87). This use of Euclidean space may be seen to reflect its privileged place in philosophical discussion, the fact that Euclidian geometry is that which philosophy accepted as an *a priori* absolute: a fixed, homogeneous and unchanging medium. Such a space is reinforced by René Descartes, propagated by the Enlightenment – Kant's use, in the name of a western metaphysical tradition, 'of the axiomatics of Euclidean geometry … the drawing of linear boundaries and homogeneous space' (Islam 9) – and continued in colonial practice.

This overlaying of authority is necessary to affirm the viability of the empire, its credibility as a power, diplomatic entity and trading station. It is also crucial to the perpetuation of colonial rule and the control of the colonial subject. For a boundary that appears as absolute cannot be undermined by local affiliations, a bounded territory must be respected as a legitimate entity: its status as an absolute undermines the preference for older communal or tribal practice. Its laws, religion, education and social practice become superior. For Edward Said, such a space begins even before colonisation in the construction of stereotypes. Yet with colonisation, however, such a space becomes manifested physically, central to the colonial claim to dominate not only the land but all that is contained within it.

Noyes' work, although less well known than Anderson's, Pratt's, Carter's and Said's, is useful in this respect in the way it extends their concerns to identify specific sites of spatial ordering both conceptual and physical. For Noyes, echoing both Said's Foucauldian comments on the role of the imperial spectator, and Mary Louise Pratt's seminal discussions of the imperial gaze, the initial colonial project of spatial ordering is caught not only in physical delineation and mapping but also in vision, as exploring territory places the colonialist in the position to engage in a panoptic practice (129). Yet this pursuit continues in the administration of the colony, in a written text that develops 'a representational technique for ensuring that any specific individual positions of subjectivity are appropriated in the service of universal representation' (223).

The culmination of such totalisation in the colony impacts not only upon the physical locality and the civil rights of the indigenous population, but also acts to support particular constructions of identity. At the centre of this book, therefore, is the assertion of the fact that what is really being negotiated in the rewriting of space is this right to identity, the prerogative to feel secure within a language and protected from violence by a set of boundaries and the laws outlined within them. Here the right to space must be seen as key to the very real, often violent, material effects of colonisation. For the colonial gaze that forms a territory does not only this; it also creates an identity for the colonised. As the recent 'mapping' of DNA illustrates, the individual is subject, ultimately, to the same classificatory practices that are used to order territory; maps are ultimately an 'archetype of representation' (Massey 106) applied to the human body itself. This is Homi Bhabha's sense that 'what is increased is the visibility of the subject as an object of surveillance, tabulation, enumeration and, indeed, paranoia and fantasy ... a fixed reality which is at once an "other" and yet entirely knowable and visible' ('Other' 156). The identity created in such a space quite often portrays the indigenous citizen as an absolute space also, with a body marked by characteristics that can quite easily not be his or her own. Status of belonging to one empire or another is accorded not on the basis of community, but on the basis of an imperial perception: a fixed boundary and a foreign language. In the colonial appropriation of space it is identity that risks being lost, as the imposition of an absolute threatens to oppress all it subsumes.

Space/Myth

What must be stressed is that this colonial utilisation of tabular space relies upon a myth. It is the *fantasy of space* as a medium that is capable of being ordered, the myth of a 'natural' territory based on geographical landmarks. Colonial spatial order is *not* natural. Rather, it is a conscious act, a purchase of an imaginary, on the part of the coloniser in order to secure power. The power of being aware of this mythical nature cannot be overestimated. For it means that such 'order' is always incomplete; it is always gesturing towards a totality that can never be achieved. Nowhere – in the colony or the imperial heartland – does the order attempted by the colonist successfully exist. What does exist, instead, is quite clearly 'a *strategy* of totalisation' (emphasis added, Noyes 129), a constructed, intentional, aim, but one that is ultimately beyond the realm of realisation.

Relating to the role of language that I am privileging within spatial appropriation, such a process may be termed, I would suggest, a colonial 'overwriting'. An associated term – overwritten – was originally used by the editors of *The Post-Colonial Studies Reader* in their introduction to the section of the reader dealing with place, where they assert that places are continually being written, and 'overwritten by the coloniser' (392). I employ the term 'overwriting' throughout this study. Capturing the sense of the territory as a text, it encapsulates the sense in which colonial treatments of space attempt to obscure an existing diversity with order. What is initially 'written' is erased, and is replaced with a new representation. Yet, in a deconstructive spirit, such erasure always leaves its mark. The original text remains – in Ashcroft's words, 'the contest of inscription is still there' ('Newness' 99). A new reality is layered over the old, which nevertheless continues to exist as a trace, akin to the silences of a written text. Such a trace exposes how unreal, how unachievable, is the order and homogeneity that the colonial division of space projects.

As comments on such elements as the silences of the text and its traces suggest, this overwriting and its indication of the unreality of colonial spatial order is perhaps best elucidated through reference to poststructuralist terminology. Poststructuralism suggests the instability of meanings, the impossibility of the stable signified, and an ever-present trace that interrogates the obvious. Colonial spatial order can be read productively within these terms. Its 'truth' is continually undercut by a trace that cannot be obliterated; its meaning is always unstable and continually refers back to that which it denies, marking the absence of an obscured diversity. The work of both Jacques Derrida and Gilles Deleuze and Felix Guattari, in particular, has a specific relevance. Colonial spatial ordering is an exemplification of Derrida's *différance* – appropriately both a spatial and temporal form (*Speech* 129) – in which there is a continual deferral of meaning that reveals difference. The colonial spatial order is the 'element that is said to be "present," appearing on the stage of presence, [which] is related to something other than itself but retains the mark of a past element' (Derrida, *Speech* 142); it simultaneously signifies not just what it is – order – but also what it obscures. Similarly, Deleuze and Guattari have been associated with a spatial project that offers an alternative to Cartesian modes of cartography and their ideological implications with a 'geo-philosophy' of fluid and disruptive spatial complexity.[5]

As a fusion of postcolonial and poststructuralist influences, Bhabha's work continually reveals this slippage in its readings of colonial discourses. Hence in his reading of nineteenth-century missionary work in India, Bhabha notes the failure of the Biblical word of 'truth', as it became culturally translated away from its original meaning:

> Here the word of divine authority is deeply flawed by the assertion of the indigenous sign, and in the very practice of domination the language of the master becomes hybrid … . The Word could no longer be trusted to carry the truth when written or spoken in the colonial world by the European missionary. (*Location* 35)

Even as the 'truth' appears to have been accepted, order secured, it is in fact indicating the trace of a different cultural tradition. Colonial discourses attempt an ordering and definition of experience. Yet while they proclaim the success of this strategy – indeed deny it even is a 'strategy' – deconstruction continually reveals a resistant trace, the ambivalence and difference that is obscured, yet nevertheless resurfaces.

---

[5] See Bonta and Proveti, and also Buchanan and Lambert, for a detailed outline of Deleuze and Guattari's spatial politics.

Space/Chaos

In spatial terms, what colonial ordering obscures is a more chaotic reality. Exposing attempts at totalisation as fundamentally incomplete continually reveals an underlying fluidity to space. Colonial absolutism may be identified as a response to this natural openness. Ironically, the colonial enterprise seems to reply upon this multiplicity, even as it obscures it in its own justifications of territorial appropriation. For Noyes, the colonial project desperately relies upon open space to begin its imperialization of space; it needs such fluidity – its own 'myth of mobility' (Noyes 162) – to justify expansion. This has been reinforced by Ashcroft, who illuminates how a discourse of newness was utilised by colonial forces to reproduce order: 'a sameness that will never be quite the same, but one in which difference will be erased ('Newness' 94).

Such awareness illuminates that chaos may be used as much in the service of oppression as a solution to it, that colonial regimes themselves may employ disorder as a means to secure power (Mbembe, 'Necropolitics' 24; Gregory 258). This reflects the growing awareness not only outside postcolonial theory, but also within postcolonial criticism, of the limits of fluidity as the basis of a model for resistance.[6] In relation to the spatial, Massey has made such a critique explicit:

> It is popular today to revel in the glorious random mixity of it all. It is taken to
> be a form of rebellion against over-rationalisation and the dominance of closed
> structures. ... Too often, though, it is a weak and confused rebellion. For one
> thing, what may look to you like randomness and chaos may be someone else's
> order. (111)

For Massey 'both openness and closure, and both classical territory and rhizomatic flow, can be the outcome of sedimented and unequal power relations' (174). Similarly, for Michael Hardt and Antonio Negri in their influential *Empire* (2000), contemporary neo-colonial power relations work precisely through chaos, rather than in spite of it. The borderless, deterrotiorialized space for them does not contribute to a more democratic world, but rather to further capitalist exploitation which thrives on destabilised political and economic relations. It allows the imperialist nations of the past to be replaced with an all-consuming and global power network which functions all-pervasively without fixed location or national identity.

This book functions not to dismiss such critiques of fluidity, but rather to complicate them by suggesting that to see fluidity functioning only in the service of western capital and its neo-colonial interests is too simplistic. What Hardt and Negri perhaps neglect (though not as much as some readings of the book might

---

[6]   Such a critique is best represented by Parry, Shohat, Ahmad, During, Dirlik and Loomba. For a comprehensive summary of these positions see K. Chowdhury 127–40. For a recent response to these critiques see Childs, Weber and Williams, 19.

suggest) is the inventive ways in which fluidity may be utilised to foster disruptive actions. Equally, their concern for the use of fluidity by global capital obscures the fact that, like colonialism, contemporary powers utilise the lack of borders to in fact construct a system, ultimately, which is defined not by chaos, but by order. Hardt and Negri state that 'in contrast to imperialism, Empire establishes no territorial center of power and does not rely on fixed boundaries or borders' (xiii). Yet this is only partly true. Despite their evocation of the evils of fluidity, Hardt and Negri's ultimate point of concern is an all-pervasive 'world *order*' (emphasis added 3). Thus despite their critique of fluidity, at the heart of this is a desire for power and control which mimics the colonial utilisation of a discourse of fluidity in the service of a very denial of the strategy employed:

> This juridical concept involves two fundamental tendencies: first, the notion of a right that is affirmed in the construction of a new order that envelops the entire space of what it calls civilization, a boundless, universal space … Empire presents order as permanent, eternal and necessary. (Hardt and Negri 11)

As the colonialist would utilise chaos to provide the mandate for settlement and political control, so the contemporary capitalist world continues its own 'civilising mission' that promises to bring stability to the supposed tumult of developing world nations. Moreover, whilst Empire, in Hardt and Negri's terms, does not attempt to fix boundaries at the level of the nation, nevertheless it does attempt to secure territory and establish centres of power which are tightly controlled. The suggestion that 'whereas colonial power sought to fix pure, separate identities, Empire thrives on circuits of movement and mixture' (Hardt and Negri 199) obscures the fact that colonial ordering relies upon an initial discourse of movement but, equally, that Empire's ultimate desire is demarcation and the perpetuation of difference.

The polarised world that Hardt and Negri present obscures these complexities. Chinese mining enclaves in Africa, the destruction of rainforests to raise cattle to supply western fast-food chains or the anticompetitive practices of land purchase practiced by multinationals such as Wal-Mart and Tesco provide just a few examples of attempts to secure land and establish territorial influence which pervade contemporary capitalist practice. This sentiment has been foregrounded by Ellen Meiksins Wood, who argues that projects such as Hardt and Negri's overlook the continued role of states and boundaries in the dominance of global capital, when in fact imperial power's dependence on territorial boundaries is more significant than it has ever been before (15). For Meiksins Wood, capitalism explicitly continues to follow the colonial project of ordering, as the nation state provides 'stability and predictability' (17) upon which capitalism relies, whilst institutions such as the IMF, the World Bank, the G8 and the WTO increasingly assume this role on a global scale (137). Similarly, for Thomas Blom Hansen and Finn Stepputat, free trade obscures the control of space through 'special economic zones' upon which such supposed fluidity relies (33). In a postcolonial context, such an alternative reading of globalisation is offered by Kanishka Chowdhury and by Robert Marzec.

For the former, directly critiquing Hardt and Negri, the 'spheres of influence' of the early twentieth century continue to dominate postcolonial societies (127). For the latter, land in the 'global village' can be inhabited only after being subjected to the rationale of purifying enclosures, made manifest in the ever-rising demand for partitions and policed borders' (23); the IMF and the World Bank support the increased incursion of multinationals, facilitating cultivation of land that mimics, rather than diverges from, the colonial project.[7]

In this context, renewed awareness of the pre-existence of chaos may provide the possibility to expose the limits of the colonial project, and thus also to challenge the hegemonic power of global capital by deconstructing the myth of western order. Thus it is not a case of fluidity fighting fluidity, as Hardt and Negri's critique might suggest, but rather of fluidity fighting the 'order justified by fluidity' that the capitalist system employs. Whilst one may agree that chaos can manifest itself in the service of capitalist oppression, this does not necessarily mean that the solution is to engage in a dialectic opposition which itself mimics the colonial mindset. Such an opposition is profoundly inappropriate when, in fact, the capitalist system's ultimate desire is for the same ordering and territorial control – trade agreements, outlaw of competition, economic enclaves – which exemplified the colonial project. Instead, an alternative rendering of chaotic intervention, one that reclaims fluidity from its capitalist associations, may be more effective; as Hardt and Negri themselves suggest 'the struggles to contest and subvert Empire ... will thus take place on the imperial terrain itself ... The deterritorializing power of the multitude is the productive force that sustains Empire and at the same time the force that calls for and makes necessary its destruction' (xv, 61). Indeed, it would be a misreading of Hardt and Negri's text to suggest that their rejection of fluidity is absolute. For by the end of *Empire* they have come to what may seem like a surprising conclusion:

> The multitude's resistance to bondage – the struggle against the slavery of belonging to a nation, an identity, and a people, and thus the desertion from sovereignty and the limits it places on subjectivity – is entirely positive. Nomadism and miscegenation appear here as figures of virtue, as the first ethical practices on the terrain of Empire. From this perspective the objective space of capitalist globalization breaks down. (361–2)

It is such potential that the texts discussed in this book attempt to capture. Chaos is negated by colonial and neo-colonial powers in order to assume effective control. Yet as the vision and language that overwrite space are constantly exposed for their failure to totalise, the hybrid and boundless space beneath the absolute continues to find a way to be asserted.

---

[7] This represents just a short summary of the interventions into Hardt and Negri's work. For similar interventions see also Petras and Veltmeyer, Boron, Münkler, and Balakrishnan.

Throughout the chapters that follow, I am going to suggest that it is the traces of this chaos that are the silences in the colonial text and the remnants hidden within the colonial landscape. They undermine the authority of the territory and the map: power structures, hierarchies and oppressions which are continually unravelled even as they are reinforced. It is also important to note, however, that I am not suggesting here, in this reading of order as continually revealing chaos, that the coloniser discovered a chaotic world which it then tamed with order imported from the imperial homeland. Communities throughout Asia, Africa, and Latin America were not any more than the nations which colonised them chaotic spaces before the era of colonization. Rather, I am suggesting that the space of colonised territories – like all space – originally existed in a fluid state, which the colonial administration attempted to order to secure its authority. The colonised space is thus no more or less chaotic than the imperial space but rather represents the impact of this process; it is not a chaotic 'Other', but rather represents the diversity of all space that is then strategically ordered and defined by imperial practice. The trace of chaos is ever-present, in all spaces. This is evident by the fact that what is revealed about colonial space is not a geographically specific reading; it is the same interrogation of absolutes that the postmodern geographer has attempted in his or her readings of linear Euclidean concepts of space, Lefebvre's comment that 'abstract space is *not* homogeneous; it simply *has* homogeneity as its goal' (*Production* 287).

Post-Space

In the chapters that follow, I illuminate how postcolonial literary texts offer an interrogatory alternative to the colonial myth of spatial order. I suggest that, through seizing the denied fluidity of abstract space and imbuing locations with a political function, postcolonial authors create space as a site of possibility and resistance. Yet what is the precise nature of this interrogatory space? And how does it relate specifically to postcolonial identity?

What is certain is that any postcolonial disruption of colonial ideas of space does not function by simply inserting its own politicised version of that static Newtonian space that exists only as a container. The anti-colonial response to colonial space has centred not simply on attempting to overlay a new conceptual space of its own in what would, itself, be an imperialising exercise. Rather, analysis of colonial discourse has focused upon the inherent flaws in colonial space that I have outlined. It has seized upon the mythic nature of order and its fabricated status, the fact that colonial order is not 'natural', but is in fact an overlaying of diverse space that is employed to reinforce colonial authority. Foregrounding a more fluid and chaotic space, I would argue, is at the centre of the postcolonial spatial imagination. Yet importantly, the deconstruction of colonial space means such alteration is not a new overlaying. Rather, it is a return to that fluidity overwhelmed by the colonial project, the diversity of all space which means that its ordering into mapped, defined locations and 'natural' territories is always an imposition.

Returning to such multiplicity is a positive removal of colonial authority. As it reprivileges a vision of space as chaotic and fluid, it does not exoticise the colonised as 'Other' in its turn towards a chaotic vision of reality. Instead, in exposing colonial spatial ordering as a myth, it opens up the possibility to identify sites of intervention, spaces in which the colonial codification inevitably breaks down and reveals its unreality. In identifying sites of interruption and failure, it is clear that colonial authority never achieved the normalisation of its order that it so desired. Foregrounding the reality of order as myth prompts a realisation of an incomplete and, ultimately, defeated project. The ability to locate the status of colonial spatial authority as unreal means its task of obscuring its construction has failed and, with it, the colonial mandate in entirety, powerfully attesting to the fact that 'colonial rule did not represent as drastic a rupture in the history of colonial societies as is often made out' (Nederveen Pieterse and Parekh 2).

Moreover, the assumption of such fluidity does not mean moving into a world of complete disorder, violence or destruction. At times in this book, 'chaos' will be used to describe the postcolonial reimagining of space. Yet when chaos is employed, it is within the context of the perception of chaos itself not as a complete breakdown of all stability, but rather as a removal of the fixed to open up new patterns of understanding and experiences. For Mbembe, chaos in the postcolonial world is juxtaposed with more positive statements of fluidity: 'Fluctuations and indeterminancy', he writes, 'do not necessarily amount to a lack of order. Every representation of an unstable world cannot automatically be subsumed under the heading "chaos"' (*Postcolony* 8). In this book, however, chaos is not to be read in Mbembe's negative terms as the opposition to positive, meaningful fluidity, but rather as the expression of it. Such usage is very much to be seen within the terms of chaos *theory*. For those working within chaos theory, chaos is defined not as interminable disorder, but rather as destabilisation that itself ultimately offers meaning. Most notable here is the work of Edward N. Lorenz, whose *The Essence of Chaos* (1993) translates chaos theory as mathematical principle into real-world contexts. In particular, Lorenz associates these quotidian examples of chaos with spatial arrangements (4): a flapping flag or a falling leaf which, even if their true randomness were removed, would still continue to appear to behave randomly. Lorenz's definition of chaos as 'seemingly random and unpredictable behaviour that nevertheless proceeds according to precise and often easily expressed rules' (ix) captures my usage of the term here. The destabilisations of space offered by postcolonial texts are not in refusal of meaning: they have their own structures to be uncovered. Yet, unlike the myth of postcolonial order, they acknowledge their instability and embrace a dynamic mutability echoed in the sensitive dependence upon which chaos relies. As for Lorenz, these spatial destabilisations are phenomena with 'variations [that] are *not random but look random*' (4). Cultural stasis, and supreme authority, is challenged, but there is nevertheless an underlying essence that may be seized upon, which can be seen as akin to what Hardt and Negri describe as the process by which 'the multitude produces itself as a singularity' (395), using multiplicity to create a subversive solidarity. Whilst this may seem paradoxical, it is central to the postcolonial experience: a challenging of colonial ways of thinking and their legacies, but nevertheless recognition of the need for enduring meaning for the very survival of colonised populations in the wake of colonial disruption.

More than any other postcolonial theorists, it is the Caribbean theorist, often drawing heavily on poststructuralist theory and unperturbed by its western associations, who reinforces this approach. In his *Poetics of Relation* (1997) Édouard Glissant offers an explicit rendering of the potential of this chaotic intervention. Resonating with chaos theory, Glissant's development of the term 'chaos-monde' signifies a chaos that is 'not "chaotic". But its hidden order does not presuppose hierarchies' (94). This fluidity instead offers a power of transformation, situated in an 'intermixing of cultures' (138) that challenges the colonial discourse of purity and unequivocal sovereignty with one of difference, contamination, and uncertainty. In its close relationship to the Caribbean slave plantation, such chaos is inherently spatial, and also directly confronts the absolute tabular and Euclidean space of colonialism as it 'renounces linearity's potent grip' (137). Similarly, for Antonio Benítez-Rojo, meaning is to be found in the Caribbean colonies not in spite of their tumult – as colonial exoticisation and a mandate for order would suggest – but instead precisely because of the diversity, the chaos, of the islands. For Benítez-Rojo there is the existence of 'dynamic regularities … within the dis(order)' (36), the essence of Caribbean vitality and strength emerging from a source that is hybrid, refractory and discordant.

Explicitly acknowledging such properties the postcolonial space refuses to follow the colonial in denying the fact that territory is everywhere constructed and provisional. Instead, space must be reclaimed for its inherent diversity, and for the possibilities for moving beyond colonial experience that it consequently contains: in Bhabha's terminology, not a negation of what has gone before, but a subversion, a negotiation. Offering, in bell hook's terms, 'spaces where we begin the process of re-vision' (*Yearning* 145), this alternative spatiality, in contrast to the authoritarian colonial discourse, is filled with heterogeneous voices and diverse experiences that emphasise difference and subjectivity. In such *postcolonial spaces*, oppression seemingly becomes marvellously transformed into resistance offering new radical perspectives, new sites of imagination and creativity, from which the colonial representation of territory can be excised and, perhaps, overcome. Situating such space precisely in the site of greatest upheaval – the margin that signifies isolation and alienation of the colonised subject – is a manoeuvre that reaffirms Trinh T. Minh-ha's strident call to action that proclaims that 'margins, our sites of survival, become our fighting grounds' (330). Subversion of the status of the minority location from which the postcolonial speaks transforms a colonial identity as victim into a postcolonial interrogatory voice and reversed gaze.

This fluid conceptual space is epitomised by Bhabha's concept of 'Third Space' (*Location* 38), his own sense, echoing hooks, of a marginal location which 'overcomes the given grounds of opposition and opens up a space of translation: a place of hybridity' (*Location* 25), where the interrogation is not a matter of simple opposition between coloniser and colonised that leaves existing patterns of order intact, but instead replaces binary oppositions with a third alternative, a means of transcending the dialectic in favour of 'a political object that is new, *neither the one nor the other*' (*Location* 25). Contrasting with the colonial obsession with order and taxonomy, what results is a space of resistance directly associated with postcolonial plurality: a site of marvellous realities that is fragmented, multicultural and constituted of both the real and imagined. In such space, as for Glissant and Benítez-Rojo, identity is cross-cultural rather than multicultural – 'the self-recognition of one civilization in the culture-bed of the other' (Bundy 38) – no longer overwriting difference, but instead commemorating such cultural multiplicity, the unification in the act of celebration itself the commonality within diversity.

I have suggested that this fluidity has a specific connection to space, as it draws upon the reality of the plantation, and the radicalism of the margin. Such connection is affirmed, however, by the fact that such chaotic re-visioning is nowhere more evident than in the work of those postmodern and poststructuralist geographers who discuss postcolonial and political concerns. For Soja, space hinges on his own particular notion of 'Thirdspace'. Such a space defies the absolute as it celebrates hybridity and difference, and refuses conventional identities created from opposition between the Firstspace and Secondspace in favour of those formed from complex processes in which numberless fusions occur. Promising 'to break open this dualism to a third alternative' (Soja, *Thirdspace* 74), this approach to physical space directly resonates with Bhabha's theoretical Third Space location. This complex space is, for Soja, neither inherently positive nor negative, focusing instead on the chaotic experience that is simply existing in space.

The transformation from acceptance of the absolutism of the colonial space to awareness of its relational status in the context of poststructuralism and postcolonialism may be seen in the writings of Foucault. Writing on space in 1975, the dominant model for Foucault is the hopeless structure of the panopticon, a vision of 'this enclosed, segmented space, observed at every point, in which the individuals are inserted in a fixed place' (*Discipline* 197). Yet, as Soja has illuminated, relatively late in his career, evident in its most developed form in the posthumously translated essay 'Of Other Spaces', Foucault moves towards suggesting a very different sort of space: one that encapsulates the postcolonial space of interrogation and multiple interpretations. For Foucault, it is called the heterotopia: blending the real and unreal, the Derridean absence and presence, as a revelatory window on the self:

> In the mirror, I see myself where I am not, in an unreal, virtual space that opens
> up behind the surface; I am over there, there where I am not, a sort of shadow
> that gives my own visibility to myself, that enables me to see myself there where
> I am absent: such is the utopia of the mirror. But it is also a heterotopia in so far

as the mirror does exist in reality, where it exerts a sort of counteraction on the position that I occupy. From the standpoint of the mirror I discover my absence from the place where I am since I see myself over there. (24)

This is a space of transformation where real resistance may occur, a fluid space 'capable of juxtaposing in a single real place several spaces, several sites that are in themselves incompatible' (25), and therefore open to constant re-visioning suggestive of new possibilities and interpretations.

Such a space, taken up in postcolonial contexts, moves towards the possibility of positive new identities in such a way that comes to define what may be seen as a process of growth. Subversion facilitates a movement away from a focus on colonialism as an immemorially disabling impact upon the lives of individuals and communities. Chaos is invoked by the postcolonial citizen – gathered from the very sources of oppression – and used against the colonial power in order to disrupt totalisations. While such chaos might seem only to open up new colonisations as it undermines the bordered territory or even the home as a defensive unit, it in fact provides powerful resistance. The authority that is gained by having absolute control of space is no longer recognised. Here the postcolonial space diverges from Said's representation of the crushing power of Orientalism. For in postcolonial space, the colonised is given the opportunity to write back, to express a clear sense of agency, and the possibility of overturning. The fact that the colonial conception of space is only ever a myth is exploited to indicate that dissenting voices can never be completely silenced.

Thus, if there is a nonlinear history at the centre of postcolonial subversions of official western historiography, so chaotic spatiality might question any colonial ordering of location. In this book it is this possibility of an interrogatory chaos that I refer to as *post-space*: where a chaotic sense of the spatial on all scales becomes a resource towards the re-visioning of the postcolonial position in society and consequent issues of identity, the possibilities inherent in postcolonial spaces as a direct result of their hybrid histories. I choose the prefix 'post' to emphasise how such a space moves beyond colonial use of space to suggest order, and beyond those earlier definitions of space discussed at the beginning of this introduction which rely upon Euclidean lines and Cartesian grids. Space here is hybrid, shifting, and reflective of the elaborate relationships that construct our sense of place in the contemporary world.

The central premise of post-space is its explicitly metamorphic function, where it is precisely through re-visioning chaos, fluidity and disorder, rather than in spite of it, that statements of resistance or survival are made. A fusion of real and imaginary is utilised to rewrite space, to reprivilege its role as a positive multiplicity celebratory of postcolonial cross-culturalism. Rather than a space being either chaos or celebration – a term in a conventional dialectic – chaos becomes survival, resistance, and even celebration. It suggests a necessary turmoil that offers the tapestry of influences and possibilities that only a fractured, multiplicitous space can provide.

In this book, such a space goes beyond the third spaces of Bhabha and Soja, in that it continually suggests a reality in which spatial transformation does not end with a shift in consciousness, but rather begins with this as it gestures towards outcomes that include active resistance and material change. While efforts at shifts in spatial representation have aesthetic resonance, I will also suggest that they may also be seen as actively being constructed in the postcolonial world today. In this way, they transcend existence as only a critical strategy or aesthetic. Therefore, post-space must be read as acknowledging the chaos inherent in both conceptual space and its realisation in material places. In contrast to Peter Hallward's recent suggestion that the creativity of postcolonial literature is intrinsically distinct from the specifics of location (xv), I argue here that, in post-space, these two logics are combined. The utilisation, for example, of the work of Deleuze and Guattari in this book must be seen to represent a significantly different usage to that employed by Hallward; I do not agree with Hallward's suggestion that Deleuze and Guattari's theory aims for an affirmation 'at a level of coherence which *excludes* that of the specific living organism' (15), but instead agree with Hardt and Negri's reading of their work as 'a properly poststructuralist understanding of biopower that renews materialist thought and grounds itself solidly in the question of the production of the social being' (28).[8]

This argument for the realisation of chaotic concepts in the physical may require some defence. Yet to utilise chaotic space to challenge the myth of colonial spatial absolutism is not simply an interest in rethinking space, but also in re-visioning physical locations. There is therefore here, shared with Massey, the assumption that 'the spatial is political' (9). This movement – from the theoretical to the real – reflects what hooks refers to as the belief that 'postmodern theory that is not seeking to simply appropriate the experience of "Otherness" to enhance the discourse or to be radically chic should not separate the "politics of difference" from the politics of racism' (*Yearning* 26). Thus the employment here of postcolonial theory comes with a full awareness of the dangers of its potential abstractions. I employ poststructuralism here not as a textual enterprise, but rather in line with Philip Leonard's argument that it is a discipline which has 'sought to trigger a shift in the understanding of regional, national, international and global identity by developing concepts that facilitate a different understanding of identity – concepts that avoid the unwitting rearticulation of a colonial or neo-colonial sensibility' (13). Yet, at the same time, there is more which is resonant here, I would like to hope, with the recent work of a cultural theorist such as Paul Gilroy in texts such as *After Empire* and *Between Camps*, rooted in specific and physical examples, than the more abstract elements of the work of Homi Bhabha and Gayatri Spivak. Indeed, Gilroy has his own version of third space – a location 'between camps' (*Between Camps* 84) – that refuses the essentialising positions of cultural purists of all ethnic backgrounds, yet at the same time, in line with the meaning inherent in chaos theory, maintains the belief in notions such as identity rather than advocating a

---

[8]   See also Bonta and Proveti, 4, 39.

complete rejection (*Between Camps* 98). I thus follow Gilroy's own project which emphasises the value of fluidity only in relation to specific contexts:

> The aim ... is not to construct a history of simple hybridity to offset against the achievements of the homogenizers and purity seekers. Instead, local and specific interventions can contribute to a counterhistory of cultural relations and influences. (*After Empire* 161)

Gilroy's work can be seen as part of a revisioning of conventional notions of hybridity by Marxist critics, who reconsider classic postcolonial usage and highlight how the term can be materially grounded. Hence, for Anjali Prabhu, hybridity can be rooted in a specific historical context and tied to the political action of the colonised; read through Glissant and Fanon, he suggests, hybridity becomes tied to Marxist theories of totality and revolution and emerges as a 'robust form of politics' (149). Translated into spatial terms, the concerns of theorists such as Gilroy and Prabhu mean that it is not enough to simply be interested in a theoretical notion of space, but that we must also be interested in how this conceptual space can be translated into a concern for the very real violences and oppressions that exist within postcolonial contexts. I thus aim to reflect postcolonial theory's own increasing awareness of the need for a more rooted model of engagement which addresses the opposition between the theoretical and the demotic in some of its work (Li 214) – what Peter Childs, Patrick Williams and Jean Jacques Weber have recently referred to as the 'hidden agenda' of postcolonial theory: 'overcoming discrimination, living diversity and pluralism, standing up for human rights and social injustice' (ix).[9]

Such an explicit political possibility situated in the real world is already beginning to be voiced. For example, in her comments on the community festivals of West Belfast Eilish Rooney captures the sense in which groups may transform real, physical space as a statement of political opposition:

> With respect to the north of Ireland, a practical example of remembering that is being creatively channelled is the transformation of the commemoration of internment (9 August 1971) from an annual, mostly male spree of rioting in West Belfast into an annual community festival (Féile an Phobail). The Féile is a productive cultural transformation, whereby the political and personal 'wounds' and achievements of the past are used in music-making and drama, and to debate and display the issues of the day. It is the achievement of hundreds of people in small neighbourhood and interest-based Féile committees. Fifty-seven other Féiles have been established ... . the Féile has become its own powerful transformation of trauma into a celebration of resilience and creativity. (222)

---

[9]   For a further example of this approach see Venn.

Similarly, for Ashcroft in *On Post-colonial Futures* (2001), possibility and transformation finds a specific context in the Caribbean sugar industry. Ashcroft sees such industry as exemplifying real change, defining 'what post-colonial transformation actually means in the lives of colonized peoples' (*Futures* 67). It may be summed up it one passage from Ashcroft that encapsulates the concept of post-space as a reconfiguring of traumatic locations into geographies of possibility, the belief that 'because sugar is the reason for the most traumatized and disrupted colonial populations, it is also the focus of the most revolutionary cultural developments' (*Futures* 73).

It is such a situation of possibility and its complex interactions in everyday life within a specific spatialisation that offers the promise of post-space. What these examples also reveal, however, is a politics whose relevance stretches beyond the actuality of colonial experience, to its legacy in the contemporary world, and in particular in relation to the post-independent state. This is what Mbembe (2001) defines as the *postcolony*, a space in which, elsewhere, Mbembe has emphasised, contemporary relations continue to be caught in processes of spatial ordering both intimately related to colonial practices, but also extending beyond them ('Edge' 261). It is also what Derek Gregory (2004) has in a broader context, in the book of the same title, called 'the colonial present': a contemporary society in which the global community 'continue[s] to think and to act in ways that are dyed in the colours of colonial power' (xv). As I discuss in detail in Chapter One, the relevance of post-space is truly postcolonial: extending its possibilities into the contemporary manifestations of the colonial experience, as they continue to resonate through they way space is both constructed and negotiated in the contemporary world, asking us to question the extent to which we have yet to exorcise the ghosts of the imperial past. For whilst Mbembe may maintain the dangers of fluidity, nevertheless its inherent ambiguity offers equally the only potential to subvert continued patterns of colonial-inspired ordering:

> What defines the postcolonized subject is the ability to engage in baroque practices fundamentally ambiguous, fluid and modifiable even where there are clear, written, and precise rules. These simultaneous yet apparently contradictory practices ratify, de facto, the status of fetish that state power so forcefully claims as its right. And by the same token they maintain, even while drawing upon officialise ... *the possibility of altering* the place and time of this ratification. (*Postcolony* emphasis added, 129)

Mbembe's final definition of the postcolony acts against any simplistic African authenticity, and announces the possibility inherent in such harnessing of fluidity, if yet unrealised: 'the postcolony is a period of embedding, a space of proliferation that is not solely disorder, chance, and madness, but emerges from a sort of violent gust, with its languages, its beauty and ugliness, its ways of summing up the world' (*Postcolony* 242). This, then, is not a contradiction of the postcolonial world of fluidity and its poststructuralist influences, but rather a mediation of such concerns within the context of a grounded materiality.[10] What is this, if not the positive disruption of intensely physical locations – the emergence of real-world positivity through trauma – which post-space represents?

Texts

The fact that the exploration of post-space following this introduction centres on the literary does not undermine its political nature. Part of my aim is to establish that literature is always central to a political strategy of the postcolonial citizen, a reflection of how storytelling is central to the narration of place as a text to be read (Ashcroft, 'Newness' 103). This reflects the history of literature playing a central role in colonial liberation (Nederveen Pieterse and Parekh 13). Moreover, I would suggest, literature is always extending towards revealing traces and exposing chaos, including that of space.

The novel dominates this study of postcolonial literary space because it is a literary form that, more than any other, has been implicated in the construction of colonial absolutes. As Said has, most famously, argued, in its realist form the nineteenth-century novel can be read as part of the imperial structure, attempting to create fixed identities for colonised peoples.[11] There are powerful correlations to be uncovered between the role of literature and colonial authority over the territory. For Elizabeth Ermarth, 'fictional realism is an aesthetic form of consensus' (ix). This consensus may be seen to parallel in fictional terms the colonial myth of spatial order, reinforcing through the novel a colonial discourse of a universal ideal of reality. What Anderson defines as the 'homogeneous, empty time' of the 'old-fashioned novel' (24, 25) is a fixing of the imagined world that creates the mirage of a common identity and a common history. As colonialism overwrites chaos and difference, so the realism of the conventional European novel reveals a similar desire for dialectical resolution – a movement 'toward the reconciliation of divergent codes' (Ermarth xii), 'toward a single goal' (Auerbach, qtd. in Gebauer and Wulf 12) – which equally refuses multiple meanings. Indeed, the construction of the realist novel as a text in which 'the basic grid is agreed upon' (Ermarth 22) reveals its affinity for the same tabular mentality that dominates colonial organisation of physical space. At the same time, as Robert Marzec has argued, the realist novel may equally through its thematic concerns be seen to have encouraged the desire for land enclosure that would drive the colonialist impulse. Whilst I am not suggesting here that the novel is simply a colonial product, nevertheless I am following these critics in arguing that it attempts to construct comparable patterns of order that make it – in relation to a strategy that is about subversion rather than opposition – a crucial site of textual intervention.

---

10   See Syrotinski 106–9.
11   For Said's argument, see *Culture and Imperialism* (1993), in particular p. 82.

Just as colonial space may be unravelled by a chaotic alternative, so the reflection of this space in the novel must be countered by new ways of imagining. In this way, the unravelling of the colonial must also be an unravelling of realism. Whilst realist texts are thus referred to in this book, I nevertheless identify one particular genre of literature as being particularly significant in terms of this interrogation of conventional realism, and that is magical-realism. Though realism continues to be used effectively by postcolonial authors and indeed, it may be argued, used to question realism's colonial connotations, it may nevertheless be observed that postcolonial writers have been increasingly drawn to magical-realism as an effective genre in which to develop colonial critique. As Jeanne Delbaere-Garant expresses, magical-realism 'is not exclusively a postcolonial phenomenon, but a much older one' (249). It does not arise out of the postcolonial condition. Nevertheless, it may be seen as a device that is strategically used by the postcolonial author, to gesture beyond the *status quo* and call into question the authority of realism and the colonial-centred history it has conventionally been used to support, posing 'an ideological, postcolonial opposition to that linear, imperialist version of history' (Merivale 331). The drift away from realism to magical-realism may be explained not only as the selection of a genre in opposition to conventional realism. In addition, this shift can be explicitly related to the movement from an earlier phase of anticolonial nationalism to independence. Rather than aiming to assert the right to secure freedom, as anticolonial nationalist fiction did, postcolonial independence literature aims to explore the limits and consequences of this freedom once it has been achieved. Therefore, the fact that magical-realism is a mode 'suited to exploring – and transgressing – boundaries' (Zamora and Faris 5), rather than securing them, draws an obvious connection with post-liberation negotiations of identity. As anticolonial nationalism is concerned with reclaiming colonised territory, so postcolonialism is concerned with exploring the marginal identity that results when the coloniser leaves; it is therefore no coincidence that it chooses to represent this exploration in a form that is not about revolution as much as negotiating survival, a genre that 'seems to be closely linked with a perception of "living on the margins"' (Slemon 408), rather than echoing the territorial concerns of earlier antinationalist texts (Szeman 4, 25).

In exploring post-space representation this book references a large number of postcolonial magical-realist authors and, additionally, realist postcolonial authors who provide interesting points of comparison or contrast. At the centre of each chapter, however, are case studies which rely on the texts of what I believe to be three authors who exemplify these literary strategies: Salman Rushdie, Toni Morrison and Wilson Harris. Focus on these authors is not arbitrary. Rather, their complex and very different relationships to colonialism and its legacies allow post-space to be explored in the widest comparative context. Focusing on the diasporic qualities of postcolonial fiction, they capture my sense of postcolonialism as an experience that exists in any location where the legacy of colonial power has been felt. Drawing on metropolitan locations, they unravel the myth of order as it exists in both postcolonial spaces and the imperial locations from which colonialism originates. In this way, they highlight the very crucial sense in which order is always an imposition, and how chaos reflects the state of space everywhere, rather than a reading which would facilitate the exoticisation of colonised spaces. Writing in English, and what are to different degrees magical narratives, their texts provide particularly powerful engagement with the elements of counter-realism and language that I have identified as central to postcolonial subversion. Finally, writing novels that move from colonial occupation to postcolonial independence, they capture precisely the sense of post-space as relevant to both colony and postcolony – to the legacy of colonial power and its very real continued operation – that is central to my concerns.

In the case of both Rushdie and Harris, postcolonial status is largely unproblematic. Though perhaps less well known that the other two authors in this book, Harris plays a crucial role; just as Rushdie and Morrison have been seen to embody the postcolonial reactions of Asian and African-American geographies, respectively, so Harris resonates with the work of Caribbean postcolonialists. Moreover, his nonfiction creates a context that is in harmony with many of the qualities of the book's post-space model and its conceptualisation of the literary form. Arguing for 'a capacity for renewal *through* and despite a compulsive character of oppression' (Harris, 'Enigma' 141), the interrogation and negotiation of repressive spaces is at the heart of Harris's writing. He is also the most inherently spatial of the three authors selected here – where 'new architectures of space' ('Profiles' 208) are central to Harris's unique interpretations of the possibilities of a re-visioned postcoloniality – and, echoing his Caribbean contemporaries, the most chaotic, with an acknowledged interest in chaos theory that this book endeavours to explore.[12]

Morrison's status as a magical-realist author is well established in recent criticism. The inclusion of Morrison here as a postcolonial author, however, may for some readers be a contentious one, and requires its own separate comment. It relies upon two factors: firstly, the assumption that the United States is in some sense a postcolonial space; secondly, the belief that Morrison's texts specifically are concerned with issues of postcolonial identity. Within literary studies, a precedent for the reading of at least some authors from the United States as postcolonial is provided by both John Cullen Gruesser and Timothy Powell. For Gruesser, Black Atlantic literature, including the work of Morrison, is open to postcolonial readings which for him draw productive comparisons with the work of authors including Salman Rushdie, although his book never draws direct comparison between these authors in its chapters (2).[13] For Powell, the postcolonial relevance of American literature is wider, acknowledging that 1776 could 'be called, in the strictest sense of the term, a postcolonial moment' (349), but also emphasising the continued colonisation of ethnic minorities by the United States after independence, its

---

[12]   For a recent example of Harris's spatial concerns see Harris and Maximin.

[13]   Gruesser's work is also directly relevant to this project in that, like my own work, he sees Gilroy as an essential theoretical lynchpin for discussing such cross-cultural activity.

aggressive colonial-style expansion, and its own neo-colonial role. It is within the terms of Powell's definition of this complex position as *postcolonial colonialism* (351) that I read the United States as postcolonial. I make an intentional choice here with such an inclusion. Reading the United States as postcolonial within the terms of Powell's and others' criticism allows detailed consideration of how the legacy of colonialism continues to penetrate society.[14] Designation of authors from the United States as postcolonial is not determined by race, or by how far after 1776 the author is writing. Rather it is a designation applied on the basis of an author's concerns with America's own unique postcolonial identity: not simply with the relationship to Britain, but with the legacy of colonialism in an independent nation.

In terms of the second factor – Morrison's concern with postcolonial issues – the precedent is even more established. It relies upon an understanding of Morrison's concern with slavery as colonial slavery, a form that was begun during the colonial period, and which continued even in independence. This means that while white Americans were liberated from colonial rule in 1783, African-Americans continued to be subject to colonial patterns of exploitation in a process that exemplifies Powell's postcolonial colonialism. It also relies upon reading Morrison's treatment of African-American identity in general as an extension of this concern, drawing on how the legacy of slavery continues to be felt in the exploitation of African-Americans even after 1865. This reading is facilitated by the fact that the critical language of postcolonial theory – key terms such as hybridity, Diaspora, difference and mimicry – are so well suited to an analysis of Morrison's texts. To read Morrison in such terms is to recognise an emerging discourse surrounding her work, substantiated by her inclusion on university syllabuses dealing with postcolonial literature, by prominent investigations by critics such as Bhabha, Gruesser and Holly Flint, and now finally a book – Sam Durrant's *Postcolonial Narrative and the Work of Mourning* (2004) – reading her fiction in such terms.

By choosing writers from three very different locations and supplementing discussion of their works with readings of postcolonial fictions from other geographies, I aim to offer a reading of postcolonial space as a representational concern that may constitute a trans-geographic counter-discourse. Reflecting this awareness of location as driving principle, the book is divided into five thematically led chapters, each focusing on one particular space that is significant in the search for a postcolonial spatial politics. The chapters that follow trace the postcolonial movement towards a relocation of spatial politics in a dynamic and diverse set of locations. In Chapter One I reassess the significance of the most prominent of these large spaces – the nation – to explore the postcolonial author's problematic relationship with the nation-state, and the possibility for a refocusing of critical readings on the representation of other spaces that this offers. In Chapter Two, I begin this rereading by examining the role of larger-than-national space in the

---

[14]   For comparable positions which have echoed Powell see Park and Schwarz.

form of the journey. I then continue by moving in the opposite direction to explore what I see as the often-undermined smaller-than-national spatial location. This begins in Chapter Three with a critical reading of the representation of cities, and their connection to – but also deviation from – national space. It continues in Chapter Four with a reading of domesticity, in which I suggest that the postcolonial author effectively challenges the colonial use of the house as a metaphor with a reappropriation of the domestic space. In Chapter Five, the movement towards the postcolonial space culminates with a reading of the body as space: a politics that is located, finally, at an intimate and personal level.

In this way, I move intentionally from the macro to the micro, hoping to reappraise both the meaning and significance of spatial locales in the light of a postcolonial politics. I want to assert, as does Arundhati Roy in the very title of her novel, *The God of Small Things* (1997), that the 'small' is at the centre of postcolonial spatial politics. Explaining the title of her novel, Roy notes:

> To me the god of small things is the inversion of God. God's a big thing and God's in control. ... This small activity that goes on is the under life of the book. All sorts of boundaries are transgressed upon. At the end of the first chapter I say little events and ordinary things are just smashed and reconstituted, imbued with new meaning to become the bleached bones of the story. It's a story that examines things very closely but also from a very, very distant point, almost from geological time and you look at it and see a pattern there. A pattern ... of how in these small events and in these small lives the world intrudes. And because of this, because of people being unprotected, the world and the social machine intrudes into the smallest, deepest core of their being and changes their life. (Roy, *Interview*)

Against accusations levelled at Roy, common to many postcolonial authors, that she is apolitical, writing 'another narrative of postmodern immorality, perversity and irresponsibility' (Kumar 69), this statement illustrates something very different: not a rejection of consideration of larger political issues, but rather a situation of these debates on the small scale.

Postmodern, poststructuralist and postcolonial, post-space moves beyond conceptions of space as fixed towards the empowerment of new possibilities. The chaotic multiplicity of everyday postcolonial oppression is gathered up and subverted into a gateway to the power of unforeseen pathways. What emerges is what Marilyn Chandler has referred to as the 'politics as well as the poetics of space' (5). An account of the dynamics of this postcolonial literary space has yet to be written. Anderson, Pratt, Noyes, Said and Carter do much to establish the myth of absolutism, but their remit is not to focus on its unravelling. Soja – extending the work of both Foucault and Lefebvre – offers a chaotic spatial model on which literary analysis may draw, but from the bounds of geographical study. Bhabha, indubitably, applies his own version of such a model to texts that do include the literary, offering an insight into the potential of chaotic spatial subversions, but situated firmly in the theoretical space, rather than the physical. In this book, I extend the work of these critics to examine how postcolonial literary representations of space, often magical and chaotic, allow the absolutism of colonial space – in very physical locations – to be exposed as myth. Seen as a postcolonial foregrounding of the multiplicity denied by the colonial space, yet ever-present, the literature of postcolonialism will be seen as the explicit revealing of the inherent confusion, disorder and chaos of space: not as negative fluidity, but as empowering destabilisation. This is its post-space. Instead of the common national scale of political resistance I offer a more dynamic set of politicised locations, a storm that is both political and literary as it disrupts the very centre of imperial structures and their postcolonial legacies.

Chapter 1
Shifting the Scales:
Postcolonial Nation

... nationalism cannot seriously be considered to be the alternative to imperialism
that it was once thought to be.

(Gikandi 7)

If, as I suggested in the introduction, the centre of post-space is a movement towards
alternatives to considering the postcolonial space in national terms, then what is it
about this 'nation' in a postcolonial context that offers such an opportunity? In this
first chapter, I want to address such a question. Using the fiction of Toni Morrison,
Salman Rushdie and Wilson Harris as case studies, it is clear that, regardless of the
specifics of geographical location, postcolonial fiction can be seen to problematise
the use of national space as the signifier of political engagement.

The relationship between the contemporary postcolonial novelist and the
nation must be set within the context of an anticolonial history that has seen ideas
of independent nationhood as integral to liberation. The concept that liberation
from colonial power has most notably been enacted on a national scale, rather than
through local politics, has ensured the prominence of the nation in postcolonial
discourses. This support for the nation, and nationalism, as the means to
independence, has prevented a full interrogation of the ways in which, in fact, the
same nation may be responsible for continuing colonial attitudes and has obscured
the common reality of the nation itself as a colonial construct: a site complicit
with, rather than in opposition to, colonial control of indigenous space.

An assertion of this complicity does not mean we should not acknowledge
the basis for nationalism as a legitimate anticolonial response. Rather, it is to
contextualise this response with an awareness of two important factors: firstly,
the colonial involvement in the construction of many developing world nations
and the implications of this for those nations as symbols of anticolonialism and,
secondly, the resistance to colonialism at other spatial scales which the focus on
national politics has obscured, often involving the appropriation of more local
subversions for the nationalist cause.

The positive nature of the idea of nation for the postcolonial imagination is
highlighted by Timothy Brennan and Laura Chrisman. In Brennan's reading, the
very fact that the nation is itself in many cases a colonial construct only adds to
the power of that nation becoming the central focus of anticolonial resistance, a
subversive rewriting of a space against its original intentions. Similarly, Chrisman
has made particularly well-argued assertions of the continued importance of the

nation as a point of reference for postcolonial studies. Directing her attention toward Paul Gilroy's *Black Atlantic* (1993) as 'anti-nationalist' (7), Chrisman argues that the demonisation of the nation is both reductive and premature. For Chrisman, the nation is central to a need to restore 'the emancipatory elements of the political sphere' (3) to what has become an over-aestheticised discipline. She argues that the loss of the political has been facilitated by an exaggerated opposition to the nation. Most recently, Elleke Boehmer has reinforced these comments from a postcolonial gendered perspective, by emphasising how the nation can equally be a libratory space for women, as much as one that needs to be associated with the perpetuation of patriarchal power structures (*Stories*, 4).

Such arguments are in many respects insightful, highlighting the continued significance of the nation as a space of subversion. What they might do more to emphasise, however, is the incomplete nature of this perceived insider subversion, and the extent to which the ultimate result of that 'subversion' has often in fact been, on a national scale, a reaffirmation of colonial power hierarchies and divisions, and, on both local and international scales, an extension of violent tensions originating in colonial divisions of territory. Recognising the importance of the nation against the rejections of figures such as Hardt and Negri does not mean, necessarily, that one must as a result maintain, as does Kaniskha Chowdhury (152), the privilege of the nation as a site of value. Associations with fascism, separatism, neo-colonialism and terrorism have revealed nationalism, in many cases, to be in the long term an extension of colonial power, rather than the libratory force of initial anticolonial rhetoric. As Ian Baucom realises, to support autonomous national identities in relation to colonised nations is also to allow a discourse of racist exclusivity that may act against these very same localities. The racial exclusions upon which nationalist principles often rely are the same exclusions that have often, in colonial regimes, been central to the exploitation of the indigenous population. The nation may have been necessary for liberation, but this is to be contrasted with its continued usefulness as a political construct (Szeman 7, 10).

The focus of Brennan's commentary – Rushdie's fiction – reveals the centrality of contemporary postcolonial authors to these debates. Rushdie, in particular, has been drawn into the centre of discussions about postcolonial literature's engagement with concepts of nationality. Aijaz Ahmad, a major critic of Rushdie, argues that a calling into question of nationalist principles can be identified at two key points in modern history. Firstly, he suggests, nationalism was rejected in Europe as a response to its Fascist connections. But, secondly, for Ahmad, there has been a more general – though not comprehensive – movement away from the nation associated with poststructuralist and related postmodern discourses. It is Rushdie's writing which for Ahmad is at the centre of this later movement, turning nationalism into 'illusion, myth, totalizing narrative' (41). Ahmad's criticism of Rushdie for this perceived enterprise is not in the name of a return to anticolonial nationalism, which he sees as equally reductive. Nevertheless, there is the sense in which Rushdie's movement away from the idea of a firm, solid nation that can be fought for is at the centre of both his subversions and, for Ahmad at least, the problems of his fiction.

What I want to suggest is that Rushdie's movement away from a solid nation, to which Ahmad draws our attention, is not, in fact, the flaw in his politics, but rather is central to his re-visioning of spatial locations: the essence of a movement from space, to post-space. Moreover, examining Morrison's and Harris's fiction within the context of these debates, Rushdie's strategy may be seen to be part of a larger movement away from the national scale. This may be seen to be a defining feature that distinguishes independence fiction from earlier anticolonial writing, in which nationalism represented the possibilities – rather than the extinguishing – of freedom. What emerges is not simply a critique of national principles, but also, more curiously (and contradicting many of the nation-centred readings of postcolonial authors), an absence of consideration of national principles that asserts some definite break. This raises two important questions. Firstly, why is there this definite break? And secondly, what does it suggest for a postcolonial spatial politics, and for the location of post-space? The answers are not straightforward: while such absence suggests movement away from national politics in some terms, a break with a specific incarnation of the nation-state is not a rejection of all that concepts of nationality represent.

Shifting Space

The role of nationalism in uniting colonised populations made the nation-state a significant banner under which the colonised could respond to empire, providing – in theoretical terms – an absolute space, the 'nation', necessary for the opposition of a much larger and more powerful theoretical totality: the colonial territory. This sense of the nation as a fixed and, importantly, timeless and natural institution that would oppose the foreign invader can be seen as a strategic construct necessary to challenge the absolutes and order which, as I discussed in the introduction, colonialism relied upon. At the centre of this strategic usage is a distinction between state and nation. Popular usage often sees nation as interchangeable with state, or even country, marking simply a political and territorial unit. And yet there are differences – a state of 'public institutions ... exercising a monopoly of coercion and extraction within a given territory' is not the same as a nation signifying 'a cultural and political bond ... all who share an historic culture and homeland' (Smith, *National* 14–15).

In these terms, the sense in which newer openly 'pluralist' nations exists is misusage. For while a state may be founded on a notion of diversity, the nation is founded on subsuming cultural difference to a communal image: a population of a nation may not naturally be homogeneous, but they are encouraged to see themselves as such, with cultural difference discouraged. This unity is obviously central to the importance of the nation for anticolonial resistance: it embodies the sense of the nation as a unifying concept capable of challenging the absolutes of colonial theory.

Yet as part of the poststructuralist turn against the nation that Ahmad identifies with Rushdie's fiction, it is clear that this absolute nation has been eroded. In the wake of the poststructuralist interrogation of reality and a wider postmodern concern with revising conventional histories, the absolute nation no longer holds. Instead, its credentials have been deconstructed in a similar way to the deconstruction of the order of colonial rule. It is now common to conceive of nationalism as a discourse constructed to achieve specific political aims, rather than the reflection of a communal feeling or spirit. In this latter reading, nationalism in many senses precedes the nation that it proclaims to defend: it is the political discourse of nationalism that forges the nation and convinces its 'inhabitants' of their belonging and shared values, rather than nationalism reflecting pre-existing feelings and loyalties. Most notable in terms of this reading is Benedict Anderson's *Imagined Communities*. For Anderson, nations are 'cultural artefacts' (4), and he is not alone in this view; for Eric Hobsbawm, writing in the same year, the nation is 'invented' ('Inventing' 14). Anderson's concentration on the nation as an imagined political community resonates with rejection of it as a fundamental concept: nations are 'administrative units' converted into 'fatherlands' (53). In conflict with the use of nationalism to serve inherent claims to a particular territory, based on notions of shared history and belonging, the nation is based on the creation of a false consciousness, and an illusory mythical past.

In postcolonial terms, such fluidity is emphasised by Homi Bhabha, for whom the nation is always 'a narration' ('Narrating' 1) at odds with its myth of timelessness. Bhabha speaks of a nation space 'in the *process* of the articulation of elements: where meanings may be partial because they are *in media res*' ('Narrating' 3). National culture is presented as 'neither unified nor unitary' ('Narrating' 4), rather it forms 'a space that is *internally* marked by cultural difference and the heterogeneous histories of contending peoples, antagonistic authorities and tense cultural locations' (Bhabha, 'DissemiNation' 299). Bhabha identifies this tension in his own terms as a split between the pedagogical and the performative, between the nation-state's casting of itself as absolute, and a need to be modern and creative in order to achieve this, constructing 'ambivalent temporalities' ('DissemiNation' 294) that deny the homogenising effects of the nation-state's official history:

> Counter-narratives of the nation that continually evoke and erase its totalizing boundaries – both actual and conceptual – disturb those ideological manoeuvres through which 'imagined communities' are given essentialist identities. For the political unity of the nation consists in a continual displacement of its irredeemably plural modern space, bounded by different, even hostile nations, into a signifying space that is archaic and mythical, paradoxically representing the nation's modern territoriality, in the patriotic, atavistic temporality of Traditionalism. ('DissemiNation' 300)

This model bears considerable similarities to J.K. Noyes's assertion of the chaos revealed in the wake of colonial totalisations of space. As colonial space is continually revealed as incapable of being maintained in absolute terms, so the nation's political unity is continually undermined in the process of its own creation. Fluidity is overwritten to provide a secure space that echoes colonial totalisation of all space.

What this understanding reveals is that the same process which enshrines the colonial territory is at the centre of enshrining the nation as a foundational concept. As colonial ordering of space is part of a discourse of colonial rule, so the previously natural bases of nations are revealed to be cultural moments facilitating the imagining of a national space with political resonance. This raises questions as to how colonialism may have fed into anticolonial nationalism. For Elie Kedourie, it is only with the influence of colonial models that discrete identities become significant. Kedourie's claim that 'in none of these [Muslim, Hindu and Buddhist] areas before the coming of European influence was a homogenous population considered a religious or political ideal' (*Nationalism in Asia* 33) may be overdramatic: yet it emphasises the extent to which colonial discourse may have brought with it a model of cultural homogeneity. Colonial programs of education may be seen to have indoctrinated indigenous populations not only into colonial language, but also colonial methods based on standardisation and absolutism, developing elites who would take on the mantle of anticolonial nationalism from the only model available: the European.

The most important context for considering postcolonial reactions to the nation, however, is the awareness of how the construction of the very national territory itself is intimately entwined with colonial processes. Nationalism has been seen to continue the colonial project of making artificial boundaries into 'natural frontiers'. As Elie Kedourie points out in his fourth edition of *Nationalism* (1993), such natural frontiers 'do not exist' (120), but are constructs designed to give the nation precedence over other administrative units. Like colonialism, therefore, nationalism relies upon the ordering of space, and the subsequent overwriting of the process of construction with a discourse of natural development. Like colonialism, nationalism obscures the chaos and hybridity underlying the organisation of space, with the sense of a simplistic and logical arrangement. In *Imagined Communities*, Anderson's description of nation building as reliant upon a 'totalizing classificatory grid' (184) again foreshadows Noyes's concept of colonial space as a regulation of territory through administrative institutions. The maps that Anderson describes as the focus of colonial state building, and latterly national borders, are the same spaces of 'geometric grid ... alignment of map and power' (Anderson 173) that Noyes more generally outlines, with the same underlying instability reflecting the fact that 'once we lift the iron curtain of geometry and geography we find neither natural space nor natural boundary' (Islam 21).

This similarity between nationalism and colonialism extends beyond the method of securing power over a given land mass to the very physical spatial reality of the territory. As part of his discussion of national and colonial similarities, Anderson points out 'the isomorphism between each nationalism's territorial stretch and that of the previous imperial administrative unit' (114), and illuminates how colonial states manipulated borders at independence to maintain existing boundaries or claim the right to define new ones. In these terms the colonial space *is* the postcolonial nation, although, as Mbembe has rightly noted, such boundaries in the contemporary world have a military, economic and religious reality that cements their continuance ('Edge' 265). For the colonised, identifying with a national selfhood may mean identifying with exactly that which destroyed a pre-existing communal sense of self – the same colonial space that negated the communities and territorial boundaries existing prior to empire.

If the nation-state is not a natural entity but a product, this undoubtedly holds implications for its impact on the national population. As Mbembe notes, the internal boundaries created by colonialism have had more damaging consequences than the actual borders between nations which exist ('Edge' 266). While 'most nation-states are polyethnic' (Smith, *National* 39), their origins around the 'myths and memories' of a 'dominant *ethnie*' (Smith, *National* 39) means continued conflicts. Inheritance of colonial models and ideals facilitates neo-colonial subjection of postcolonial states, encouraging valorisation of the west and also corrupt, military regimes which are as elitist as preceding imperialists. Inheritance of colonial boundaries calls the unity of nationalist territories into question, often revealed as based only on superficial shared opposition to colonialism – a strategic response – rather than on the ethnic, cultural or linguistic terms. This leaves such spaces – without deep-seated unity or time to construct a false consciousness of such unity – 'still born' (Smith, *National* 108). Such an understanding is supported by readings of individual postcolonial geographies. Both Crawford Young and Rupert Emerson stress how the reorganization of African political space classified groups with no respect for local definitions, as 'colonial boundaries arbitrarily imposed in the course of partition cut across ethnic lines, taking no heed of the problem of future nations' (Emerson 93). Young provides examples not only of the divisive effects of this change on existing groups such as the Tutsis and Hutus, but also asserts his belief that colonialism in fact created tribes through its administration. Inferred here is a suggestion of 'divide-and-rule' tactics on the part of colonial administrations, pitting groups against each other and developing some in favour of others.[1] For Emerson, Nigeria illuminates these principles: a nation formed by opposition to colonialism, where division and secessionism has led to claims for a federal state and intractable problems (354–9). Yet Nigeria is not an exception: Emerson discusses further examples including Burma, Ceylon and Indonesia (112), stressing the failure of democracy in heterogeneous populations (221).

It is this transference of not simply colonial borders, but also a colonial mentality, that is so powerfully evoked by Mbembe's invocation of the 'postcolony'. As Massey states, there pervades in contemporary society a 'nostalgia' which, in my analysis, is revealed to be a longing for the colonial myth. Thus Massey explains

---

[1]   See C. Young 81, and also Moore-Gilbert 197.

how, against the increasing awareness of shifting borders and fluid patterns of social movement across space, 'there is still often alongside it an assumption that once (once upon a time) those boundaries were impermeable, that there was no transgression. This is an attitude, a cosmology, reflected in all those nostalgic responses to globalisation which mourn the loss of old spatial coherences' (65). It is thus no surprise that Mbembe's analysis of the postcolony reveals precisely this continued desire for spatial ordering:

> The government related, of course, to a territory that constituted the colony. The colonial territory had its space, its shape, its borders. It had its geological make-up and climates … . There were, above all,the people who inhabited it … it is these people who were labelled natives. They constituted the raw material, as it were, of government. They had to be enclosed in relations of subjection … . 'Politique indigene' set out how to dispose of this raw material, how to increase it, what laws to impose on it, what punishments and penalties and tortures to inflict on it, what services and contributions to compel it how to extract as much as possible from its labor, and in what conditions to care for its subsistence. (*Postcolony* 32–3)

As in Foucault's world discipline moves from executioner's block to prison, so Mbembe offers the postcolony as an example of sameness within difference. He could not be more explicit, arguing that 'not only the state forms but also the colonial rationality sketched above were quickly reappropriated by Africans' (*Postcolony* 40). This, then, is not simply a matter of the transfer of territory into the contemporary period, but also a transfer of attitude which has a legacy beyond the immediate nationalist period into the present day. For Mbembe, the postcolony only increases regimes of order: there has been movement only towards violence rather than peace, with conflicts over land ownership leading both to newly ordered national territories, and spaces under militia control with no official government representation (*Sovereignty* 155). It is not simply about neo-colonial influence, but rather of the realisation of that continued mentality and practice which Fanon warned against so strongly in *The Wretched of the Earth*: the independent nation becomes its colonial antagonist, even when that antagonist has ceased in simple form to even exist.

Shifting Scales

What critiques of the nation suggest is a desire to engage with the political through alternative locations, but also to reflect a political world in which power is frequently held not in the nation itself, but in more diverse forms, reflecting Hardt and Negri's belief that '*the decline in sovereignty of nation-states … does not mean that sovereignty as such has declined*' (xi). So if the nation is to be complicated as a site of political allegiance, then what is the alternative? Underlying the readings of postcolonial writings which follow is the suggestion that other scales can take the place of the national as sites of political significance. This is more that simply recognising the national reflected in other locations. Instead of this metaphorical usage, what I proffer is an alternative which recognises that clinging to the nation as the site of political significance is itself something open to critique. Anthony Smith is one of only a few critics to note this problem. He asks us to consider 'how flexible can the concept of the nation be without losing its fundamental features, particularly those of common culture and history?' (*National* 146). Extending from this, I want to do more than suggest that spaces of conflict in the postcolonial novel are simply metaphors for national tension. Thus this project moves beyond the literary readings made by Baucom, whose recognition of 'the struggle for Englishness as the struggle to preserve, possess or hybridize a certain sort of space' (39) and focus on smaller and more diverse spaces – 'Gothic architecture, the Victoria Terminus in Bombay, the Anglo-Indian Mutiny pilgrimage, the cricket field, the country house, and the zone of urban riot' – is in the service of reading them strictly as 'synecdoches of the nation's space' (4). Instead, I ask, why need the nation – if it is time-bound and illusory – be the focus of political engagement in such narratives? Need it be the focus of anticolonial resistance, or might this be located elsewhere?

This is the greatest value of the work of a critic such as Paul Gilroy: its encouragement to the reader to think outside the national frame when 'neither political nor economic structures of domination are still simply co-extensive with national borders' (*Black Atlantic* 7). Here movement away from the nation is not necessarily a removal of politics, but a quest for resistance that must be undertaken elsewhere. Chrisman's argument against *The Black Atlantic* is that it denies politics when it favours aesthetics over national movements. Yet it is particularly oppression Gilroy is interested in, and while his notion of 'nationalism' is narrower than that provided by Chrisman – defined only in its desire for cultural homogeneity and not by the heterogeneity that such totalisation inevitably denies – it seems that his definition of 'politics' is more expansive. In this way, it is Gilroy, ironically, who is more connected to the complex reality of resistance politics, and to a harsh, everyday reality which is not a simple matter of institutional policy, but also of cultural and social behaviour. Such broadening of the definition of resistance – 'a philosophical discourse which refuses the modern, occidental separation of ethics and aesthetics, culture and politics' (Gilroy, *Black Atlantic* 38–9) – suggests that other forms of protest against power structures may be successful, offering an alternative to a nation-centred approach.

The support for such shifts in thinking is more notable than might initially seem obvious. For Gilroy, an alternative scale to the national is the transnational, a focus already explored in ideas of cultural hybridity, and amply supported in the acknowledgment that 'intensification of globalization processes has weakened the traditional nation-state' (Guibernau 175). Gilroy's argument is reinforced by Jurgen Habermas, for whom there is now a '"post-national" self-understanding of the constitutional state' (134). For Isaac Deutscher, the scale of political affairs today makes the nation-state 'ridiculous and out-lived' (40). Hobsbawm perceives that the history of the future 'will inevitably have to be written as the history of a world which can no longer be contained within the limits of "nations" and "nation-states" as these used to be defined' (*Nations* 191). Rushdie himself, significantly, is part of this debate. He echoes Gilroy in his proclamation that 'the frontierless nation is not a fantasy' ('Notes on Writing' 67), but is instead evident in the rootlessness of postcolonial authors which means that 'if writing turns repeatedly towards the nation, it just as repeatedly turns away' ('Notes on Writing' 67). This process of more global identification manifests itself in less celebratory, more pessimistic, terms in Hardt and Negri's *Empire*. For Hardt and Negri the nation-state has been replaced by global power concerns which need to be seen as the new manifestation of imperial power systems in the postcolonial world. That Hardt and Negri call such a system of power 'Empire' profoundly illustrates how such a new spatial reality may be compared to the actions of imperial nations in the colonial period. Whilst this book calls into question some of the profoundly pessimistic associations of Hardt and Negri's book, nevertheless their reflection on the significance of the global for how oppression functions in the postcolonial world only highlights even more urgently the need to address this spatial scale.

At the same time, there is equal support for movement towards smaller, rather than larger, scales of engagement. In 'The Time and Space of Everyday Life' (2004) Ian Burkitt argues that personal interactions should not be divorced from the study of institutions in social analysis. Indeed, echoing the notion of post-space, he suggests that whilst the latter are attempts to fix time and space, the former offer alternative, more diverse, models of social and political exchange. Equally, Gilroy initially sees smaller spaces as less tied to an ideology of difference, as 'regional or local subjectivities [that] simply do not articulate with "race" in quite the same way as their national equivalent' (*There Ain't No Black* 54), whilst, similarly for Hardt and Negri, their concern for global power structures is developed through the impact of these structures on the individual (24). Current distinctions between 'the modern nation-state' and 'something more ancient and nebulous – the *natio* – a local community, domicile, family, condition of belonging' (Brennan 2), suggest a desire to return to smaller, more traditional, concepts of nationality. Khilnani sees Indian nationalism challenged by the 'reinvigoration of regional politics' (190). In his reading of Indian historiography, Dipesh Chakrabarty argues that everyday life has often been subsumed into nationalist discourse, preventing it from being judged on its own terms; moreover, the intimate has been neglected, presenting Indian history as 'public without private' ('Postcoloniality' 232). In these terms, against the public, 'other constructions of self and community, while documentable in themselves, will never enjoy the privilege of providing the metanarratives or teleologies ... of our histories' (Chakrabarty, 'Postcoloniality' 232). For Katherine Verdery 'the size requirements of viable nationhood are decreasing' (44), adding to the sense that nation is taken up conveniently when what is in fact at stake is a smaller, more communal identity. Ernest Gellner, for example, notes that while social control and removal of difference meant 'nations were assumed to be the permanent real categories of the social world' (121), individuals 'have more earthly concerns, and if they rebel it is seldom for a culture' (120). Similarly, Henri Lefebvre's representational space 'has an affective kernel or centre: Ego, bed, bedroom, dwelling, house; or: square, church, graveyard' (*Production* 42) that illustrates life centred not on national identity, but on personal interaction. In relation to Mbembe's postcolony and Derek Gregory's colonial present, this need to engage with personal scales is equally apparent, as 'the apparatus of state finds ways of getting into its subjects' most intimate spaces' (Mbembe, *Postcolony* 121), and power is not produced through geopolitics and geoeconomics alone .... It is also set in motion through mundane cultural forms' (Gregory 16). In terms of literature, for Ahmad, the bleakness of Rushdie's representation of the nation of Pakistan in *Shame* (1983) lies in a politics 'narrowly conceived' (151) that neglects 'more diverse ways of allegorization' (289). In these more 'diverse ways' the government is not taken to be the nation (297), but must instead be captured in the lives of the populace.[2]

Finally, it can be considered that both scales, coterminously, may be embraced. This reflects Massey's definition of space as 'the product of interrelations; as constituted through interactions, from the immensity of the global to the intimately tiny' (9), and David Harvey's call for 'a political movement at a variety of spatial scales' (52), including 'households, communities, and nations' (75) as interrelated locations. Indeed, in many critics it is possible to find a divergence from the nation on dual scales: both larger and smaller. For Guibernau, there are both smaller territories that desire political autonomy (16), and also the possibilities of a 'global state' (19). For Bhabha, new types of agency may be found at the site of the margin. This theoretical space, which locates itself as an enclave within the dominant nation, will 'contest claims to cultural supremacy, whether these are made from the "old", post-imperialist metropolitan nations, or on behalf of the "new" independent nations of the periphery' ('Narrating' 4). Yet this margin, smaller than the nation, will forge a 'transnational culture' (Bhabha, 'Narrating' 4). In a British context, Stephen Reicher and Nick Hopkins point to the importance of both larger 'non-national politics' (68) and also 'individual and local difference' (101). Finally, and perhaps most interestingly, Gilroy's earlier concerns with first smaller and then larger scales has been replaced by a concern with multiple scales of engagement, asking in relation to cultural practices, 'Are they local or global forms?' (*Between Camps* 178):

> These modest aspirations can be connected to the idea that we should take the *scale* upon which the calculus of human difference is to be judged more carefully into account. The shift away from a Euclidean geometry (which operates within closely bounded scalar limits that are anything but natural) and its analytic

---

2   Rushdie, I would argue, if read against the grain of Brennan's influential text, is already making this transference to the personal in *Midnight's Children* (1981).

Cartesian successor, which links perception to a deterministic rationalism, and toward a fractal geometry problematizes the questions of scale and scaling in a radical fashion offers a useful analogy here. Bodily scale is certainly important, but it is not the only possible basis for calculation and interaction. Varieties of solidarity other than the local and the national assert their presence and have to be placed within an explicit hierarchy of scales with multiple patterns of determination. (*Between Camps* 217)

So why now turn to this particular form of resistance? On one level, it is possible to suggest that this is the wrong question. Reading him as a nationalist, Bruce King notes the detail in which Chinua Achebe narrates Ibo life (68), and yet this is not only a concern with colonially-marked national space, but also with more regional identities. In this way, it is not that spatial focus has changed over time, but rather than the way of defining it has become ever more nuanced. Yet there also is a case for suggesting that this spatial practice *is* different, that it marks a decisive break from past approaches. Ironically, such a break may not be the invention of a new, postmodern form at all, but rather a return to pre-nationalist consciousness. In 'The Imaginary Institution of India' (1993) Sudipta Kaviraj highlights the actions preceding full-blown nationalism as small-scale resistances that have latterly been obscured in the history of large-scale movements. For Kaviraj, 'it is an error to think that until nationalism in the latterday sense arrives, there is no political consciousness' (10). What exists are 'utterances [that] are political, although no overt, external political acts follow immediately from them' (Kaviraj 11). Yet in terms of small-scale protest, Kaviraj believes that, in relation to the individuals involved in such resistance, 'in some ways their rejection of a colonizing western rationalist civilization often goes deeper and is more fundamental than that of later nationalists; but they simply do not see the end of colonial subjection as a historically feasible project' (7). The postcolonial narrative may have returned, for good reason, to precisely these forms. For while it must be acknowledged that 'the centre still tends to operate politically through the medium of the nation state, or nation-state alliance' (Moore-Gilbert 197), in an era when racism is often not simply a problem with governments, but with deeply imbedded cultural norms – that often cannot be, for the individual, challenged by reforming legislation – protest may in fact exist more profitably at other spatial scales.

Shifting Fictions

It is this context – the cultural and spatial continuity between empire and the nations formed in response to independence, and the possibility of an antinational alternative based on divergent scales – that can explain the motivations behind criticism or rejection of the nation in postcolonial literature. Increasing acceptance of the nation-state's provisional, and culturally constructed, status, and the fact that colonialism is no longer seen as a distinct phase to be followed by nationalism, means that the postcolonial commentator can no longer unquestionably support or herald the arrival of the nationalist regime. By examining in more detail the relationship of each author with their 'home' nation or nations, it is possible to find an explanation for their reluctance to centre their fiction on such spaces.

1. Wilson Harris: Guyana and Britain

While many of Harris's novels deal with Caribbean or South-American culture, few reference his 'home' nation of Guyana explicitly. Ralph Premdas argues that the 'highest aspiration of the Guyanese child is not to be a physician or a professor but simply to escape by migration' (193). Migrating to England in the early 1950s, this socially conditioned desire for escape might alone explain Harris's reluctance to address national space, responsible for the central narrative voice of the nomadic migrant consciousness across many of his fictions. Yet absence of the nation in Harris's work indicates far more than this desire for migration. It also reveals a critical and problematic interaction with Guyana's national status which is directly relevant to the relationship between nation and colony.

The complexity of Guyana's national history offers important indications as to Harris's possible problems of interaction with the territory. Guyana terms itself a nation, formed under the banner of '"one people, one nation, one destiny"' (B. Williams 20). Yet it is a space defined by repeated alteration of its identity under imperialist systems. Shaped from three Dutch colonies – Demerara, Essequibo and Berbice – Guyana was unified in 1831 as a result of British seizure of these territories. It is unlikely that even the original colonies would have made successful nations, with their own tribal affiliations and cultural customs. Amalgamating three already diverse populations was therefore only likely to increase conflict. Through slavery and indentured labour, the British introduced new populations to Guyana with their own nationalities. This resulted in significant Indian and black Guyanese populations, both overwhelming demographically the indigenous inhabitants.

In this construction of the Guyanese colony, we can find much evidence for processes that resonate with the construction of colonial space indicated by J.K. Noyes. Indeed, in his study *Masters of All They Surveyed: Exploration, Geography, and a British El Dorado* (2000), D. Graham Burnett provides an account of Guyana heavily influenced by Noyes's theories, though he receives shamefully little credit in the text.[3] Burnett moves beyond Noyes in his distinction between the official use of maps and their creation, in an attempt to absolve surveyor Sir Robert Schomburgk from his role in imperial aggression. His findings, however, reach the same conclusion. What emerges is 'a region called terra incognita that Europeans

---

[3]   Burnett makes six references to Noyes in his index, most of them footnotes. However, there are more references to Noyes in the text than this, and there should be far more given Burnett's reliance on Noyes's material. Compare, for example, the quotations below from Burnett with my introductory epigraph.

turned into a mapped and bounded colony' (Burnett 3). Yet such a territory continually reveals its own instability, the surveyor's 'expansive, nomadic and boundary-transgressing technique ... a highly ambiguous boundary ... the tension between boundary making ... and boundary crossing' (Burnett 16, 255).

In these terms, when Guyana gained independence in 1966 it did not provide a model of the classical nation. As Premdas points out, 'state and nation were not coterminous entities' (183), but instead revealed a population united only by 'a shared struggle to uproot the colonial oppressors' (27). This is despite the fact that Guyana did, in principle, offer the possibility of a multi-ethnic state, either in an integrated form or, less attractively, in a more extreme federalist configuration, which was indeed suggested briefly in 1961. The partnership of Cheddi Jagan and Forbes Burnham had been the firmest indicator of this potential, but their alliance quickly made way for traditional nation building. Attempting to form a 'stable, putatively homogeneous brew ... state-as-nation' (B. Williams 4), the nationalist discourse surrounding independent Guyana – like the colonial one preceding it – denied diversity in favour of an illusory unity. Educational texts aimed at Guyanese children, for example, such as Vere T. Daly's *The Making of Guyana* (1974), stressed independence as an opportunity to create a national mythology, where 'our national heroes would no longer be men like Sir Walter Raleigh' (195), forming a concept of the Guyanese nation that obscured racial disharmony.

Because, however, racial politics have dominated Guyanese history, the mythical nature of a unified, unquestionable nation is more obvious than elsewhere. Existing as a nation in conflict with its neighbours and internally divided, unified Guyana is in fact built on immense civil unrest. Throughout the nation's independent history, black Guyanese at times have supported both movements towards a West Indian nation and also Black Power calls for pan-African union, whilst Amerindians attempted in 1969 to secede and join Venezuela. By the 1980s the possibilities for cross-cultural politics seemed lost forever when Walter Rodney, leader of the WPA, a cross-cultural alternative to the dominant PPP and PNC parties, was assassinated. The role of colonialism in such cultural stratification exceeds the consequences of settlement. What Premdas calls a 'colour-class ... stratification system' (14) was introduced by the British, dividing occupations along racial lines, a policy that made it near-impossible for independent Guyanese to unite. Premdas goes as far as stating that 'the colonial state *deliberately* spawned an ethnically segmented social and cultural fabric' (emphasis added, 183), creating separate ethnic groups so defined by race that they would never unite as one nation. To compound such factors the integrity of the Guyanese nation has been threatened by colonialism even after independence. It was initially 'dependent on its former colonial master' (Manley ix), and its constitution was suspended on the election of a left-wing government in 1953, indicating that 'self-government [was] tolerated only where it worked within patterns acceptable to the imperialists' (Emerson 319). Adapting at speed to a plural population a European model that was meant for less defined social groupings, and to develop over centuries, means that Guyana epitomises the problems of postcolonial nationalism.

One way in which literature has challenged this colonial connection has been to explicitly critique Guyana's nationalist politicians. For writers such as Andrew Salkey, this has been an identifiable aim. Harris's novels, however, are of a different emphasis, which – I want to suggest – illustrates precisely the movement away from national scales that I have indicated. It would be wrong to give the impression that Harris ignores issues of nationality entirely. At a conference on Commonwealth literature, Harris mourns the loss of national identity, and the trauma of colonisation:

> The Ibo in Nigeria are a terrifying example of the engulfment which can suddenly overtake a people within a *trauma* of helplessness – external conquest, internal collapse. There is reason to believe that the earliest forms of tragic art were born out of a necessity to compensate such losses within the human psyche. ('Interior' 145)

Similarly, in his novel *Jonestown* (1996), Harris reflects upon the rigid identity imposed by alterations in the naming of Guyana, where 'it may seem inevitable or convenient to submit to one frame or name but, in so doing, cultures begin to imprison themselves, involuntarily perhaps, in conquistadorial formula that kills alternatives, kills memory' (9), as the Guyana that results is what 'British colonizers framed' (9). This adds to the possibilities of reading *Jonestown* as national critique, the authoritarian figure of Jonah Jones standing for the corrupt elites ruling Guyana since independence.

However, even in these cases, Harris quickly moves away from discussion of the nation to wider issues of humanity. This supports the view, espoused by Michael Gilkes, that Harris sees Guyana 'as only part of a larger historical and geographical reality' (22). Ultimately, what this offers is not a focus on the nation-state, but rather movement towards wider, more universalised interpretations. In his conference paper, Harris ultimately explores not nationalism, but the role of the individual:

> With the mutilation and decline of the conquered tribe a new shaman or artist struggles to emerge who finds himself moving along the knife-edge of change … a task which is profoundly personal. ('Interior' 145)

In terms of *Jonestown*, what is retrieved through a breakdown of absolute identities is not in any traditional sense a nation, but rather dissolution of false territorial borders, not in favour of ethnic solidarity, but a transnational perspective:

> Hidden textualities of pre-Columbian and post-Columbian place are hinted at in the word 'Guiana' … . 'British Guiana' became 'Guyana' in 1966. A link was implied with an older frame one may perceive in Spanish maps of the region encompassing the 'Guianas' and Venezuela and South Brazil. Cross-culturalities running through 'Guianas' and 'Guyanas' are invoked. (9)

With each space here indebted to another, the nation dissolves, and it is for this reason also that Harris can write of Venezuela and South Brazil without any mention of border disputes. For, instead, Harris offers a cross-culturality transcending current conflicts. His concept of Guyanese identity moves beyond the nation, either in terms of Guyanese borders, or in terms of ethnic grouping: every influence remains as a force to be utilised and amalgamated into the human consciousness.

Kerry L. Johnson's work on Harris is particularly illuminating in this regard. Johnson sees Harris as constructing 'a postcolonial identity that is an alternative to national identity' ('Muse' 74) where 'restrictive nationalisms are subverted' ('Muse' 88). Her reasoning for Harris's rejection of the nation stands as an excellent general model for the problems of postcolonial interactions with the nation-space:

> The nation, then, has been defined as the desired 'first world' result of 'first world' imperialism, thus making it an understandable target for criticism by the postcolonial writer, or as a concept that binds 'third world' writers to a restrictive form of 'third world' nationalism. (Johnson, 'Muse' 74)

Reading *The Carnival Trilogy* (1985–90), Johnson interprets Harris as an intensely political author, seeing his constructions of the body as related to a 'body politic' ('Translations' 124). Yet this politics is distinctly non-national, moving towards 'a cross-cultural history of global proportions … beyond the limited frames of a solely national identity' (Johnson, 'Translations' 124, 142). Indeed, it is both larger and smaller scales suggested by Johnson's work, which resonates strongly with the concept of post-space deferral away from national concerns. What exists is on one level a body, on another level an international community, but on no level a nation. However relevant the political analysis, to ignore this perspective in Harris's work is to underestimate the originality of his vision. And whilst Johnson's comments may be pertinent, they exist within a field that is more reluctant to take on Harris's own message in readings of his fiction. Robert Carr, for example, provides a detailed and fascinating reading of *The Guyana Quartet* (1960–63). Yet his tendency towards metaphorical interpretation, seeing the novel as a work of the 'micro-nation' (143), where 'estate=state' and 'coast=nation' (134), denies the more honest reality – that Harris is not deferring his interest but is, rather, not concerned with the nation at all.

For Harris it is not critique that is the intention, but re-visioning of national identity into a fluid, specifically cross-cultural humanity. For this reason, and here I again would take issue with Carr's reading, Harris *does not* promote reform of a nation that, even were this successful, would not transcend its borders to achieve such an aim. Even close association with the Caribbean to encourage regional integration as attempted in the 1950s and 1960s would alone, for Harris, be unsatisfactory. It would build, undoubtedly, what was cast as a 'West Indian nation' (Manley 30), but would reflect neither the diversity of Guyana's population nor its history and unique geography. The entire Guyanese project to put 'their categories in order, their hyphens in place' (B. Williams xiii) is anathema to Harris's ideals.

Harris's reflection on English cultural traditions since his arrival in Britain in the 1950s means that it is also possible to identify how, in terms of Britain, too, Harris may relate to space in such a way as to interrogate national identity. In *Da Silva da Silva's Cultivated Wilderness* (1977) Britain is reduced to London, a heavily circumscribed locale consisting only of Kensington; in *Black Marsden* (1972) it is Scotland, again reduced to the city of Edinburgh. What this absence of the national in favour of the local ultimately reveals is an indubitable paradox. In *Da Silva da Silva's Cultivated Wilderness*, narrow focus on London facilitates an international vision:

> Da Silva painted the lake, he painted the buried rivers that flowed beneath the London streets, he painted a canal in ancient Tenochtitlan on which Montezuma sailed and it was as if they all moved together and were one principle of advancing, complex, shadow or light within the mystery of a tidal body that vanished to reappear again where one least suspected it. (15)

Similarly, in *Black Marsden*, Scotland becomes a space suggesting a 'combination of naive and complex features [that] was true of kings whether in pre-Columbian America or pre-Renaissance Scotland or Europe' (11) and Edinburgh, while mapped by Harris more extensively than any other city, is coterminously globalised and removed from specific socio-historical context:

> Goodrich made his way from the Market Cross towards St. Giles, then past the old Parliament ... . Then along the Royal Mile ... . There were shops with wares and items from many parts of the world ... there remained a strange brooding mixture of presentness and pastness embracing all historical seasons inserted into the place. (35)

In his Edinburgh home, the central character Goodrich proclaims that 'the globe itself seems to be at our fingertips' (46); walking along the city streets, names blur and Goodrich finds himself in a space that seems 'to reach also farther south into the South Americas' (62). In the long dream sequence at the novel's centre, these associations become more profound. Entering a symbolic 'Nameless Town' stripped of its identity, Edinburgh permeates space through 'features which may have been plucked from the loneliest reaches of the Highlands of Scotland like transplanted snow' (72). In the case of both novels, Harris's imagery creates a location with much more diverse, international resonances. Due to its representation, the local in fact leads to an awareness of scale much broader than the supposedly overarching nation-state.

In contrast to his vitality, the hopeless figures Goodrich encounters in *Black Marsden* suggest to him a demoralisation that might stand easily as a metaphor for the failure of national politics, and as acceptance of its hegemonic practices:

It was a depressed feature. Robust as he was he lacked authority. Physical as he was, he seemed devitalized economically, beaten into shape by a kind of perennial regional hammer, the hammer of depression. Solid as he was he seemed depleted of both a will-to-power and a will-to-revolution. (69)

It is in this novel that Harris makes one of his few references to national space, to 'the proverbial nation-state ... to consolidate the proverbial middle class' (81). Here the nation-state is indelibly linked to the conventional – 'the proverbial' – and to the social elite as it is represented in the 'middle class'. Thus a tension emerges in the novel: between the bureaucratic national elite creating a space whose identity has been robbed by colonialism, and the fluid locales managing to survive within this structure, offering new ways of seeing. As the nation is replaced by smaller scales, so these scales give way – perhaps in a manner the cohesion-preoccupied nation never could – to much larger and all-encompassing perspectives. Such representation denies both any reading that would see the urban space act metonymically for the nation-state in any definitive sense, and also the very specificity of the nation as the location of identity-formation and political negotiation.

2. Toni Morrison: The United States

Toni Morrison's relationship to the nation is undoubtedly less clear cut than Harris's transcendent and cross-cultural perspective. Undoubtedly, Morrison's novels engage – through ideas of slavery, racism and black identity – with themes integral to America's general understanding of its own concept of nationality, and, additionally, to ideas of black nationalism. In particular, through her historical novels – *Beloved* (1987), *Jazz* (1992), *Paradise* (1997) and *Love* (2003) – Morrison encourages reappraisal of American history in terms of its exclusions and violences, and deconstruction of the myths of the American nation. Morrison's connection of these national myths with slavery, as a practice that is brought to America by colonialism, creates a negotiation of national space that identifies Morrison at the centre of postcolonial critique.

Yet, like Harris, Morrison does not engage *specifically* with institutional politics, but instead enacts a shift in representation to other scales of reference. Focusing on the personal, Morrison sees national debates in microcosm in the lives of individuals: only in two later novels – through the myth of the founding fathers in *Paradise* and the context of the civil rights movement in *Love* – has she begun to focus more directly on the wider events framing these issues. Yet even with this acknowledged move, Morrison still maintains an approach which means her texts are never simply national allegories. In both *Paradise* and *Love* the political shifts slowly into the background, ultimately overwhelmed by powerful personal stories, and at the same time by significant global contexts. The myth of the founding fathers makes way in *Paradise* for the personal narratives of the women who form the novel's core whilst, similarly, the civil rights context of *Love* becomes overwhelmed by the intense relationships between the central characters and, indeed, the haunting voice of the novel's female narrator. At the same time, the younger generation of men in *Paradise* move beyond local identifications and look towards international models of black identity.[4] And, as for Harris, criticism acknowledges this shift. For example, Katrine Dalsgard's reading of *Paradise* begins by outlining Morrison's representation of American exceptionalism and its relationship to national Puritan mythology, yet ends with a movement away from national frames of reference: where the text 'does not imply that Morrison offers an alternative African American ideal' (237), and where the achievements of its women are seen to be 'independent of African American national aspirations' (245).

To understand Morrison's relationship to the nation, it is first necessary to appreciate the specifics of American nationalism, and its relationship to ideas of absolute space. The United States firmly established itself in national terms immediately after the War of Independence; it defined itself explicitly as a nation in 1789.[5] Thus, as I outlined in the introduction, in strict historical terms – though it is for other reasons problematic – the United States may be viewed as the first of the new postcolonial nations, formed in response to independence from colonial power. On many levels, it can be argued, the United States challenges the understanding of nations as homogeneous. Its motto of *E Pluribus Unum*, and its basis in migration, seems to offer support for cross-culturality, though only by disregarding the issue of the Native American population. Yet as Anderson points out, differences between North and South in the independent United States severely question its existence as a nation at all (64). The South's attempt to secede, and the indubitable loss of their cultural preferences – however distasteful – as a result of civil war defeat suggests distinct divisions and the obscuring of particular cultural beliefs post-1865. In these terms, the postcolonial tensions of the United States appear little different from their developing world successors.

Moreover, against its motto, the United States has from its very beginning expressed the desire for difference to be subsumed by 'a more homogeneous "national character"' (Wilson 4). As early as George Washington, freedom was conditional on the need of Americans to 'sacrifice their individual advantages to the interests of the Community' (Washington, 'Circular' 118), decided by the dominant social group. Difference was gradually eroded:

> The name of AMERICAN, which belongs to you, in your national capacity, must always exalt the just pride of Patriotism, more than any appellation derived from local discriminations. With slight shades of difference, you have the same Religion, Manners, Habits and political Principles. You have in a common cause fought and triumphed together. The independence and liberty you possess are the work of joint councils, and joint efforts; of common dangers, sufferings and successes.' (Washington, 'Farewell' 141)

---

[4]   For an insightful reading of global contexts in *Paradise* see Flint.

[5]   See Anderson 69n.

Such a statement places the popular representation of the United States under erasure. There is little room for diversity in such 'slight shades of difference'.

Equally, supporting the connections between colonialism and postcolonial nationalism, the independent United States adopted almost entirely the colonial boundary without question. Regardless of its claim for self-determination in 1776, and its later expansion, the United States would fight a civil war based initially on a desire to protect the territorial boundary as an absolute, the North fighting against anything that 'would destroy the Union' (McPherson vii). It seems of little concern that this territory was only an absolute because of colonialism, and little attention appears to have been given to the possibility that true independence might mean not maintaining boundaries, but dissolving or redefining them.

What is of greatest significance, however, is that as well as maintaining colonial boundaries, the independent United States maintained colonial practice. This is precisely what is referred to by Powell as the United States's '*postcolonial colonialism*' (351), but also is evident in critiques of contemporary racist politics in the United States such as the one offered by Gilroy's *Between Camps*. With particular relevance for Morrison's fiction, slavery can be read as a postcolonial continuation of colonial practices, leading to divisive attitudes on race perpetuated into the present. For the slave population, independence from Britain held little worth because the new nation truly was simply the colony in alternative form. Freedom for slaves was not considered necessary for nationhood; after revolution the Union was an 'absolute' due to 'seemingly irreversible bonds of national unity' (Wilson 3). Only in the 1840s did the image of 'a nation founded in freedom about to be irretrievably lost to the evil of slavery' (Wilson 16) develop. Yet even after 1865, segregation undermined this national doctrine; how could the United States be a nation based on freedom and equality when free movement was denied, and equality did not exist?

As a result of this situation, many African-Americans felt increasingly divorced from the nation-state. They were increasingly frustrated with the fact that segregation still denied them equal status. It is this frustration that ultimately took its form in the rise of black nationalism, the suggestion that while African-Americans might belong to a nation, that nation was not the United States but was instead an Africa that could be developed into a 'great independent nation or empire' (Fredrickson 153). Indeed as early as 1919 Marcus Garvey argued 'that blacks had no future of equality or self-determination in a strictly American context' (Fredrickson 155), looking immediately for the deconstruction of absolute national borders in the concept of 'a freedom that has no boundary, no limit' (Garvey, 'Speech' 285). W.E.B. Du Bois suggested in 1947 that by staying in the United States, African-Americans were 'a nation within a nation' (Fredrickson 287).[6]

It is this history which suggests the problems for Morrison when engaging with national issues. Indeed, we may see the absence of the nation in her novels as a reflection of the absence of black figures in the official history of the construction

---

[6]   This comment has also been made in relation to Native Americans: see Stuart 3.

of that nation, a 'national mind' that in its early stages of nation building was preoccupied with 'the architecture of a *new white man*' (Morrison, 'Black Matter(s)' 312). Drawing on the use of naming in a way that echoes Harris's concerns, Morrison, in her nonfiction, seems to express this sense of exclusion explicitly:

> For in this part of the twentieth-century, the word American contains its profound association with race ... . American means white, and Africanistic people struggle to make the terms applicable to themselves with ethnicity and hyphens ... . The American nation negotiated both its disdain and its envy in the same way Dunbar did: through a self-reflexive contemplation of fabricated, mythological Africanism. ('Black Matter(s)' 318)[7]

African-Americans are not what the official, institutional American nation-state is, but the Other against which it is defined. They are the black for its white, the slavery for its freedom, where the concept of 'the rights of man' became 'inevitably yoked to Africanism ... . Nothing highlighted freedom – if it did not in fact create it – like slavery' (Morrison, *Playing* 38), part of a whole host of structuralist oppositions based on stereotype and assumption.

In terms of Morrison's fiction, this relationship has two principle effects. Firstly it means that, on one level, Morrison does not concern herself with the American nation, but is interested instead in an African-American community. This community, itself, is at times seen instead in national terms, resonating with the ideology of black nationalism. Secondly, as a result of this, Morrison paradoxically also does engage with the American nation, by pointing to its exclusions, and the inability of African-Americans to challenge a nation built on institutional racism. Her silence on the nation, and the alternatives she proffers, must in themselves be seen as a comment on that which goes unspoken – on the overwritten black presence at the centre of American national identity. It is through focusing on personal, individual interactions that Morrison highlights how, on an everyday, unexceptional level, African-Americans are engaged in the construction of identities that shape the American nation:

> It [the black presence] is there in every moment of the nation's mightiest struggles. The presence of black people not only lies behind the framing of the Constitution, it is also in the battle over enfranchising unpropertied citizens, women, and the illiterate. In the construction of a free and public school system, in the balancing of representation in legislative bodies, in jurisprudence and the legal definitions of justice. In theological discourse, in the memoranda of banking houses, in the concept of Manifest Destiny and the narrative that accompanies the initiation of every immigrant into the community of American citizenship. ('Black Matter(s)' 322)

---

[7] This opinion foreshadows that later expressed in *Playing in the Dark* (1992).

Tracking the importance of black communities means that Morrison's narratives do not take Harris's cross-cultural direction. Instead, in narratives such as *Jazz* and *Paradise*, black nationalism emerges as a possible alternative national identity. Interestingly, however, such projects themselves seem to be as flawed as the American nationalist endeavour. As the nationalist follows the colonial, and is flawed because of this, so black nationalism is represented by Morrison as following the nationalist (and therefore, by a chain of association, the colonial, too) and is subject to the same absolutes and exclusions. The microcosms of black nationalism presented in the Harlem of *Jazz* or the Ruby of *Paradise* are riddled with the same inequalities that preoccupy the American, colonialism-influenced model, replicating the class divisions and narrow prejudices of American society. No longer fighting white prejudice, the exclusive black community is represented as damaged by the hierarchies it transplants from its oppressors.[8]

Denied access to national discourses and damaged by their own, Morrison's characters frame identity in inclusive terms: they form their sense of self not in relation to the American nation, or a class-ridden black nationalism, but rather in relation to their own communities, to a 'neighbourhood' ('Unspeakable' 389). As a reaction to the pervasive nature of national ideology, authority is challenged not through public protest, but at the level of the personal. The political agency of African-Americans is focused on personal lives, surviving even when not institutionally recognised, and without the dangers of mimicking the American national model. This, for example, is the role of the convent in *Paradise* – functioning as a feminist politicised community for the women excluded from Ruby – or the hotel in *Love*, which offers respite from the racist exclusions of the outside world, and, in doing so, is a statement against it. Indeed, Morrison sees no distinction between these two types of writing, following political issues 'within very deep personal lives', choosing 'response to the world' instead of 'political' to define her work.[9] Morrison reflects national issues in all their forms, but her most powerful speculation is on the similarities between these nationalisms: whether US nationalism or black nationalism. The natural conclusion of such representation is the need to ultimately reject the colonialist's terms in favour of a different, less baggage-laden, political scale.

3. Salman Rushdie: India, Pakistan and Britain

I conclude, however, with Rushdie, because what is offered by his writing is a relationship with the nation at its most complex. As Brennan's *Salman Rushdie and the Third World* (1989) indicates – reading *Midnight's Children* (1981), *Shame* (1983) and *The Satanic Verses* (1988) as a triptych of national fictions with each novel devoted 'to a single national creation' (119) – Rushdie's fiction has been

---

[8] For a reading of *Paradise* which engages with these concepts see Michael, in particular p. 151.

[9] Answers given to audience questions, University of East Anglia, 6 Dec. 2003.

strongly connected to readings of the nation-state. These readings add much to our understanding of Rushdie's fiction. Yet, on another level, I would suggest, they risk simplifying his relationship to and, indeed, over-identifying his fiction with, this location. While in *Shame* and *Midnight's Children* clear metaphors exist which connect personal lives to national events, Rushdie himself warns against 'the writer who sets himself or herself up as the voice of a nation' ('Notes on Writing' 66), and against allegorical readings of his novels.[10]

Brennan's interpretation persists because of its intellectual rigour and persuasive argument; he makes a convincing case for Rushdie's criticism of nations, where '"India" can act as abominably as the British did' (27), and for the presence of a multiplicitous postcolonial identity with 'a hierarchical structure of tongues, customs and complexions' (40). Reading *Shame* and *The Satanic Verses* he argues credibly for the former's 'mockery of national fiction' (134) and critique of Pakistani state absolutism, and for the latter's exposure of the 'the repressive apparatus of the British state' (160) to form a 'more oppositional' (147) text. Yet Brennan's work is also riddled with contradictions. He argues that the nation is what 'the Third-World artist is very often either consciously building or suffering the lack of' (4): there is no suggestion that it might be the nation that the 'Third-World artist' is suffering *from*. Despite following Anderson in viewing nations as 'imaginary constructs' (8), the nation is nevertheless presented as a unifying project that provides a 'uniformity and specificity' (25). This representation carries worrying connotations, seeming to mimic colonial desires for order and control. Yet most significantly, Brennan's hint at the *absence of the nation* in Rushdie's novels – relating more closely to the strategies of Morrison and Harris that I have identified – desperately needs further explication. Discussing *Midnight's Children* Brennan notes that 'the story of Indian nationalism is erased from the book that documents its sad outcome, and the most dramatic illustration of Rushdie's argument is an absence' (84). In focusing on the nation so specifically, Brennan has little space to look at what Rushdie is diverting our attention towards *instead* of the national space.

It is significant in discussion of Rushdie that the failure of colonial boundaries to accurately represent the needs of communities is nowhere more evident than in the partition of India. Lord Mountbatten's involvement in drawing up these boundaries meant the British government was heavily implicated in the partition disaster, yet the borders of the Indian nation and the British role in their construction are also problematic in other ways. India typifies many of the general arguments about the fate of postcolonial nations. On independence, India was immediately established as a nation, yet to secure its future it was driven to create precisely the illusion of naturalness and timelessness indicated in those theories which stress the nation's imagined status. As Sudipta Kaviraj notes, India 'had to create a sanctioned, official history of itself' (4), overwriting a diverse population with one based on homogeneity. This took the form of a process of 'immemorialism' (Kaviraj 8),

---

[10]   See 'Interview with John Haffenden' 40–41, 'Interview with John Banville' 154.

encapsulating national myth making. What resulted was an absolute. In contrast to the 'fuzzy' (Kaviraj 20) communities of the past, the nation was represented as fixed and defined.

In the desire for a 'conventional, European-style nation' (Nandy, *Creating* 57), this approach to nation-building can be seen to build on models passing directly over from colonial rule. Here a connection between Noyes's colonial space and the nation cannot be clearer. India is hybrid, what Partha Chatterjee calls 'confederal' space (*Nation* 113), overwritten by homogeneous nationalist discourse. What results are fixed boundaries and an 'enumerated' (Kaviraj 26) population connected to 'a world securely distributed into tables' (Kaviraj 30), echoing the colonial rule of the nation that is described as 'mapping, tabulating and classifying ... that by an Act of Parliament in 1899 converted "India" from the name of a cultural region into a precise, pink territory' (Khilnani 155). Despite attempts to alter and modernise, the Indian constitution inherited colonial governmental practice and administrative structure. A new group of middle class elites aimed to replace colonial rule with their own, following British constructions of Indian history and practices of ordering and classifying the population, 'capable of ordering into a single hierarchy all its subjects' (Cohn 180).

Such a process was not without cultural or physical loss. For Ashis Nandy, those involved in the encouragement of Indian nationalist feeling were convinced 'the Indians had to be pummelled into a single nation through the ideology of Hindutva' (*Creating* 60). Here the construction of an official history takes on ominous undertones, the construction of the Muslim as an Other – 'the foreign ruler and aggressor' (Chatterjee 77) – from which the Indian identity could be formed in opposition. Significant in terms of Rushdie's postcolonial fiction, however, is the fact that only in the 1970s when his writing first emerges does India become centralised and caught up in communalism, exacerbated in the 1980s and beyond by the rise of the BJP which has been interpreted as 'committed to a negative programme, designed to efface all the signs of non-Hinduness' (Khilnani 189). For Satish Deshpande, this is a monumental transformation, from the potentially inclusive Hindutva, and Nehru's economic nation that 'could identify as "other" only the shirker' (185), to Hindutva's rearticulation post-Nehru as an exclusive definition based on 'those who possess ... and those who don't' (180).[11]

It is the rise of this ideology that Rushdie objects to in *Midnight's Children*. There is a significant difference between such a rejection of the nation and the deconstruction of states themselves. What the narrative rejects is an absolute, colonial-influenced nationalism: it does not reject India as a state. The India that Rushdie nostalgically creates, imagines, and maintains is not one in which India is a 'nation' if we take that to mean a unified, cohesive and homogenous space. Certainly what is frequently defined as 'nationalism' was at the centre of India's claim to independence. Yet the element of this that Rushdie positively engages with, an India that for him 'means plurality' ('Interview with David Brooks' 77),

---

[11]   For the complex effects of nationalism in India see Chakrabarty, 'Introduction'.

would in fact be better termed 'statism' rather than 'nationalism'. 'Statism' would be read as Gandhi's and Nehru's campaigns for a secular India. It would be based on the former's 'faith in unity' (qtd. in Read and Fisher 271), resulting in the desire to form a nation defined by its hybridity – '"one nation before the advent of Islam, it must remain in spite of the change of faith of a very large body of her children"' (Gandhi, qtd. in Read and Fisher 350) – and the latter's desire for a history that charted 'a space of ceaseless cultural mixing' (Khilnani 169). In this diversity, it would be in direct opposition to the nationalist project to affirm a singular cultural history. This issue of terminology is made more complex by Rushdie's own use of 'nation'. For when Rushdie talks of India as a nation, the properties he imbues that 'nation' with in fact have more in common with the attributes of a political state; his distinction is between what he sees as the true Indian nation of diversity, and its current homogeneous form. Hence in his discussion on national literature:

> For many of us it meant 'versus'. South African writers – Gordimer, Coetzee – in those days of apartheid set themselves up against the official definition of the nation. Rescuing, perhaps, the true nation from those who held it captive. ('Notes on Writing' 65)

While there is a great difference between South Africa and postcolonial India, it is clear here that Rushdie's idea of a 'true nation' is a national consciousness in opposition to social division and the politics of difference. Such a 'true nation' has a unity based on tolerance of multiplicity: it would be better termed a state than retaining associations with a nationalist discourse it is in such opposition to.[12]

In such terms what is missing from *Midnight's Children* is not the historical rise of nationalism, as Brennan suggests, but statism: missing because Rushdie wants to separate the positive idea of a diverse secular state from the homogenising demands of nationalism, which Rushdie critiques in *Midnight's Children* as based on false mythology and fabricated history. In his nonfiction, Rushdie has been quick to express his dislike for nationalism in this form. He has openly expressed disappointment that India's independence 'has not been the promised golden age of freedom' ('India's Fiftieth' 175), and concern about the rise of communalism as 'the most dangerous thing happening in the country' ('Angels' 84). He also notes the colonial role in this nationalist failure, seeing Muslim secession as unnecessary. Vocal about support for its alternative, what Nandy calls 'society's traditional ability to live with cultural ambiguities and to use them to build psychological and even metaphysical defences against cultural invasions' (*Intimate* 107), Rushdie sees in India the creation of 'the most innovative national philosophy' ('India's Fiftieth' 179).

Examining Rushdie's representation of Pakistan, the distinct nature of his critique of the nation as a nationalist construct becomes clearer. Historically, here

---

[12]   For this representation of the Indian nation state as a consciously hybrid and diverse project, in contrast to its recent nationalist history, see Srirupa Roy.

the identity of one nation was literally overlaid with another as, in the making of maps, 'Indian notes would remain in use, but were overprinted with the words "Government of Pakistan"' (Read and Fisher 471). It is, for some, the epitome of an absolute, overly determined space, as Kedourie's reading emphasises:

> So we see all the problems, fears, and aspirations of the Indian Muslims … transmuted and simplified into a nationalist ideology which requires that Indian Muslims shall be called Paks, that Paks shall be called a nation, that the Pak nation shall be considered a nation-state, and that this nation-state shall be deemed to have lived from of old in a territory known as Pakistan. Such are the triumphs of doctrine. (*Nationalism in Asia* 30–31)

Responding to this, Rushdie sees a homogenising, religious state, a space he describes as one in which 'democratic institutions … have never been permitted to take root' complete with elites that 'loot the nation's wealth' and 'draconian versions of Sharia law' ('Pakistan' 321). Pakistan is presented in *Shame*, therefore, in the context of this vision: individuals 'hung upside-down by the ankles and beaten' (28). What Rushdie critiques here is explicitly an exclusive national space, rather than a political state.

At the centre of *Shame* is the magical deferral of Pakistan into an unnamed locale, the location of a fable. Much more might be indicated by Rushdie's magical deferral in this novel than Brennan identifies. For Rushdie's choice of form for his national critique makes a point that is of great relevance to the postcolonial novelist's concept of the nation as a site of political negotiation. While fantastical re-creation is subversive, deferral in fact signifies the limits on actual campaigns against the nation. Rushdie feels the need to point out that such an absolute space cannot be challenged directly: it represents a 'closure of possibilities' in contrast to the 'multiple possibilities' ('Interview with John Haffenden' 49) of India. Towns must simply be referred to by their initials, and the novel must declare that 'the country in this story is not Pakistan' (29). Of course, while what all this really does is draw the reader's attention to the fact that it *is* Pakistan, it also suggests something else. For while according to *Shame* the greatest thing about seceded nations such as Bangladesh is their 'hopefulness' (86), recourse to fantasy indicates Rushdie's sense of *hopelessness* that the nation cannot be reformed, *cannot be in any sense other than the fictitious* drawn away from an totalitarian path: that in terms of critiquing Pakistan the only entrance remaining is the backdoor of magic; that realism is impossible. The subversion gets through, but there will be no discussion of the political real-world to follow that is not conducted in secret. The horrors can only be stated if they are phrased in such a way that they politically counter nothing: the things that the author 'might have to put in' (69) a realist novel but can be listed here only because their fantastical construction provides the administration with a defence that they are 'not really describing Pakistan'. Ahmad recognises this when he notes Rushdie is incapable of imagining 'a real possibility of regenerative projects on the part of the people' (149).

In this sense, *Shame* must not only be read as a critique of the nation-state, but also as the significant beginnings of the postcolonial author's realisation of the limits of resisting that nation. Rushdie's Pakistan is a perfect manifestation of the bleakness of Mbembe's postcolony. The novel is concerned, unlike *Midnight's Children*, not with recounting the vast history of colonialism and its consequences, but only with what must be seen as an irrevocable end to the nationalist dream. Thus what Andrew Teverson righty says in his countering of Ahmad's critique of the novel – that Sufiya Zinobia's journey is irrelevant because the novel is 'not about those processes of development but the tragic end point – or end-game – that results from the failure of these processes' (143) – is equally true of the novel as a whole. The mirror of Pakistan's Zia and Bhutto in Harappa and Hyder, with its violent machinations and political intrigues, reflects Mbembe's 'Necropolitics' (2003), in which the biopolitics of control of the body to secure state power has been elevated to control through death. Equally, the revenge of Sufiya Zinobia, trapped in madness, embodies the stifled expressions of a nation unable to effectively counter national authority, a rebellion not on the level of state revolution, but at the level of the corporeal – creating a Beast that is the 'most terrible uprising' (143). Zinobia is 'barbarism grow[n] in cultured soil ... savagery ... concealed beneath decency's well-pressed shirt' (200). It is thus not despite but rather because of its fantastical exaggerations that Rushdie's novel so effectively engages with the postcolony. It effectively captures Mbembe's very real world of grotesque bodies, as we find 'phantoms ... images connecting shame and violence' in countries 'entirely unghostly' (117). As Harappa/Zia is the official representation of such power – 'subjugation of life to the power of death' (Mbembe, 'Necropolitics', 39) – so Zinobia represents the movement of this influence out into society as a degrading and ultimately all-pervasive character. The nation can be nothing but a mirror of the order of colonialism – it offers nothing but violence and corrupt military rule – only a fairy tale will topple these dictators (257) and, as Teverson rightly notes, 'there can be only destruction, and despair' (144). Of course, this bleakness is a matter of timing: written when Zia was still in power and martial law still in place, from this perspective the novel cannot look outside of its own timeline to the potential for a more positive national space. Yet, at the same time, it also marks a wider awareness. If a solution is to be found that releases the people from a stifling past-laden existence, then it must be found not through nationalism, but in other spheres. It is a realisation that suggests the need to look for other spaces in which resistance might be more effectively undertaken.

Continuing this argument, the 'limitations of resistance' (161) Brennan points to in *The Satanic Verses*, I would suggest, are limitations at the level of nation-state politics. Thus not just colony and postcolony, but also post-imperial space demands alternatives to national politics. Brennan begins this project when he notes that 'simple slogans of anger directed against the British state give away too much' (162), yet does not follow the assertion comprehensively through to its logical conclusion. Arguing we are continually directed towards 'current events' (85) against the characters' lives, Brennan oversimplifies the relationship between a structuralist nation – the public – and the individual lives – the personal – that Rushdie presents. Rushdie's relationship to Britain is informed by a larger context than Brennan allows, formed by the specifics of late twentieth-century British race relations and filled with an appropriate darkness, violence, and sense of depression.

It is through British culture as it is represented by the work of theorists such as Gilroy that *The Satanic Verses* must be read. For Gilroy, English nationalism is made through the 'biological and cultural' (*There Ain't No Black* 45). Whilst British territory may demographically be heterogeneous, it will never admit the Diaspora into the 'nation'. This is because the very construction of this nation rests on a need to deny its heterogeneity, a 'cultural insiderism' (*Black Atlantic* 3) that is precisely the nation's creation of a myth of historical unity. It is this same reality that Rushdie presents in *The Satanic Verses*, illuminated by his essay 'The New Empire in Britain' in which 'divide-and-rule' (138) is transferred from the colonies to the home nation. In such a space, what matters is not the diverse cultural reality, but the overwriting of this multiplicity that the victim of nationalism must face at the hands of common representation and ideology.

Reading the novel in such terms prompts me to question other, more celebratory, interpretations. This is the case even when such readings may be immensely attractive to the theory underlying this discussion. For example, in relation to the theory of post-space, a reading of *The Satanic Verses* such as Baucom's, which finds in the text the potential for positive disorder – reading the novel's riots as a space of 'pleasure' (192) and 'redemption' (193) that creates a 'national community of belonging' (195) – is extremely alluring. It strikes at the heart of the possibility of chaotic disorder to form the basis of liberation upon which post-space rests. Yet to accept such arguments is also to occlude the fact that what actually exists is not a national community, but a local, urban community that Baucom identifies with national issues in line with his allegorical readings, in much the same way as Carr metaphorically reads Harris's *Guyana Quartet*, but which may in fact be more usefully considered in local terms. Baucom's argument that because events are read as local 'does not mean that they were not also English events' (196) betrays his desire – and also reflects the desires of others – to adapt Rushdie's text to a particular reading. Whilst there is nothing wrong with doing so – indeed, this is the work of much literary criticism – it does fuel a particular association that continues the privileging of the nation as a site of political action and resistance.

This is evident by the fact that here Baucom is not alone. Simon Gikandi, too, follows Brennan in casting *The Satanic Verses* as a novel concerned with nationality. Whilst, again, this produces insightful reflections on the relationship between Rushdie's writing and the construction of a postcolonial British subject, it equally obscures certain thrusts in the narrative. Gikandi's argument that the novel marks a 'desire to call all totalized explanatory systems into question' (206) fails to acknowledge the problematic of such relativity, the fact that the text in fact moves far closer in its conclusions to Gilroy's more pessimistic position. Gikandi sees the inability to shake off nationalism in such texts as a 'problem' (207), indicating how 'even when we reject the nationalist myth of return, we are – unconsciously, perhaps – restaging it' (200). In his reading, Gikandi sees the ending of the novel as the most damning section in this regard, dismissing it in parentheses by stating that 'the whole momentum of the novel, *at least until its closure*, is toward the transcendence of such categories' (emphasis added, 210).[13] Yet such argument, even if we agree with it, can equally be reconfigured as Rushdie's self-aware acknowledgment of the problems involved in attempting to overturn such old and established categories. The ending *is* a failure – but not a failure of the novelist, rather of the characters: an intentional failure that, in line with Gilroy's theory, illustrates the monolithic power of national ideology, which cannot be dismissed with a magical-realist flourish. In its core, the novel does exactly what Gikandi and Brennan suggest it does. Indeed, it disrupts the nation in ways beyond their comments.[14] Yet in the ending their readings choose to obscure, the novel resonates with Gilroy's awareness of the limits of subversion in the middle of a reborn nationalist rhetoric.

In these novels, therefore, the nation clearly is on at least one level the subject of discussion, though not in the way that the vast majority of current criticisms suggest. Rather than simply destabilising the nation, Rushdie's novels in fact point more readily to the problems of this endeavour: his engagement with national issues represents an 'ideological ambivalence' and 'refusal to propagate myths of renewal' (P. Chowdhury, 1, 158) that deeply calls into question the future of the nation space. When nationalism has come to represent immigrants as 'an illegitimate intrusion into a vision of authentic British national life that, prior to their arrival, was as stable and as peaceful as it was ethnically undifferentiated' (Gilroy, *Black Atlantic* 7), and has been on numerous occasions challenged to no effect, there may be a multi-cultural society but – without unity – no nation. This applies whether the context be the postcolonial state (India), the postcolony (Pakistan) or the post-imperial (Britain). For Rushdie postmodern chaos cannot raze such walls; the challenges to the nation in *Midnight's Children*, *The Satanic Verses* and *The Moor's Last Sigh* (1995) all end in the victory of official forces; success on a national scale can be achieved in *Shame* only by recourse to escapism, an avenger who disappears to become only 'the collective fantasy of a stifled people' (263). As for Morrison, this awareness of national limitations has taken Rushdie's fiction,

---

[13]   A similar criticism might be made of Homi Bhabha's interpretations, which see Rushdie as aiming to 're-define the boundaries of the western nation' ('DissemiNation' 317), yet neglect to reflect upon the limited success of this endeavour, failing once again to engage with the novel's problematic conclusion.

[14]   For example, it is strange that Rushdie's corruption of language in the novel, while commented upon by Bhabha, is left separate from focus on national critique by these other critics: it is in the hybrid, polyglot English spoken by his central characters, suggesting the possibility of a nationwide deconstruction of an English protected by a 'disciplinary regime' (Baucom 28), that Rushdie comes closest to a national post-space. Baucom is among those who, despite this comment, virtually ignore Rushdie's use of language.

too, in different directions. Rushdie's novels after *The Moor's Last Sigh* have as a rule become increasingly disassociated from national themes. The territory is much less significant in *The Ground Beneath Her Feet* (1999) and *Fury* (2001), although in a recent novel, *Shalimar the Clown* (2005), Rushdie does return to the theme of the nation in his exploration of Kashmir. It seems no coincidence that it is in these later two novels that diverge from the nation that Rushdie provides more optimistic endings, whereas the ending of *Shalimar the Clown* returns to the depressive, hopeless conclusion of *The Moor's Last Sigh*, with a violent revenge reminiscent of *Shame*. Part of the project of this book is to trace the beginnings of this movement in those texts which appear to be about national issues and to suggest that, rather than these later novels (*Shalimar the Clown* excepted) marking a stark departure, they in fact realise the movement away from the national scale which is the unrealisable aim of Rushdie's earlier fiction. Rushdie's own comment that 'in the best writing, however, a map of the nation will also turn out to be a map of the world' ('Notes on Writing' 66) is suggestive of such readings. It is quite the reverse of Brennan's reading: a nation as metaphor for human events, rather than human events as metaphor for the nation.

The fact that, within three diverse geographies, the nation can be seen to have been problematised, and postcolonial authors have reacted to this, can be seen as indicative of a wider postcolonial response. For a large number of novels, Mbembe's postcolony is starkly evident in violent, corrupt and hierarchical societies which have moved little from the colonial model. In *The God of Small Things*, Roy exhibits anger at the neglect of intimate experience, the fact that 'personal despair could never be desperate enough. That something happened when personal turmoil dropped by at the wayside shrine of the vast, violent, circling, driving, ridiculous, insane, unfeasible, public turmoil of a nation' (19). In a shift in attention to 'small things', Roy presents us not with idealism, but with a real world strategy. In her expression that the 'personal is political', she revises the notion of political engagement and 'refuses to fall into the cliché of representing the nation as a duty of the postcolonial author' (Alexandru 165, 175). Osella and Osella, for example, in their study *Social Mobility in Kerala* (2000), note the ways in which change has frequently been developed at the level of 'everyday reality' in which, in contemporary Kerala, caste distinctions may be 'challenged, reversed, discarded or openly toyed with' (221). They identify this as a 'micro-politics', the beginnings of which may be registered in the tentative, but powerful, first steps of Roy's characters in asserting the importance of their personal lives. This is echoed by Vikram Chandra's *Red Earth and Pouring Rain* (1995), in which the spatial ordering – 'the planting of certain iron rods in the ground' (469) – is challenged ultimately not by wars (which invariably fail) but rather by magical bodies, and the feeding of these bodies with magical foodstuffs, affirming cultural hybridity against the colonial process of classification.

Equally, for Michael Ondaatje interrogation of the nation is a prominent theme. In *Anil's Ghost* (2000), telling the story of the Sri Lankan Civil War, the potential of national markers is rejected, undermined by the fact that '*The National Atlas of*

Sri Lanka has seventy-three versions of the island' (39), foregrounding the failings of conventional geography. Instead the Sri Lankan consciousness is literally embodied: in the sculpture of a head of one of its Civil War victims, formed from the damaged stone of a ravaged landscape. This is part of a wider strategy in the novel moving away from national scales towards regional geographies and personal sites, what David Farrier usefully refers to in his reading of the novel as a '*renewed intimacy with the local*' (83). Thus, according to Chelva Kanaganayakam, although the novel is political and engaged with Sri Lankan national politics, it nevertheless offers 'a carefully articulate ambivalence about its project' (5) that denies a 'unified reading of the nation' (19) in favour of other spatial scales. Ondaatje had already privileged such a theme earlier in his career: in *Running in the Family* the boundaries of colonial Ceylon are questioned by the artificial nature of mapping: the narrator's brother has 'false maps ... translations ... mythic shapes' (63). Against these abstractions, it is only in a physical journey to explore the personal spaces of his own Ceylon family that the narrator comes to know his past. Such a journey challenges the maps, calling into question the nation as a cohesive entity:

> Ceylon falls on a map and its outline is the shape of a tear. After the spaces of India and Canada it is so small. A miniature. Drive ten miles and you are in a landscape so different that by rights it should belong to another country. (147)

Most recently, a similar approach to Ondaatje's has been taken by Chimamanda Ngozi Adichie, whose novel *Half of a Yellow Sun* (2006) follows Ondaatje in illuminating the failure of nationalist discourse in the wake of violent internal tensions. Telling the story of the Biafran War from the perspectives of soldier, female indigene, and foreign sympathiser, Adichie offers a fictionalised version of the accounts of failed colonial map-making in Nigeria privileged by Emerson and Mbembe in particular, complete with Mbembe's 'categories of people' and their differing fates: refugee camp, battlefield, survivor or victim, civilian or combatant ('Necropolitics' 34). In the history written by Ugwu, houseboy turned soldier, not only are these definitions complicated, but the present conflict is located in a history of colonial ordering, the desire of the British to 'preserve Nigeria as it was' on independence, regardless of ethnic identities (155), encouraging the anti-Igbo sentiment that fuels the tensions decades after independence (166). Nigeria's leadership, we are told, is 'too interested in aping the British' (205). Adichie's novel blurs the easy distinctions between postcolony and neocolony – a nation in which independence has lead to colonial mimicry, but at the same time is reinforced by continued colonial influence, which is itself part of larger racialised power structures. Thus Ugwu writes:

> about the world that remained silent while Biafrans died. He argues that Britain inspired this silence. The arms and advice that Britain gave Nigeria shaped other countries. In the United States, Biafra was 'under Britain's sphere of interest'.

In Canada, the Prime Minister quipped 'Where is Biafra?' The Soviet Union sent
technicians and planes to Nigeria, thrilled at the chance to influence Africa without
offending America or Britain. And from their white-supremacist positions, South
Africa and Rhodesia gloated. (258)

Unlike the earlier pro-Biafran position of Achebe, Adichie however refuses
to see the establishment of a new homogeneous nation as the answer: African
nationalism itself is no solution to the problems of colonial absolutes. Whilst
Biafra's patriarchs, such as Kainene's husband Odenigbo, continue their mission,
its women and young people challenge its logic:

'The white man brought racism into the world. He used it as a basis of conquest.
It is always easier to conquer a more humane people.' 'So when we conquer the
Nigerians will we be less humane?' Kainene asked. (402)

Adichie reflects the difficulty of reversing the postcolony's repetition of
colonial forms; to institute fluidity is neither easy nor straightforward. The battle
for Biafran independence represents how such new states may equally succumb
to oppressive practices, 'a new form of organizing power resting on control of the
principal means of coercion (armed force, means of intimidation, imprisonment,
expropriation, killing) ... emerging in the framework of territories that are no
longer fully states' (Mbembe, *Postcolony* 92). In the new Biafra, ethnic tensions
continue to prevent harmony; Ugwu, raping a young woman, is not exempt from
the crimes which are associated with his 'enemies'. As for Rushdie, the nation
itself is a false prophet (embodied in the yellow sun of the Biafran flag that gives
the novel its title) – an illusion to be followed with disastrous results. Economic
turmoil, rape, murder, corruption: all accompany the official waging of war, with
violence that pervades society. Adichie's novel thus captures Mbembe's assertion
of the belief that war is the most decisive manifestation of 'absolute, sovereign
power' ('Sovereignty' 148): a 'putting to death' which is the ultimate expression of
control over the individual. The fusion of capitalism and neo-colonialism creates a
'new geography of conflict' with the result of 'violent attempts to immobilize and
spatially fix entire categories of population, notably in the interests of waging war'
('Sovereignty' 150). The control of the individual body is the means by which
the space of the territory itself is ordered: a 'new form of governmentality, based
on the proliferation of extreme situations and predatory practices, attacks bodies
and lives only in order the better to control the flow of resources, objects, and
commodities released by the process of economic informalization' ('Sovereignty'
151). This, like *Shame*, is a state of 'necropolitics' – embodied in war as the
ultimate expression of a political state in which death is the means by which power
is secured, and the nation ultimately defined (Mbembe, 'Necropolitics' 12). The
control of populations which Mbembe sees as essential to war ('Necropolitics'
14) is highlighted by the ethnic cleansing Adichie recounts. Her characters live
Mbembe's Africa: trapped in a territory created by and dominated by the British,

riven by disease and death, and subject to not just death but also rape, forced removal, and disappearance.

A new hybridity based on state, not nation, Adichie suggests, can be the only answer. Thus Ugwu, who will eventually become the voice of his people, finds his inspiration not in the political discourses surrounding him, but rather in the writings of Frederick Douglass (396), a cross-cultural transference from slave back to the African homeland. This acceptance of change and celebration of fusion is embodied in the lives of the characters themselves, with their interracial relationships, and refusal to be defined by ethnicity. Whilst war rages around them, these individuals find solace and solidarity in the maintenance of their personal spaces – homes and bodies in particular – which are frequently invaded by the ravages of conflict. Kainene and her sister Olanna walk together, their steps 'in harmony' (390). And, after Kainene's disappearance, it is this connection which remains, encapsulated in Olanna's final words of the novel. Rather than in national belonging, the personal is ultimately where meaning resides.

Presenting, in Roy's words, a history that 'would lurk for ever in ordinary things' (55), small spaces are for many postcolonial authors the important beginnings of communal resistance, a coming together that can only begin in the experiences of individuals. As authors undertake essential movements away from national scales directly related to specific geographical contexts, an alternative for politics located at other spatial scales develops. In the chapters that follow, discussion will illuminate how the productive chaos of post-space can be identified at these other spatial scales. Even when order ultimately wins on the large scale, personal subversions may act to subtly undermine absolutes at more easily accessible levels, so that regardless of oppressive national discourse, actions at more intimate levels affirm the possibility of agency. This is reflected in Jean-François Lyotard's belief that 'no one, not even the least privileged among us, is ever entirely powerless over the messages that traverse and position him' (15). Focused against pervasive systems of inequality ingrained in social attitudes, the strategies postcolonial authors undertake are located not only against the state, but also at these more basic communal levels. Such spaces may be more open to re-visioning and transformations as 'the spaces between nations … are not yet spaces of belonging … but are in the process of being created from the myriad Diasporas and migrations' (Westwood and Phizacklea 40). It is at these alternative scales that change seems more often possible, an initial movement that precedes reform in the same way that Kaviraj highlights the movements preceding independence.

Chapter 2
The Fulcrum of Instability:
Postcolonial Journeys

So: a moment, but, I believe, a crucial and revealing one, because it was neither a beginning nor an end, but a middle, a time that felt close to the fulcrum of history, a time when all things, all the possible futures, were still (just) in the balance.

(Rushdie, *Jaguar* 13)

In the previous chapter, I reviewed the central place of the nation in commentaries on postcolonial literature, and offered as alternative a reading of both political theory, and of postcolonial fiction, focused instead on political engagement at alternative scales. The rest of this book is concerned with how those alternative engagements are realised by postcolonial authors, and their consequences for how we conceive of postcolonial novelists' engagement with space. I begin such exploration by considering how one representation of the 'larger-than-national' – the space of the journey – may offer its own politicised potential. If the nation is to be, as Frantz Fanon and pan-nationalist movements suggested, and as contemporary critics of the nation speculate, only a stage in the creation of an international coalition, then how might such a theme be represented in literature; how do we capture a spirit of the global in a medium that relies on setting and place as a central tenet of narrative? This chapter suggests that the postcolonial author continually wrestles with such questions, attempting to capture a sense of action – and resistance – on a scale larger than the national, yet at the same time caught in the significance of place in order to reflect the geospecific impact of colonisation.

The representation of larger-than-national spaces can be seen to be embodied in the journey: a motif that is taken up by postcolonial authors as a representation of transnational and unbordered engagement with space. As Edward S. Casey has elucidated, the journey and the concept of place are intimately entwined, where 'places provide the changing but indispensable medium of journeys' (274). Moreover, the passage of the journey offers an example of chaotic space, presenting engagement with 'heterogeneous' and 'in-between places' (Casey 275) that may challenge stable constructions of place. However, whilst Casey sees journeys as important because they reaffirm the importance of place, for the postcolonial author, I want to argue, journeys are so important precisely because they relieve many of the tensions of fixed locations. For the postcolonial author the journey represents the possibility to escape the limits of national space. It is a metaphor for a world in which movement, facilitated by air travel and global communication networks, undercuts national belonging with an international perspective. This has led to powerful pronouncements of the centrality of the journey in postcolonial writing, such as John Phillips's assertion that 'the post-colonial writer is grounded on the paradigm of travel, an identity produced disjunctively, out of fragments, in travel' (76). As almost a *non-space*, beyond the confines of boundaries and mapping and therefore approaching something far more fluid, indefinable and chaotic, the journey is a fitting beginning for exploring the concept of post-space.

To invoke such an image, however, is far from unproblematic. If the colonial enterprise is founded on the desire for an absolute space, then at the heart of this endeavour is the sense of an absolute journey. Movement is not only a way for the colonised to escape the confines of the nation through migration; it is also a necessary feature of the coloniser's practice of conquering territory: it is by its very nature a transferral of bodies and resources from one space to the other. Violent travel such as indentured labour or slavery exposes the very unequal ways in which postcolonial citizens themselves experience movement. The travel of the postcolonial writer, or voluntary economic migration, is very different from the harsh experiences suffered by exiles or those seeking asylum. Moreover, even in the case of voluntary migration, travel is often undercut by the stark difference between the hopes and ideals embodied in such movement, and the reality, which is often cast in terms of disappointment, poverty, and prejudice.

In many ways the act of movement can be read as a metaphor for the entire colonial practice. It is a journey that relies upon an assumption of chaos, of the exotic, in order to facilitate free, boundless movement, only to then conceal this with measurement and a sense of final destination, a need for order that is required to justify colonial control which is embodied in the colonial preoccupation with frontiers and map-making. As the travel narrative is shown by Mary Louise Pratt to be a mental capture of territory, as 'imperial eyes passively look out and possess (7), so it exemplifies the same processes identified by Noyes as central to the construction of colonial space generally. Such journeys have become the focus of numerous narratives, both in the form of colonial fictions and travel writings. Thus any postcolonial narration of the journey stands in relation to such texts. In the case of fiction, as early as Daniel Defoe's *Robinson Crusoe* (1719) the novel comes to exemplify the journey as representative of colonial methods. Movement utilises a sense of chaos, only to ultimately bring order and control. Syed Manzurul Islam's description of Defoe's novel as the story of a traveller who, 'haunted by the footprints of the other, is driven to a singular obsession: he draws circles, constructs fences, erects walls in an endless pursuance of boundaries' (2) is a concrete example of Noyes's definition of colonial movement as involving 'strategies for mapping universal principles' (164). Crusoe attempts to exploit what he sees as an untamed wilderness, in fear of 'savages' and 'wild beasts', using such assumptions to validate his use of the land, the need for 'securing my self' (Defoe 76). Yet he obscures what he discovers, justifying his actions with religious zeal and a focus upon supposed progress, defining the seasons and working the land in a process that reduces his discovery to his own version of the England he departs from. It is this that is reflected in powerful critiques of Defoe's narrative such as

J. M. Coetzee's *Foe* (1986) and Derek Walcott's *Pantomime* (1980). Such texts, in their own unique ways, emphasise both the racial and patriarchal power – the silencing of difference – exemplified in the telling of Crusoe's story. *Pantomime* reverses the Friday–Crusoe dynamic by offering a contemporary relationship in which the black slave becomes the master. This can be seen to directly relate to the conceptualisation of post-space as a negotiation via the trauma of colonialism, rather than in spite of it: for Helen Gilbert, the play aims 'to dismantle the binary oppositions on which imperialism depends' (129) and reveals in Walcott's work how 'colonialism, despite – and even because of – its brutalities, thus becomes a kind of alchemy' (128). Equally, *Foe* exposes, through a silenced Friday figure and a female narrator, the cultural politics at work in Crusoe's narrative.

Even when not explicitly based on aggressive expansion, the colonial traveller can be seen to advocate a fixed space based on classification and definition as the solution to supposed backwardness in order to justify the crossing of autochthonous boundaries. As Pratt has illustrated, the motive behind even scientific missions was to define and control: a 'European knowledge-building project ... specified plants and animals in visual terms as discrete entities, subsuming and reassembling them in a finite, totalizing order of European making' (38). This sense of ordering means that travel writing is no more than fiction a realist account of the space it documents, 'about as "natural" a kind of text ... as any book one can think of' (Said, *Orientalism* 93). The topography as uncovered via movement reflects the European gaze and its portrayal of the indigenous territory as something to be appropriated. Hence in discussing Richard Burton's *Lake Regions of Central Africa*, Pratt is keen to point out that from the narrative 'what Burton sees is all there is ... . Thus the scene is deictically ordered with reference to his vantage point, and is static' (205). Indeed, while the colonial journey may be seen as a process of travel in the literal sense, it is not necessarily one of movement in the sense of representing change, making the colonial journey into a paradox centred around the colonial traveller's transferral of their own values to a new setting. The colonial traveller is continually denying the fragility of new constructions of belonging: the tumultuous nature of relocation is quickly lost.

Yet despite, or perhaps because of, this colonial provenance, the postcolonial novelist appears to find the journey a useful motif, whether the movement represented is internal or migratory, an indication of forced displacement or a voluntary journey of discovery. What is this relationship between the colonial movement and the postcolonial pursuit of the same event? Perhaps it is not the same event at all. For what we find in the postcolonial narrative is often a new kind of journey: one with no final arrival or departure, without the desire for settlement but instead filled with the potential of constant, chaotic movement. Such a journey may mimic the colonial travel that precedes it but, as it does so, it will strategically unravel the very principles that such an original journey is based upon.

The Absolute Journey: Geometric Immobility

It would be fallacious to suggest that the postcolonial writing of the journey is a simple rejection of the colonial travel narrative. In many ways the narratives discussed here all borrow from and mimic a colonial sense of the journey. In this sense, such representations acknowledge the colonial desire for order and its classification of space through movement.

In Wilson Harris's *The Guyana Quartet* the colonial journey forms an intertextual backdrop that supports Fernando Galvan's assertions of a modern genre of travel writing as metafiction, a postmodern referentiality that encompasses both fiction and the travel writing genre proper itself. This is evident in the continued reference to *The Guyana Quartet* in Harris's other novels, such as *Heartland* (1964), so that *The Guyana Quartet* is itself an intertext. It is also present in the reference to earlier models of the journey that preoccupy the narrative. Considering the first novel of the quartet, *The Palace of the Peacock*, the journey of Donne and his crew through the interior of Guyana is framed with awareness of both the totalising force of colonial expeditions into the Caribbean and specific journeys into Guyana and their portrayal via travel narratives. T.J. Cribb has linked this narrative to classic narratives of exploration and, through this, to *Robinson Crusoe* as 'one of the crew is called Schomburgh ... an actual descendant of one of the brothers Schomburgk who explored Guyana in the 1840s', where 'translation ... compares ... with Robinson Crusoe' (108). The journey towards the Palace that forms the central narrative provides an echo of the colonial pursuit of El Dorado – 'Carroll who reappears at the end of the book within a corridor in ancient El Dorado' (Harris, 'Quetzalcoatl' 186) – and with the English economic pursuit of this ancient city under the leadership of Sir Walter Ralegh. Interestingly, V.S. Naipaul has described El Dorado as the typical colonial space: conquered on the basis of a myth and on a notion of the exotic and yet with the ultimate aim of veiling this uncertainty with order, with the need for 'common linke of affinitie, lawe, language, or religion' (Keymis, qtd. in Naipaul, *Loss* 43). Indeed, Ralegh's journey was not only imperial in aims, but also in its writing, an early example of colonisation of the narrative itself as his own account of the journey meant that 'the Spanish Empire was over and the El Dorado legend was fixed: it was Ralegh's' (Naipaul, *Loss* 29). The direct legacy of this appropriation of space through writing would be the realist novel: Cribb's assertion that Defoe believed that he himself was a descendent of Ralegh.

The leader of the expedition in *Palace of the Peacock*, Donne, typifies the colonial adventurer, the new conquistador whose actions echo those of the sixteenth-century Spanish conquistador. He relates to Guyana's space as one who is a socialised product of imperialism, mimicking colonial desires to map and seize territory as he believes '"rule the land ... . And you rule the world"' (23). As 'the colonist', Donne must rely upon a fluidity of space in order to facilitate this appropriation, declaring 'every boundary line is a myth' (22) in the same way that the colonial adventurer declares empty space to aid and legitimise colonial expansion. Yet he also follows what I have termed in the introduction a colonial overwriting, where chaos is literally overlaid with an absolute space, nevertheless – like a written text – retaining a trace of what lies underneath. It is a fitting irony that is exposed by Harris in one short passage: relating to Donne, the narrator reveals that 'the country ahead was mysterious and little known he said. A long series of dangerous rapids marked the map in his hands' (76). Here Donne relies upon the unidentified territory for his adventuring, but it must be an unknown that is mapped, and mapped for him so that he may take the role of knowledgeable guide and rightful owner. The journey in this sense is a microcosm of the nation as it mimics the colony, an unstable construct fixed as natural and eternal even as it reveals the trace of its instability. When the crew travel, they always move in the wake of a history of colonialism. This is indicated by Donne who 'had conquered and crushed the region he ruled, annihilating everyone' (27). He is the epitome of 'balance and perspective' (51); the rational identity that the colonial assumes on movement through foreign landscapes becomes echoed in Donne's movement through the indigenous interior. It is no coincidence that Donne must lose his sight at the end of the journey to be redeemed. For what he loses is that very colonial ability to take possession and create order through vision.

This scenario acknowledging the territorializing colonial journey is repeated across *The Guyana Quartet*. In *The Far Journey of Oudin* Oudin materialises in Ram's world in order to 'found a conception of empire' (139). In *The Whole Armour*, Abram's initial dream of wandering is a vision in which 'every private notice and fable and boundary against the sea stood in the turmoil of the foreshore as in a graveyard of sculptured history and misadventure' (243). Such a landscape is fixed to a colonial past, a past that is 'sculptured': not a natural flowing of events but that which is defined from outside, 'shaped' (*OED*). This is a Guyana that is formed in the wake of travelling and must suffer, as it first appears, the legacy of such movements, representing 'dogmatic kinship and approval, formal and narrow … traditional yoke and narrow intention' (275, 290). Such a journey space is represented through a metaphor of a linear geometry, as 'the ground was criss-crossed by dead memory – the floor of an ancient jigsaw' (281) which, as I argued in the introduction, correlates to a colonial uniformity of space. Following the colonial example, authority defines the fluid indigenous population as the exotic: it must be controlled and measured 'until every passion had cooled' (320).

In the final book of the Quartet, *The Secret Ladder*, Harris's self-referentiality marks continuum with the earlier text, a journey that once again reminds of Sir Walter Ralegh and the search for El Dorado, where 'Fenwick had named his dinghy *Palace of the Peacock*' (367). Fenwick, the government surveyor, may be read as a thinly-veiled Wilson Harris – who began his own movement through Guyana during such a career – and he epitomises a movement through the interior based upon measurement, the surveyor as 'an anchor of imperial expansion' (J. Black 137), mapping the river basin. As Fenwick 'remained staring up curiously as if he saw an introspective ladder of climbing numbers rather than actual feet and decimals placed on a strip of vulgar wood' (357) the linearity of this journey is powerfully evoked. Mapping the river as an absolute scientific space, gauging the water levels, Fenwick's mental disposition is similarly fixed by his experience. There is a mental ladder he must climb – parallel rungs leading in a univocal direction – as his physical journey progresses concomitantly. In this way, Fenwick embodies the colonial traveller, measuring physical geography, charting and mapping territory. Analysing one particular passage, Fenwick's journey on land, illustrates how such an experience of travel is reinforced. It is carefully constructed by Harris at the level of language, in order to build a sense of the overwhelming power of the colonial overwriting of the diverse landscape with a myth of absolute space:

> Fenwick passed under the men's resthouse and picked up a *narrow* track which ran *parallel* to the river for nearly a *hundred yards* or two through the bush. This brought him to another and *smaller* clearing in the *centre* ... . Fenwick had to bend to enter the camp at the *side* facing the trail. The *frame* had been laid out inconveniently in this respect, at *right angles* to the river, in order to utilize the only *stable* piece of ground. One open *triangular face* therefore looked *straight* upon the river – rather than upon the trail – while the other confronted a wall of bush. (emphasis added, 362–3)

This strategy betrays the desire for the absolute always underlying Fenwick's own movements. The land is mapped, it is geometric and it is secure, the perfect surveyor's space. Thus there is irony in Fenwick's statement that "'I am not the Colonial Secretariat, thank God ...'" (364), an ellipsis that marks Fenwick's unconscious collusion in that he proclaims to abhor. It eventually becomes explicit: when Fenwick dreams, he imagines a 'conquest of space' (432), and what results is an absolute at the level of Fenwick's own body as 'his feet ... grew cold as stone ... unable to move a single step in any direction' (434). The timing of this prohibition, the cessation of movement at the most personal level, is no coincidence. It is not only when Fenwick is faced with his own death, but also when he comes closest to representing the colonist, monitoring the land against Poseidon and the power of the sea and the indigenous land rights that he represents. Here Harris's reflection on absolute colonial movement is encapsulated: a complex ordering of space that infiltrates the very bodies of those who journey, revealed by Harris through subtle use of language.

In its focus on mental stasis, what Harris's representation of the journey neglects, however, is the very physical legacy of colonialism in terms of journeying: the way in which Mbembe's postcolony may be captured in movement across space. Toni Morrison, in contrast, stresses this legacy: a pattern of abuse and trauma that results not simply in travellers whose identities reflect the colonial legacy of mapped and totalising journeys, but also in journeys that still mean confronting colonialism directly. In *Beloved*, Morrison moves into the past to directly confront the colonial journey, shifting time frames facilitating representation not only of the legacy of slavery but also a return to it. The journeys of Sethe and Paul D.

exemplify an America in which colonialism continues through slavery and racism, even while existing within what is, after independence in 1783, a postcolonial nation. This returns us to a connection with the absolute nation-state as a space that continues to embody colonial patterns, a reflection of the fact that 'decolonization proved less disruptive of frontiers than colonization had done' (J. Black 145–6). The boundaries and laws that restrict movement in *Beloved* are the same laws and principles that defined America as a newly colonised space, North American colonies where slaves' movements were closely controlled, continuing so that although white Americans would gain freedom in the war of independence, African-Americans in the North would have to wait until 1808 for the same liberties, while those south of the Ohio River would have to wait until after the Civil War, and then still with a racist legacy.

Morrison herself writes fiction with an awareness of such historical patterns, what she calls the American 'fear of boundarylessness' (*Playing* 37). Sethe's journey attempts to provide a realistic account of the slave-runner's traumatic flight, her story based on the real narrative of escaped slave Margaret Garner. Using the fragmented nature of memory to guide her narrative technique, caught in her nonlinear time of 're-memory', Morrison's recounting in *Beloved* of Sethe's journey to freedom illustrates the restricted movement under slavery. Preoccupying the inhabitants of Sweet Home, it is the feeling that 'one step off that ground and they were trespassers among the human race' (125).

Sethe's celebrated flight is problematised by its colonial implications, the need for a life of movement that is *not a choice* which is embodied in Paul D.'s commitment to 'Move. Walk. Run. Hide. Steal and move on' (66) as his only security because 'if a Negro got legs he ought to use them. Sit down too long, somebody will figure out a way to tie them up' (10). This exemplifies the contrast that must be made between the celebratory journeys of the postcolonial writer, and the harsh realism of postcolonial journeys of necessity. *Beloved*'s own narrative, 'her long journey back' (206) from which memories are invoked, shows how the legacy of such movement continues to haunt society, but it also explores colonial authority's impact on the slave population. 124 Bluestone Road becomes a metonym for the slave ship of the Middle Passage, guiding its inhabitants on a mental journey towards the same imprisoned existence with 'no room for any other thing or body' (39), its sounds described by Morrison as echoing 'the sounds in the body of the ship' ('Opening' 92). Beloved is the slave, powerfully evoking the source of Sethe's isolation, a restriction at the level of the body as she is described as 'always crouching' (210). However, in her manipulation of Paul D.'s body she too is also the colonist. The capitalised statement that 'SHE MOVED HIM' (114) turns Paul D. into 'a rag doll' (221) meaning that Beloved controls the movement of others as much as she is, herself, controlled.

Beloved's desire for this power reflects how all three generations of women in the novel are attracted to fixed boundaries. Sethe mourns a lack of physical locatedness as she reminisces about her childhood (30). Baby Suggs recounts a slave past in which 'men and women were moved around like checkers' (22).

Denver's best feeling is being 'relieved and easeful like a traveler who had made it home' (55). Such representation challenges any simple equation of post-space desires with postcolonial experience. But in Denver's experience it also points not just to the restrictions of slavery, but also the problems of movement in a post-slavery society. Morrison has in other texts extended this image to explore in more detail how, even with perceived freedom, movement continues to be problematic. In *Song of Solomon* (1977), for example, all the characters dream of flight:

> Truly landlocked people know they are ... they cannot claim a coast. And having none, seldom dream of flight. But the people living in the Great Lakes region are confused by their place on the country's edge – an edge that is border but not coast. They seem to be able to live a long time believing, as coastal people do, that they are at the frontier where final exit and total escape are the only journeys left ... the longing to leave becomes acute. (164)

The lake is a metaphor for both the central character of Milkman and the wider freed African-American community. It reflects a pain that is neither *no* freedom, as slavery prescribed, nor *total* freedom – as they face the sea as a reality only to be faced as a last resort – but rather *the possibility, the dream,* of freedom, with 'memories of the sea ... themselves landlocked' (164). Morrison here makes a distinction between privilege and the power of the journey, between the real quality of freedom and only an illusion of it. This distinction is embodied in the juxtaposition of the two central women in the book, Ruth 'well read but ill traveled' and Pilate, who 'had read only a geography book, but had been from one end of the country to another. One wholly dependant on money for life, the other indifferent to it' (140). Any journey without an accompanying freedom refuses any empowering consequences; simply moving is not itself empowering because of violence that underlies travel.

In a contemporary setting, however, travel must also be seen within the context of wider processes of global movement, and the impact of this movement on the colonial connotations of the journey addressed. With Salman Rushdie's *The Satanic Verses* the journey shifts to be related to the migrant experience, cast in a contemporary setting that initially seems very different from the kinds of travel recounted by Harris and Morrison. Ironically, this relocation to the experience of migration does not undermine, but rather increases, the sense of an underlying power relationship in movement that echoes colonial travel and reflects its implications. What may be seen as subtle motifs in Morrison and Harris – images of geometry and restriction – are for Rushdie the guiding images through which he translates the significance of his characters' movements. Walking through London, Chamcha finds himself restricted by a city epitomised by its 'poise and moderation' (37) while, in his migrant dreaming of Jahilia, Gibreel encounters a metaphorical journey to God that is one of 'certainty' (240). To rely on the most fundamental symbol of logical travel – the A–Z – is only to mimic the colonial traveller. Gibreel 'would redeem this city: Geographers' London, all the way from

A–Z … . The atlas in his pocket was his master plan. He would redeem the city square by square' (322, 326). Yet to do so – square by square – is to be caught in Euclidean, geometric strategies that replace the human with the abstract. As a result, when Gibreel really does fly over London, achieving emancipation from London's racist oppression through travel, he cannot subvert such freedom to move it away from its colonial privilege; it is not a migrant's flight, but the flight of 'London's conqueror' (425).

There is, therefore, a strong contrast emerging between those journeys that are chosen and freeing and those that are enforced or enforcing: it is to the latter that the imagery of geometry and the sense of absolute space are inexorably attached. Indeed, it is not the fast pace of air travel, which *The Satanic Verses* so memorably opens with, that exemplifies this experience, but rather the train with its predetermined path: a 'happy predictability of parallel metal lines' (190). This restrictive journey, represented in the train, is a pattern throughout Rushdie's narratives: Saleem's oppressive train journey in *Midnight's Children*, Morares's 'crawling two hour journey … end of the line' (142) in *The Moor's Last Sigh*, the violent train travel in England that prompts the narrator of *Shame* to begin his story.

This harsher, less romanticised side of Rushdie's narratives promotes a very different sort of desire to that with which he is often associated. Moving through a Thatcherite London in *The Satanic Verses*, Rushdie's central characters reflect Michael Keith's reality in which 'the black body is interpellated through the street' (367). This is not a postmodern craving for shifting borders, but rather the longing to receive the rights and privileges that come by being seen no longer as a wanderer, the 'thirty temporary human beings, with little hope of being declared permanent' (264) that represent the contemporary postcolonial migrant's reality. Such contradictions should not be seen as the failure of Rushdie's postcolonial journeys, but rather, akin to his interaction with the nation, as an acknowledgement of their complexities and their divergence from the sort of simplistic postmodern readings that associate journeys with unproblematic fluidity. Revathi Krishwasnamy, for example, casts Rushdie exactly within the terms of this sort of stereotype of postmodernism. She sees him as an apolitical 'itinerant intellectual' (125) who has contributed to the view of postcolonialism in general as a detached and apathetic discipline in some ways complicit with a metropolitan centre and globalising, aspecific generalisations, suggesting that the author's migrant narratives promote the 'de-linking of distress from dislocation' (137). Yet Rushdie's reflections of the journey powerfully counter such claims. They illustrate that Rushdie, like Morrison, is acutely aware of the very different and power-laden experiences of journeying.

This sense in which the postcolonial novel's use of travel diverges from any simplistic postmodern model becomes explicit in *The Ground Beneath Her Feet*. Despite the novel's ostensibly postmodern setting, when Darius Cama dreams of travel, it is not movement forwards to a new, globalised world, but movement backwards to a colonial ideal:

> Whenever he dreamed, he dreamed of England: England as a pure, white
> Palladian mansion set upon a hill above a silver winding river, with a spreading
> parterre of brilliant green lawns edged by ancient oaks and elms, and the classic
> geometry of flower beds orchestrated by unseen master gardeners into a four-
> seasons symphony of colour. (86)

The image of order is returned to: journeys made by 'Pilgrim Children' (251)
in the '*Mayflower*' (250) continually remind us of travel's association with a
chequered colonial past. Even as Rushdie attempts to capture postmodern life,
reflecting on the airport, the hotel and popular culture, the idea that travel can be
exclusion is not abandoned. The acknowledgement that 'few Indians travelled for
pleasure in their own country, even to Kashmir' (136) makes the narrator Rai's
frequent movement not a model of the norms of postmodern reality, but instead
an exception in a world where travel marks exclusion and is dominated by power
hierarchies. The fact that Vina's 'darkness was not Negro darkness, they were
Indians from India and didn't need to be discriminated against, they could ride on
the bus along with the regular kids' (105) shows the importance of travel but also
its intrinsic hierarchy that means that movement here itself becomes indicative of
a political act:

> Back then it wasn't easy to travel if all you had was an Indian passport. Inside
> this passport some bureaucrat would laboriously inscribe the few countries you
> were actually allowed to travel to, most of them countries that had never crossed
> your mind as possible destinations. All the rest – certainly all the interesting
> places – were off limits unless you got special permission. (178)

The journey is always implicitly linked to a political context: a shadow of
suffering that appears to accompany Rushdie's migratory trio regardless of
celebratory assertions of individual identity or distance travelled. To have the
freedom of travel, as Vikram Chandra also illuminates in *Red Earth and Pouring
Rain*, is to be in a position of privilege that distinguishes you from the struggles of
the indigenous inhabitant:

> Sanjay would see a party of English who had come to look at the last of the
> Moghuls, and on their faces he would recognize that same look, that smugness
> and impatience that is given only to those who are travellers, who are powerful
> because of their ultimate indifference, that faintly smiling detachment of the
> tourist. (260)

It is the abstraction of the traveller – his disinterest – that allows his unproblematic
engagement with space: the colonialist's status as traveller is not incidental, but
integral to his violence. In the wake of this colonial past, the journey represents not
a simple escape from power structures, but movement that is inherently implicated
in how such constructs function. The journey captures the colonial control of space,

and how this embodies a contradiction, continuing even in what is seemingly a fluid structure. It is in reclaiming this fluidity from its colonial appropriation that the postcolonial novelist offers a very different representation of movement.

The Chaotic Re-play: Unravelling Forms

Thus whilst these journeys reveal the inherent simplicity of an ideal postmodern movement, they are also contextualised by a coterminous acknowledgment of the necessity of movement, and its alternative potential. Morrison is clear that it is strong walls, in the wake of a prohibition of any movement or freedom and equality outside them, which are ultimately imprisoning. The psychic legacy in *Beloved* that causes Sethe to proclaim 'whatever is going on outside my door ain't for me. The world is in this room' (183), is a reminder of movement denied. Similarly, Rushdie is also clear that just as the migrant's experience of movement can be damaging, so the stable, too, can be 'hegemony' (*Satanic* 334) in its closing down of opportunity. It is not simply a case of finding movement, but of the quality of that movement, offering multiple, ultimately very different, representations of journeying. Such recognition offers the possibility for an alternative kind of journeying: one which is neither postmodern free play or colonial repetition, but is instead an interrogation of both these extremes.

In her book *Killing Rage: Ending Racism* (1995) bell hooks has suggested that while travel is 'fascinated with imperialism … theories of travel produced outside conventional borders might want the Journey to become the rubric within which travel, as a starting point for discourse, is associated with different headings' (43). This posits the potential for a journey that is not a simple repetition of colonial travel practices but which also, in its recognition of travel's colonial connotations, is not a postmodern simplification, either. There is a sense in which while focusing upon the journey itself may be a political statement – a subversion of the sense that such narratives are 'one-way traffic, because the Europeans mapped the world rather than the world mapping them' (Clark 3) – postcolonial narratives may be more than an attempt to emulate the colonial journey, or to show the continued legacy of its movements. This representation may be described productively in terms of what Anuradha Dingwaney Needham has termed 're-play' (53): an imperfect repetition designed for subversive purposes. Here the use of the colonial journey is seen as a mimicry of the colonial method of representation, evoked in order to reveal its ironies and facilitate a deconstruction, acting in a way that is 'displacing, unsettling, or interrogating' (61). The journey frames itself with the colonial only to reveal it as a fallacy, and to expose the multiplicity always underlying the absolute. Centred upon a disruption of the linear space it initially posits, re-playing the colonial journey may be seen to reflect both the fragmented identity of the migrant and the disruptions of travelling in colonially marked space. The journey echoes Noyes's revelation that the colonial tabular space is always a structural device that obscures its chaotic origins, where the 'establishment of borders … leads to an ever increasing segmentation and fragmentation of space ... the necessity of crossing, a constant violation of the boundaries it has created' (162). What is hidden and obscured by colonial overwriting – the instability of journeying and its endless process – is foregrounded and exposed by the postcolonial rewriting.

Such a strategy may be seen as part of postcolonial literature in all its forms, whether realist or magical-realist. Representing a mode of postcolonial literature that, at least on the surface, is antithetical to the form employed by Rushdie, Harris, and Morrison, a writer such as Naipaul nevertheless also engages in a re-play of the colonial journey and while some critics – most notably Robert Nixon – have failed to see irony in Naipaul's narratives, read through this re-play they may be seen as an important critique of the colonial position. In Naipaul's *The Enigma of Arrival* (1987) the unnamed narrator has a cultural image of London as the province of Waugh, Maugham and Dickens to which he feels he belongs and, like Chamcha, he hopes to remake himself as a colonial subject. Travelling to London and making a career as a writer, he rejects as material those with similar backgrounds to himself in favour of metropolitans. Yet on his arrival the reality falls short of his literary creation and he experiences doubt and confusion as 'the grandeur belonged to the past ... . I had come too late to find the England, the heart of Empire which ... I had created in my fantasy' (130). This experience reveals the chaos underlying the narrator's absolute constructions, and the fact that colonial England is a mirage.

Yet the narratives I focus on here take re-play in a direction that extends beyond Naipaul's representation, towards a post-space that writers such as Naipaul gesture towards but are ultimately incapable of, or unwilling to, realise. This reaffirms the argument I made it my introduction, that in gesturing beyond the realms of the *status quo*, it is magical-realist narratives that represent a particularly powerful engagement with resistance. For Naipaul's narrator – despite the destruction of his preconceptions, and a return home that echoes Chamcha's – his initial sense of 'decay' and 'death' (23) never really seems to disperse. This provides critique – a rejection of the colonial – but little possibility and few strategies for survival. In contrast, the narratives here suggest that the door is never closed to the journey escaping the confines of its initial characteristics.

In this sense, enacting a magical-realist re-play of the colonial journey creates a space of positive disjunction; the gap between the original narrative and that which echoes its content and structure opens up a location in which new representations of space, and new experiences of movement, may be asserted. This gap, created by the re-play, may in itself be connected to significant postcolonial models. Most notably, it resonates with Bhabha's notion of the 'time-lag', a variant of Bhabha's third space that associates a disruption with the 'not-there' (*Location* 198), those moments undefined or undermined by conventional discourse. Time-lag is particularly applicable to the journey: for Phillips it is defined as that space where 'the movement across spatial boundaries challenges the stability of subjective identity' (69). Indeed, despite the fact that it is a disruption of linear *time*, Bhabha himself describes time-lag as 'a *spatial movement* of cultural representation' (emphasis added, 'Postcolonial' 59). Thus through this disjunctive time-lag, it is a new space that opens up; into the absolute space enters a journey of spatialised hybridity, a version of Bhabha's radical alterity that emerges in the cross-cultural space. In line with chaos theory, such chaos is not disempowering. Rather, it is a problematic, subversive, and ultimately positive renewal.

While Phillips may see the need for origins and a fixed location in such a theory as problematic, it in fact confirms the potential for a post-space journey where there must be *location as well as dislocation*: a postcolonial narrative that is a negotiation between the postmodern and the colonial position. It also resonates with the understanding of chaos as something which offers ultimate – if provisional – meaning. Positive disruption of linear distance should not be seen simply as a literary metaphor. It may also be read, for example, in Gabriel Gbadamosi's description of his own movements through Brixton, London:

> Put your foot down hard on the accelerator and the road to Brixton market pulls London, Africa and the Caribbean into itself, eating up the distances between them as shouts, traffic signs and pumping music get blurred and pulled apart, or merged, by fast cars accelerating into the wind. (185)

What is presented here is neither the disassociation from the political so often ascribed to postmodernism, nor a repetition of colonial order, but rather true magical-realism: a journey that is Janet Wolff's 'destabilizing … from *a location*' (232), a complex interaction of discourses within the context of real life.

While I shall limit my application of re-play and its associations with the time-lag to this chapter, it is a concept that will continue to be resonant in later chapters, most notably because it is a factor that is deeply imbedded in the notion of the postcolony. Not only is the colonial journey performed before it is unravelled, so it might be that postcolonial cities, homes and bodies receive treatment to which this term is also applicable. Such re-play, however, has specific connections to the journey that motivate my use of it here, reflected in Phillips's discussion of the difference between colonial and postcolonial travel writing, which 'in the first case challenges but ultimately supports notions of stable identity and in the second threatens them irredeemably' (64), revealing the chaotic constructions that always underlie stable representations. It is this connection that makes the journey a central *fulcrum* of post-space, that upon which the postcolonial re-visioning of space turns as it provides 'the point against which a lever is placed to get purchase' (*OED*). It is not the colonial movement that emerges, but rather something quite different, not simply that produced in relation to the imperial but a new expression and a new affirmation. In this sense, the postcolony ceases to function: colonial repetition is disrupted and disordered.

Harris illuminates the postcolonial propensity for re-play; in his call for the past to be viewed as constitutive of 're-sensed spaces' ('Enigma' 147) which are 're-visualised, taken up at another level, rehearsed profoundly at another level to release new implications' ('Literacy' 28), his discussion accurately mirrors Needham's interpretive framework. It is in the name of partial attempts to complete this project that Harris re-plays not only the colonial journey, but also the travel narratives of those writers he believes came close to subverting rigid belief systems, those writers who 'came to that frontier but never crossed' ('Composition' 28). This leads to invocations across the quartet of texts including Joseph Conrad's *Heart of Darkness* (1902), Herman Melville's *Moby Dick* (1851) and Dante's *Inferno*. Here Harris offers a strategy that is echoed by more recent postcolonial texts: Karen King-Aribisala's *Kicking Tongues* (1998), for example, in which the author seizes upon Chaucer's *Canterbury Tales*. Built around the tales of forty Nigerian travellers, *Kicking Tongues* highlights the inequality of the journey. Tales such as 'The Tale of The Woman in Purdah' provide the opportunity to emphasise how ordinary travellers suffer at the hands of government privilege. Equally, 'The Air-hostess' represents Nigerian identity as subject to the whims of western standards, particularly in terms of its definitions of beauty, as the Nigerian air-hostess must fulfil these definitions to meet the demands made by business class travellers:

> Nigerian airways was carrying too much of a load
> And the fat Nigerian air-hostesses were carrying
> Too much of a load
> It was the wrong image being toted to the rest of the world
> And the rest of the world was the Western World
> On whom business and business
> Class
> Depended (72)

With class and dependence emphasised, the global hierarchies implicit in travel are exposed. Yet *Kicking Tongues* also seizes upon *Canterbury Tales* because it offers an incomplete potential: a journey filled with hybrid voices that might be reworked from an African perspective to challenge the inequalities of Nigerian society, offering 'otherness ... Third Dimensions' (7). As for Harris, such a journey acknowledges the colonial English culture it is based upon, filled with references to English folk and fairy tales. Yet – through both prose and verse – it also powerfully interrogates the purity of these images with a retelling through African voices and circumstance.

King-Aribisala offers a rare of example of a truly national fiction: the journey is explicitly concerned with interrogating Nigerian government, infrastructure, and political corruption:

> Bus is stage of country Nigeria.
> Nigeria is Bus is stage.
> Nation leader is bus driver is nation leader.
> Leading-leader-leading, leading the not so easily
> Led. (163)

It seems on this scale that the colonial legacy will be ultimately transformed; it is a journey 'In sojourning for truth/Across this mighty land of ours ... Hoped for redeeming-hope' (6). Yet what the text also offers is the sense of the journey as an important first step in that transformation – as not just metaphor, but as microcosm of the changes that need to be enacted on larger scales. For Harris, where the nation is never mentioned, the journey is itself the means towards the challenging of colonial ways of thinking. In *The Guyana Quartet*, it is *Heart of Darkness*, rather than *Canterbury Tales*, that provides, in particular, this inspiration. It is used by Harris as a model for his own novel, not only thematically – 'to transform biases grounded in homogenous premises' ('Frontier' 86) – but also in terms of its very linguistic construction. What this reveals is how, even within colonial imaginaries, writers were unravelling the absolute space and attempting to reveal its mythic and unreal status. If these projects were limited by the authors' own biases, as in the case of Conrad, what Harris recognises, nevertheless, is their movement towards such a project and their attempts to reveal the underlying fluidity of conquered space. Harris assumes Conrad's 'addiction to the adjective' ('Frontier' 91) as integral to the effective challenging of accepted representations of the non-western world.[1] Leaching words of signified meaning, in *The Guyana Quartet* oppositions are transformed into harmonies. The 'solid wall of trees' may consist of both 'ancient blocks of shadows and ... gleaming hinges of light' (28). In this sense, the re-play is constructed at the level of linguistics, using the very language employed by the British regime which came to be Guyana's final colonisers. A host of oppositions may be weaved into one description, presenting a continual oscillation of extremes:

> He *ascended* higher ... . He *slipped ... supported* by death and *nothingness* ... .
> It flashed on him *looking down* the steep spirit of the cliff ... . He *stared upward*
> to *heaven* slowly as to a new beginning from which the false *hell* and function
> crumbled and *fell*. (emphasis added, 101)

Perhaps the most powerful sense of this shifting is that we are asked to experience space, as do the crew, not through sight but rather by sound, 'transported beyond the memory of words' to sight formed by the 'glorious music' (113):

> I mention this because at first sight the consuming of bias is a puzzling notion but
> when perceived as a reversal or looping of the cannibal bone-flute into 'sound
> yet sight' ... it promotes inwardly changing or transformed building blocks of
> space. (Harris, 'Author's Note' 11)

King-Aribisala, too, in *Kicking Tongues*, offers such linguistic play: what is travelled through is a 'seeming aridity of sound' (208) that fuses the aural with the

---

[1]   The best reading of Harris's relationship to Conrad is still his own: see 'Frontier'.

sense of touch. It is an artistic strategy, a synaesthetic shift in the very basis of how space is perceived, which is inherent in a literary deconstruction of binaries.

This use of language suggests that, imbedded in the narrative's very structure, the re-play is coterminous with the absolute. Even as we are reminded of colonial narratives, we at the same time have the sense that these narratives are being reworked, interrogated by a magical-realist alternative. While the crew in *The Palace of the Peacock* make one journey during the novel, it is clear they have on many levels made the same journey before: the resurrection of Sorrow Hill, the narrator 'reliving Donne's first innocent voyage' (27), and Donne himself retracing past wanderings. Performativity re-enacts the event, epitomising movement of a living landscape and a sense of re-visioning. A nonlinear environment means one feels 'past, present and future in one constantly vanishing and reappearing cloud and mist' (44). Such patterns defy the colonial travel narrative's need for return; the passage itself is privileged, rather than any destination, a sense of the significance simply of moving through space, rather than moving for a purpose. Arrangements such as these mean that this is not a simple, singular re-play. For not only is the colonial journey revised, but the reconsideration that results is itself never certain. What emerges is an endless re-visioning that continues nevertheless to engage as an anticolonial response as it affirms a challenge to colonial ideas of absolute movement, a being 're-membered' (Harris, 'Absent Presence' 101) which resonates with Morrison's own project.

For Harris, his response to *Heart of Darkness* is a re-play aimed at realising Conrad's unfinished project, rather than an action that would support Achebe's now-famous critique. For novels that, instead, address Conrad's silencing of the indigenous population we would need to consider alternative re-plays, such as Abdulrazak Gurnah's *Paradise* (1994), in which a Harrisesque fusion of timeframes allows a contemporary journey of trains and trucks to be welded to an exploration of European expansion into the African interior resonant with nineteenth-century colonial ambitions. Here, not only is both Arab and European exploitation of Africa exposed, but the sense of the exoticism of the interior is repeated for subversive purpose. Making such a space one of chaos for both the indigenous and the European – for the central character of Yusuf an experience where 'fear ... rose in him at these silent hours in their travels ... so near the edges of the known world' (158) – forecloses European othering with a universal experience of the unknown resonant with Harris's own humanist tendencies. Moreover, giving the inhabitant of the interior a voice allows a coterminous reversal of this assumption, as the interior proclaims the visitor to be the true representative of 'evil and calamity' (160). What emerges is exactly the colonial overwriting: a space of heterogeneity becomes demarcated as 'the government had brought order to the land' (171). As districts are formed, the power to fix and define is clear. Yet, positivity and this destruction exist alongside each other: the journey which is 'the terror' (180) for Yusuf becomes in a re-visionary moment at the same time 'like the gates of Paradise' (180–81).

Framing narratives in such re-visionary terms has the effect of moving them away from the colonial quest. In *The Guyana Quartet*, the journey to El Dorado, re-played, loses its status as the pursuit of economic gain. It is replaced by a spiritual quest that reveals the tumult underlying colonial movement that the colonist attempts to overwrite and deny, as the crew travel not only through the Guyana of cartography, of 'colonial conventions' (24), but also through what Alan Riach refers to in relation to Harris's writing as 'interior states of geography' (Harris, 'Interview' 41) which are a mirror of and manifestation within the psyche of the trauma of movement into the unpredictable. Donne's rampant imperialism is, by his encounter with the Palace, merged into a more complex and multiplicitous being, a recognition of hybridity which – in line with chaos theory and the idea of meaning within instability – is paradoxically the pathway to an achievement of completeness:

> He had stopped a little to wonder whether he was wrong in his knowledge and belief and the force that had divided them from each other – and mangled them beyond all earthly hope and recognition – was the wind of repetition and superstition, and the truth was they had all come home at last to the compassion of the nameless unflinching folk. (109–10)

As the boat of *The Palace of the Peacock* resonates through its journey with the movements of peoples to Guyana and with the Middle Passage, it opens up not only a reflection of the past, but also a rereading of oppression, what Paul Gilroy has seen in the ship as key to subjugation and yet also to 'projects for redemptive return to an African homeland' (*Black Atlantic* 4). As chaos represents the possibility of alternative readings, so agency is inserted into the Middle Passage that is cast not from the perspective of the slave-runner, but from that of the seemingly dispossessed slave. Seizing the possibility of this disruption of colonial narrative – James Clifford's awareness that 'the recurring break where time stops and restarts is the Middle Passage' (264): the time-lag – Harris inserts a magical element into Gilroy's space of cultural exchange. This means that a shift to new identities, or movement back towards those lost on the journey, is literally realised to extend beyond Gilroy's metaphorical usage. The Middle Passage becomes a nonlinear journey with the possibility to close the distance of miles between plantation and homeland.

Indicated in the text through numerous Anancy references, the crew's voyage thus suggests what Harris defines as a 'limbo gateway' where, spider-like, the 'limbo dancer moves under a bar which is gradually lowered until a mere slit of space, it seems, remains ... so that a re-trace of the Middle Passage from Africa to the Americas and the West Indies is not to be equated with a uniform sum' ('History' 157). This idea of limbo space as a challenge to colonial dislocation is one that has developed through Harris's fiction. By 1970, in *Ascent to Omai*, it is explicitly featured as the central character of Victor follows a journey to the town of Omai via an 'Anancy trail' (23). For Victor, the limbo dancer represents a bodily transformation that has the possibility to transform circumstances: 'Limbo dancer ... *Spider transubstantiation. Trickster substantiation.* Metamorphosis of the fall. *Deliverance and protection*' (26). This is also a spatial manipulation – Victor remembers the limbo dancers of his youth as 'dancing under a horizontal pole through what seemed the keyhole of space' (29). Whilst this later novel foregrounds the limbo journey, even in the earlier *Guyana Quartet* its beginnings are clear. The closing of miles and of time is perhaps nowhere more visible than in Schomburgh's physical encounter with the resurrection of previously obscured elements:

> The boat seemed to gain momentum as though every effort we made carried a new relationship within it ... . He remembered it all now with a shock as he sat staring from the bow of the boat ... . The nervous tension of the day – that had now rooted him in the bow – had broken every barrier of memory and the tide came flooding upon him ... beyond life and death, past and present. (64–6)

Schomburgh sees seemingly lost spaces as he travels through the interior: as the oldest crewmember, he comes to relive a distant and yet suddenly vivid past.

This pattern of re-play, which leads to a disjunction opening up possibilities for resistance, is supported throughout the quartet. Oudin's journey undermines any sense of absolutes without alternative; an everlasting re-play is again affirmed in what is 'a crucial rehearsal, a rehearsal that would be repeated once again over thirteen dreaming years' (206). Rather than the mapped, what Oudin encounters is the disjunctive forces of the time-lag, a gap in representation that means space refuses to be defined by the traveller's gaze:

> The air had gone still, one of those incredible intervals well known to experienced bushmen and travellers, when the mosquitoes fly into nowhere and nothingness ... . One listens in vain, watching the phantom of the bush coming alive in its unearthly detachment, and its muse of utter motionlessness. (213)

An 'interval' of 'nothingness', what is faced is a disruption of the diachronic as time slows, becoming location as 'a clouding of space was the only movement of time' (213). Yet while this gap in linear representation is threatening, filled with 'impending horror and despair' (213), it also suggests an ambivalence, something 'both agreeable and disagreeable in their journey' (215).

Once again, this opens up a direct connection to the positive chaos of post-space. The significance of Oudin's rehearsal is an echo of Donne's awakening as Oudin announces 'he no longer wished to serve and to rule anybody' (218). Interestingly, it is also, through the character of Beti, for the first time a journey with a female voice. This reflects the disjunction between female and male colonial travel, and what is, for Harris, a masculine colonial enterprise that may be unravelled in part by female agency. Despite the implication of female travellers in the colonial project, for Harris it seems that gendered discourse is one way to undermine colonial narratives. Beti moves towards the centre of the narrative as the one on whom 'the initiative in continuing the journey rested ... she was equal to him after all' (215, 218). Seen in the wake of Sethe's journey this shift is itself a powerful lesson, centred on choice: Beti's right to decide, to 'migrate' (230).

In *The Whole Armour* all is once again performativity. As 'all time remained in one serial fused moment like an inescapable waking rendezvous with death and life' (305), a nonlinear process is affirmed. Yet as Abram begins in 'a land that was nowhere' (243) that is also victim of a 'sculptured history' (243), at once space is thus in one passage of description revealed as marked and colonial but also – as this space is re-played – a location for a disruption of this space and an opening of possibility. There is 'an air of uncertainty' (259), not the colonial border but a 'horizon ... beginning to shake and quiver into bright refracted pieces' (265). Such description is exactly the colonial movement uncovered: multiplicity returning to an absolute that is now pretence as the pieces 'constantly returned vibrantly together again' (265). Yet as 'uncovered', it reveals the potential for alternative agency. All movement lies in the wake of Harris's own liberation time-lag, 'the bridge that stretched across limbo – from the "dead" to the "living"' (295). And all is once again based on a clear alternative to colonial mapping. The very intertextuality of *The Secret Ladder* means it repeats this iterative journey, reversing Donne's movement as Fenwick and his crew approach not spiritual death, but rather trace backwards towards the moment of creation as they affirm 'In our end...our end... our end...our end is our beginning...beginning...beginning' (464). We are no longer in the colonial absolute but rather in the 'waking dream' (367) of possibility, a liminal 'threshold' (405) which Harris's subtle play with language makes clear as everything is 'very neat and tidy *on the surface*' (emphasis added, 386). The fact that Fenwick's statements are often ellipsed and bracketed – literally – suggests provisionality in order to undercut their authority and credulity.

In the wake of such disruption 'conquest of space' becomes 'enduring fiction' (432) and it is fitting that here, at the quartet's conclusion, the role of limbo and time-lag in such revelation is more explicit than ever, a journey where 'time itself would be unable to follow' (455). Rather than his absolute mathematical certainties, Fenwick is filled with ambiguities as space unravels under such a reawakened presence. He is aware that 'the truth was he could not shake off the conviction of a dual net of ancient spirit and helplessness – divine pride and human fallibility' (398). The fact that it is 'a treacherous rehearsal of possibilities' (436) means that Fenwick's travelling encapsulates the idea of post-space. The experience is 'treacherous', but exactly because of this – rather than in spite of it – it becomes filled with possibility.

Harris's purpose is to highlight the postcolonial potential and latent positivity that he views as *always* existing in the spaces described by the travel narrative. It is the revelation for the crew in *Palace of the Peacock* that 'in reality the territory they overwhelmed and abandoned had always been theirs to rule and take' (114), a political call to reclaim which undermines any sense of the poststructuralist narrative as disconnected. What emerges instead is exactly the new spatial politics

I identified in the introduction that, as with Rushdie, counters those criticisms of Harris as 'escapist and irrelevant' (Poynting 103): a positive flux of the everyday that stands as relief to the representation of postmodern fragmentation as simply a nihilistic characteristic.

Such a process need not be coterminous, however. In *Song of Solomon* Morrison begins with an absolute journey, highlighting the overwriting of the past and its significance as Milkman 'watched signs – the names of towns that lay twenty-two miles ahead, seventeen miles to the east, five miles to the northeast. And the names of junctions, counties, crossings, bridges, stations, tunnels, mountains, rivers, creeks, landings, parks and lookout points' (228). Journeying into the unknown, exoticising the characters he meets and initially mapping his territory – as nothing more that the physical landmarks that will lead him towards riches – Milkman is the new colonist. In what is more of a conventional *Bildungsroman*, the unravelling in this case only comes later, as Milkman reconsiders his motives and actions. Against his initial certainty that his journey will result in financial gain, Milkman comes to realise that 'there was nothing' (253). Milkman's assertion of this fact can be seen to take on multiple, parallel meanings. It suggests, on the surface, failure of the quest. It indicates Milkman's confusion. Negatively, it points to a cultural void as Milkman is dislocated from the environment he encounters. Yet, positively, it foregrounds a replacement of limited, defined-in-advance economic possibility with the open potential of the time-lag. It is this latter meaning that is evident ultimately in the text.

In order to explore this new way of moving Morrison literally changes the method of travel. She returns her character to walking, a movement that – despite its connotations of limits – Morrison associates elsewhere with awakening and resistance, the gendered walk in *Paradise* where 'it was women who walked this road. Only women' (270). Such a strategy has been emphasised by both writers and artists, by Iain Sinclair, for whom walking, within the familiar terms of psychogeography, has its own 'strange geometry of unconnected elements' that facilitates a 'means of recovering memory' ('London's Orbital'), and by photographer Hamish Fulton, who has constructed a project where the 'walking journey' forms 'art about specific places and particular events not present in the gallery' that represent, rather than the object of moving such as mode of transport, the experience.[2] This is not the fast pace of postmodern travel, but something slower. It suggests that, for Morrison, the post-space journey must be linked to the very physicality of movement.

Milkman's walking returns him to the land not as a mapped space but – reminiscent of Harris – as a living revelatory force, complete with a chaotic presence. When Milkman is told 'buses go there? Trains? No. Well, not very near' (260), following a 'winding path (which they called a road)' (287), he encounters the denied and unmapped spaces outside dominant American traditions. By the

---

[2]   Comments from exhibition guide and catalogue for *Walking Journey*, Tate Britain, 2002.

end of the narrative Milkman no longer denigrates his heritage. Instead, accepting it in all its complexity, he celebrates those strategies that have facilitated African-American survival. Echoing Harris in an invocation of music as a gateway that undermines a journey based on sight – foreshadowed at the novel's opening as Mr Smith 'heard the music, and leaped on into the air' (15) – the meaning of the Negro spiritual 'Solomon done fly' awakens Milkman. He finds his interest in his past growing, and finds conclusion to the journey not in treasure, but in divine awakening. It is the spiritual that Ronald Segal has emphasised as central to slave resistance, the dream of freedom that expresses flight to a space without territory:

> Sometimes I feel like
> A eagle in de air …
> Spread my wings an'
> Fly, fly, fly. (68)

Here Morrison's own limbo gateway emerges. Solomon's story of flying 'right on back to wherever it was he came from' (322) as one of the 'flying African children' (321) folds space and denies linearity. Milkman realises that 'if you surrendered to the air, you could *ride* it' (336), enacting a mental journey to African ancestry as he is aware that Pilate's acceptance of her complex heritage means 'without ever leaving the ground, she could fly' (335), a woman who transcends the colonial measurement. It is neither a repetition of the trauma of the colonial journey any longer, nor simply a rejection, but rather an evocation of the passages of resistance obscured by a classification as victim. The need for this past to be uncovered through the journey if it is to have any positive benefit draws parallels with Harris's desire to present lost experiences accessed through the landscape. Also connecting Morrison to Harris, the endless nature of this movement obliterates any sense of idealised return as Milkman realises that 'he had thought this place, this Shalimar, was going to be his home. … But here, in his "home", he was unknown, unloved, and damn near killed' (271).

Such a text foreshadows *Beloved* in stressing how, however traumatic the journey is, it nevertheless opens up a space of possibility in which the absolutes preceding it are unravelled. The extensive physical journeying in *Beloved* provides its own important opportunities for revision, which does however reinforce the coterminous unravelling of *The Guyana Quartet* and illustrates how such a strategy is employed in a very different postcolonial context. While Sethe's fugitive movement is in many ways a typical slave narrative against the apparent fixity of colonial borders, this very same narrative undermines other colonial expectations of the journey. As Beti provides a potentially subversive gendered discourse in *The Guyana Quartet*, so Sethe's role as a female traveller may be seen to extend this concern. Sethe's story breaks with the convention of male slave narratives. Yet Morrison's choice of focus also subtly undercuts the entire gendered field of colonial travel writing. It places Sethe in the same position as real-world female travellers, not only Margaret Garner but also the small number of female travel writers in the eighteenth and nineteenth centuries who have been seen to challenge the assertion that 'the masculine heroic discourse of discovery is not readily available to women' (Pratt 213). Interestingly, Morrison makes specific narrative decisions to support this subversion; Margaret Garner was never separated from her husband – indeed he was present at the murder of his child – neither was she assisted on her journey by any female.[3]

Bearing this in mind, Morrison's choice of a white female as Sethe's accomplice forms an intentional counterpoint to male travel narratives. In this alternative journey space, conventional black/white division is gradually undermined by gendered alliance. The oppression shared by Amy and Sethe, based on the limits of female movement, represents what Janet Wolff suggests are the possibilities of travel for destabilising the absolutes of patriarchal culture, uniting them regardless of the colour line.[4] Beyond this gendered reading, Sethe's act of anticolonial resistance through movement marks an alternative to the colonial journey that, as I have examined, the text also acknowledges. In the wake of its traumatic consequences it is easy to undervalue Sethe's achievement. Yet her refusal 'to believe that she had come all that way, endured all she had, to die on the wrong side of the river' (90) – when such rivers are 'very important in the creation of colonial, state and county boundaries in the United States' (J. Black 134) – marks an important statement of strength as, crossing the boundary, she – at least for a moment – denies the power it signifies.

Sethe's remembrances that dictate the narrative are, in the wake of this disruption of colonial travel, consumed by such alternative ideas of journeying. Throughout the novel her recollections begin with movement: she is 'hurrying across a field ... walking on two feet meant for standing still ... spinning' (6, 29, 159). What such a song and dance recreation of the past indicates is also a rewriting, a re-play that acknowledges the role of the author and the text in documenting movement, as Morrison has Sethe herself retell the journey: implicitly sensual, fragmented and without conventional spatial markers, capturing the movements of slavery in a revisionist form that emphasises the unpredictable and personal. This subversion is cemented by the fact that through their storytelling Denver and Beloved themselves make Sethe's own journey into a re-play, a *mise en abyme* twice removed from a narrative of colonial reference points. Multiple journeys open the way for multiple dislocations, and for multiple potential meanings.

It is in these terms that Morrison presents her own re-play of the Middle Passage that equals Harris in terms of magical possibility, and once again extends beyond Gilroy's discussion of the slave-ship journey. Morrison's use of the ship not only presents the idea that such a space presents a transformation of identity: Gilroy's sense of the ship as perhaps the premier 'contact zone' (Pratt 6) facilitating cultural change as it provides 'micro-systems of linguistic and political hybridity' (Gilroy, *Black Atlantic* 12). It also suggests that it may be a transformed narrative, where

---

[3]   See C. Wolff 429.

[4]   See J. Wolff 232.

seizing the ambiguity of a space without clear national or cultural affiliation means opening up possibilities and potential for denied agency. Beloved voices the journeys of those who died on the slave ships; she resurrects their stories, which have seemingly drowned in the water with them. This resonance of the past in the present, released through movement, unites Morrison and Harris in the Derridean sense that the erased always leaves a trace of its existence, what Casey in his reading of journeys refers to as '*co-habitancy*' (291): the way in which the journey opens up the possibility of the fusion of human and land, natural and cultural and – most significantly – the contemporary traveller and his or her ancestors. In this fusion of time-frames, there is again utilisation of space outside linear history and privileging of temporal disjunction, evident by the fact that, for Bhabha, Beloved's presence is 'profoundly time-lagged' (*Location* 254).

The passage Beloved recounts is, in contrast to her mother's narrative, a colonial journey, but it is a journey significantly altered in its telling. Rather than closing space down into occidental History, Beloved's narrative releases a space, the trace of a denied voice, no longer the documentation in official figures that reduces individuals to silenced statistics, but instead a magical voicing of the erased. While the details of Beloved's passage and the form in which it is narrated suggest only negative chaos, the remembrance of the reality of such a journey – undoctored by the colonial narrative or its forms – has a powerful and ultimately empowering impact. Indeed, Beloved's death has much in common with Milkman's own escape in *Song of Solomon*, in that it suggests her trauma is a return to the African heritage she later appears to represent, that Sethe 'saw them coming and recognized schoolteacher's hat, she heard wings … . She just *flew* … dragged them through the veil, out, away, over there where no one could hurt them' (emphasis added, 163). Beloved gives the traveller of the Middle Passage movement, makes her an independent traveller, walking silently in an action that cannot be curtailed by either colonialist or patriarch. However much Beloved is 'not a story to pass on' (274 etc.) this silent movement will secure her remembrance, will ensure that her story is reinscribed, drawing its own trace on the landscape, even as it seemingly disappears. It will be re-played in the movement of others, just as Beloved herself is a re-play:

> the rustle of a skirt … the knuckles brushing a cheek … . Down by the streams in the back of 124 her footprints come and go, come and go. They are so familiar. Should a child, an adult place his feet in them, they will fit. Take them out again and they disappear again as though nobody ever walked there. … Beloved. (275)

Thus it will be a journey made available for the future, a narrative of survival even in death that, like those uncovered by Harris's crew, will stimulate awakening.

It is Rushdie, however, that Needham has in mind when she introduces her notion of re-play, and together his main figures of Gibreel and Chamcha in *The Satanic Verses* embody a chaotic experience of movement standing as counterpoint to the colonial journey to create order. Focusing on a globalised celebration of movement, Rushdie juxtaposes the linear metaphors of the train journey with a narrative of air and skyscapes that epitomise fluidity. In such journeys, space is open, free, the 'most insecure and transitory of zones, illusory, discontinuous, metamorphic' (5). Thus if the colonial journey is one of geometric regularity and measurement, then its re-play undermines this. All measurement is relative, all geometry a fractured form that goes beyond its Euclidean structure. Gibreel and Chamcha's flight is an explicit subversion of linear distance:

> How far did they fly? Five and a half thousand as the crow. Or: from Indianness to Englishness, an immeasurable distance. Or, not very far at all, because they rose from one great city, fell to another. The distance between cities is always small; a villager, travelling a hundred miles to town, traverses emptier, darker, more terrifying space. (41)

In a global, metropolitan world, distance is marked not by miles, but by a relative access to popular culture, industrialisation and economic viability.

It is this image – of the re-play as chaotic disjunction from absolute travel – that provides a positive version of postmodern movement within a postcolonial context. As Chamcha and Gibreel merge into one increasingly fluid identity, so in *The Ground Beneath Her Feet* movement and uncertain identity are entwined in the belief that 'I don't have to choose … I don't have to be this guy or that guy … I'll be all of them' (303). And as the colonial image of England is firmly consigned to the past, deconstructed as Ormus, like Chamcha, finds his stereotypes unlike reality, 'utterly lost amidst buildings you recognize … a delirious enough experience' (289), so the western mirage of colonial order is stripped away. It is replaced with a whirring hive of chaotic activity serving to disorientate, where 'maps are wrong' (352), exaggerated in skyscapes where, 'drugged by flight' (253), 'the airplane terror and doubt' (354) means that 'Ormus Cama's head starts pounding' (268).

The applicability of time-lag to such movement is substantiated by the fact that Ormus literally does enter an alternative reality, a mirror of his own, yet with subtle differences that mark a rupture in the ordinary fabric of time. Ironically, it is this alternative reality that is in fact the 'real world'. The reality that the characters – and its readers – exist within is in fact revealed to be the dream. There is even in such representation an explicit acknowledgment of a poststructuralist leaning, in 'heterotopian tendencies, his forays into alternative realities' (537). Such marvellous journeying across worlds, a *mise en abyme* of displacement, parallels Foucault's displaced perception and mirroring:

> The video snowstorm vanishes. In its place is the image of a doll in a chair, holding a circular mirror, in which is reflected a rectangular mirror, which in turn contains the reflection of another doll. (509)

Unlike in previous Rushdie novels, death fails to hinder journeying – a world that is 'not cyclical, not eternal or immutable, but endlessly transforms itself' (145) – personal journeys unfinished, held in suspended animation by mortality that refuses to yield conclusions. Despite Spenta's assertion that Virus 'must surely return' (39) from his inward journey he never will; Gayomart's passage is 'finished before he began' (35), a 'finishing' which asserts an existence that means death is no barrier to his involvement with Ormus and his own, independent, journeys. Whilst Casey asserts that every journey must reach a conclusion (289), the postcolonial narrative defies this finality.

As both loss and the potential for transcendence of this loss, the journey here comes to epitomise all those that have preceded it, a double-edged experience, 'swung moment by moment between elation and despair' (7): the fulcrum that captures the ambivalent construction of a post-space that would form positive value from trauma, without ever deleting the significance of oppression. Even in Rai, the most reluctant of travellers despite 'a name that travelled easily' (18), such a paradox – a mediation of free movement with belonging – is always present. For Rai admits that while 'a kind of India happens everywhere ... if I'm honest I still smell, each night, the sweet jasmine-scented ozone of the Arabian Sea' (417). Indeed, it is ultimately Rai, the least obvious candidate for post-space experience in the novel, who comes to express the importance of the journey most succinctly, in a voice which could be used in itself to sum up the foundations of the notion. He expresses the belief that 'there is *thrilling gain* in this metamorphic destiny, *as well as aching loss* ... which kicks in *only under extreme pressure*. When we are faced with the Immense' (emphasis added, 441, 461).

Such duality indicates how post-space might function as a strategy enabling the colonised identity to be subverted into a resource for empowerment, without reducing in any way the recognition of its oppressive reality. The migrant's loss is not dismissed but, rather than accepting a status as victim, the postcolonial citizen may seize what is valuable in a past that cannot be altered. For it is only through facing the oppression that is the legacy of colonialism, the flux of the cross-cultural and postcolonial journey, that you find possibility:

> Suppose you've got to go through the feeling of being lost, into the chaos and beyond ... . You stepped off the edge of the earth, or through the fatal waterfall, and there it was: the magic valley at the end of the universe, the blessed kingdom of the air. Great music everywhere ... . It feels better than 'belonging' in your lungs. (177)

It is in this sense that we can read Phillips's evocation of 'the space for transformation, the traces of which are found only in the ruins of some master discourse' (79), discussing – unsurprisingly – Bhabha's time-lag and migrant travel.

As the narrative is continually replaying, acknowledging 'we have been here before' (464 etc.), Rushdie explicitly emphasises the re-memory function evident in other postcolonial narratives. Indeed, we may find parallels between much of Rushdie's representation of postmodern travel and narratives such as those of Harris and Morrison. Despite the postmodern bias for the speed of air travel, Rushdie too seems to share Morrison's affection for walking as holding its own nonlinear, chaotic potential. The confusion of London movement is reinforced in *The Satanic Verses* by the journey of Ayesha and her pilgrims which, seemingly ending in death, reflects the tumult of the migrant's journey. It is a unification in the act of walking which places the migrant in the position of the modern pilgrim, a 'drowning' (507) that expresses the act of wandering with blind faith into unknown territory, but also – reflecting the ambivalence of post-space – the potential for a different, positive reading of the same event as 'they walked to Mecca across the bed of the Arabian Sea' (507). Yet it is also a powerful political assertion of the right to movement, a defiant gesture in the wake of the fact that 'the policing of the pavement during the 1970s and early 1980s meant that the streets were unavailable for the kind of leisurely idling associated with *flânerie*' (Procter 101). The need for such walking as an important cultural and spiritual experience is affirmed again in *The Ground Beneath Her Feet*. It is as Ormus 'walks the city streets' that he comes closest to poststructuralist deconstruction, finding '*UnFOld Road*' (289).

So who are such travellers: what might we call those who encapsulate hook's distinction between colonial travel and the postcolonial journey? To conclude, I would like to suggest a possible answer. Reading together two key passages of *The Satanic Verses*, Rushdie seems to present a model of postcolonial movement. The traveller is not to be seen as the exile, for whom there 'is a dream of glorious return' (205). Yet neither is he the migrant, who 'can do without the journey altogether; it's no more than a necessary evil; the point is to arrive' (94). Rather, it is the nomad, 'rootless as the dunes, or rather rooted in the knowledge that the journeying itself ... [is] home' (94), to whom we must aspire. This approaches what John Erickson, in a recent lecture entitled 'Magical Realism and Nomadic Writing in the Maghreb', has referred to as the 'nomadic thought' of the postcolonial novel. Whilst we should be aware of the dangers of taking such a position, acknowledging Caren Kaplan's argument that 'recourse to the metaphors of desert or nomad can never be innocent or separable from the dominant orientalist tropes' (*Questions* 66), nevertheless it is possible to claim nomadism, in the spirit of Gayatri Spivak, as a useful, theoretical position: a strategic nomadism. It is this nomad who may not only arrive at a destination, as does the colonist, but may truly move, creating the journey of deterritorialisation where the fluid and polyvocal movement of the nomad makes it 'deterritorialized par excellence' (Deleuze and Guattari, *Plateaus* 381). As the nomad is that whom the colonist would halt as 'it is a vital concern of every State not only to vanquish nomadism but to control migrations' (Deleuze and Guattari, *Plateaus* 385), it is nomadic space which is the gap of possibility of both the re-play and the time-lag. Smooth and 'qualitatively different from the State space' which is 'gridded' (Massumi xiii) to resemble Noyes's tabular colonialism, nomadic movement is implicitly anticolonial.

If there is one image to define the identity of the traveller who enacts the re-play, then the nomad seems the most appropriate. For in a world without firm meaning, postcolonial authors suggest it is through movement that we forge identity, creating the ground beneath our feet as 'footprints are the only fixed point … made real, step by step' (Rushdie, *Ground* 268): not abandoning identity but rather finding it in unfamiliar places. Presentation of the chaotic journey of the migrant or colonial citizen suggests more than simply a hopeless situation as a victim; movement within a world of grounded possibilities, however problematic, provides personal acts of resistance. In terms of post-space, this means looking towards those spaces where the chaos denied by the pressures of national institutions breaks through in movements that escape its mappings. Fluid and discontinuous, the postcolonial representation of the journey gives post-space a more mutable quality than it would have were it rooted simply in the land-locked. It is the freedom of the journey, its status as an unbordered space open to interpretation, its focus as the ambivalent site where identities are negotiated, that makes it the pivot – the fulcrum – upon which post-space turns. Yet while the openness of such a journey may provide the possibility inherent in post-space, it also raises important questions rather than any definite resolution. For the journey is always in tension with and reliant upon the other spaces – cities, homes, and bodies – that, without location, it stands seemingly in contrast to. Thus as critics posing alternatives to the nation have turned to both micro and macro spaces as interrelated, so investigation of the journey suggests a relationship to smaller spaces that must be pursued. It is to a fuller exploration of these issues, and these other more intimate arenas, that I now turn in order to unravel the postcolonial post-space.

Chapter 3
The Ambiguous Utopia: Postcolonial Cities

Most utopias forget that utopia is nowhere.

(Spivak, *Critique* 318)

The journey, it seems, might represent postcolonial movement to the larger-than-national space. What space then represents a shift towards a smaller-than-national location? An answer may perhaps be found in the form of the city, a space that is often seen to be represented so as to act metonymically as a reflection of national tensions and yet may also be seen to offer its own specific geopolitics. In this chapter I trace the complexities of the relationship between the postcolonial novelist and the city, in particular asking whether there is a difference between dreams of the city and its lived, material reality. On the one hand, the city seems to offer possibilities for spatial resistance absent in national space, rooted in a way that is impossible in the fluid spaces of the journey. Yet it is nevertheless questionable whether – so tied to national politics – it can ever be a truly welcoming space for the postcolonial individual. In the wake of continued mass migration and movement towards the metropolitan centre, such critique of the utopian impulses driving urban settlement presents a powerful counterpoint to the contemporary city's celebrated status as an icon of postmodernity.

Utopian Cities

The epigraph to this chapter is not only a clever play on words – 'utopia' comes from the Greek 'not a place' (*OED*) – but is also an observation of importance for studying postcolonial cities. The city is inherently tied to utopian discourses: to urban space not as lived, material reality, but as dream. Despite various representations of the horrors of the industrialised city, the city has also been *at the same* time a space of projection: of personal desires and communal hopes. As works as diverse as Augustine's *City of God* (426), Plato's *The Republic*, Thomas More's *Utopia* (1516) and William Morris's *News From Nowhere* (1890) validate, it is in the city that the utopia is so often situated; according to Anatole France, historically 'it was Utopians who traced the lines of the first city' (qtd. in Mumford, *Story* 22).

These utopian discourses have particular relevance to how postcolonial novelists interpret urban space. As the colonist justifies imperial seizure of territory in ideal terms of adventure and freedom so the city-utopia is often the focus for similar yearnings. In both cases these ideals are in stark contrast to lived reality. As colonial space overwrites the freedom necessary for territorial expansion with ordering and division, so the utopian city succumbs to similar processes. In envisaging an alternative to a failed imperial Rome, St. Augustine imagines a city that embodies 'forms of authority' (Sennett 7). Thomas More's conditions 'are pretty far from being ideal and humane' (Mumford, *Story* 72), whilst the ideal city of Plato's *Republic* is an enclosed space that, although fluid on the inside, creates an inside/outside division where the 'borders are the borders of a purged discourse' (Ophir 75). Even Morris's *News From Nowhere*, seemingly suggesting a classless and harmonious society, relies upon denial of social mobility and individualism. Such contradiction – between fluidity and the order required to achieve this – is central to both the utopia and to the colonial space. Mumford's acknowledgment in reference to the utopian city of 'a paradox; namely, that in order to ensure freedom it is impossible to practice laissez faire' (*Story* 139) is echoed in 'the myth of unrestricted mobility' which hides 'spatial stratification and organization required by the State' (160, 161) in J.K. Noyes's representation of colonial spatiality.

Thus we have an explicit chain of associations: the utopia is connected to the city, the resulting city-utopia has clear similarities with wider colonial spatial practices. This connection to real-world settlement is particularly significant, in that it suggests utopian desires not as the unreality that their advocates often saw, but instead as indicative of the desires and subsequent control processes existing in real urban spaces. Is there any difference, we must ask, between utopian and colonial visions of the city?

Whilst Mumford connects city and utopia, and works such as Paul Carter's *The Road to Botany Bay* and Felix Driver and David Gilbert's *Imperial Cities: Landscape, Display and Identity* (1999) connect city and colony, few connections have been made between utopian cities and colonies, and none has traced the postcolonial novel's response.[1] Yet both colonial space and the utopian city share a preoccupation with ordering. The delineation found in both colonial space and the utopian city is – and this seems obvious bearing in mind the close relationship between colonial space and colonial cities – a key feature of colonial urban planning. The features Paul Carter associates with the grid plan of the colonial city, 'the notion of authority or the idea of control ... a *traditional* solution' (210), straight lines which 'bounding the traveller, they colonize even him' (222), are the same containment structures of the utopian city in which 'a new exercise in solid geometry' is used to 'impose measure and order' (Mumford, *City* 201). A stronger

---

[1] It falls to Jacobs, in her discussion of largely postcolonial rather than colonial cities in *Edge of Empire* (1996), to bring utopia, city and colony together: for her 'it was in the name of the ideal city that many of the most comprehensive colonial territorialisations and displacements occurred' (20). One recent study, Ralph Pordzik's *The Quest for Postcolonial Utopia* (2001), does examine in detail the utopia in relation to postcolonial literature. Somewhat strangely, however, Pordzik makes no connection between utopia and urban space.

connection is made between the height of colonialism, the city, and the utopia, by Mumford, though he would not put it in such terms:

> In the course of the next three centuries the adventure of exploring and ransacking strange countries loses its hold upon men's imagination ... they are subordinated to another type of conquest – that which man seeks to effect over nature ... . In this new world of falling water, burning coal, and whirring machinery, utopia was born again. It is easy to see why this should have happened, and why about two-thirds of our utopias should have been written in the nineteenth century.' (*Story* 114–15)

What is the historical situation that Mumford describes if not the rational, urbanising phase of imperialism?

Desired City

This connection between colonial cities and the utopian ideal city presents opportunities to explore how postcolonial novelists engage with an urban space of idealised desire; to investigate whether the relationship between colonial nation and postcolony is replicated on the urban scale. Salman Rushdie's representation of the urban seems to offer a direct challenge to the privileging of the city as a space of unrealised possibility. Whilst the Bombay of *Midnight's Children* may initially suggest magical potential that resonates with utopian idealism, the relationship to utopia is in fact ultimately interrogated. The fact that Bombay is constructed entirely as nostalgic remembrance, where 'most of what matters in our lives takes place in our absence' (19), draws it closer to classical utopia as a nostalgic force that denies its own longing for the past, a space that, while created to suggest futurity, in fact looks backwards.[2] Yet this view simultaneously calls into question urban utopias: its nostalgia is also a return to what, for the postcolonial inhabitant, is an imperial history. In these terms, Saleem's idealisation of Bombay is in fact representative not of a tangible possibility, but instead of the unrealisable dreams of the postcolonial citizen, whose past is corrupted permanently by the imposition of colonial rule. This is Rushdie's only ideal city – recurring in its description as 'Wonderland, Peristan, Never-Never, Oz' (55) in *The Satanic Verses,* and in the nostalgic remembrances of Malik Solanka in *Fury* – and in all cases what it acknowledges is hopeless impossibility, rather than a repetition of colonial attempts to realise the utopian in the real-world. For the real spaces created outside this special and problematic relationship, the utopia in its idealised form is far from view.

Through representation of urban space in *Jazz*, Toni Morrison, however, does engage directly with the notion of an ideal city. References planted within the

---

2   See, for example, Lefebvre, *Writing*, 143–4.

text indicate the specifics of the novel's urban setting. To an American reader, or one with knowledge of Harlem, the association is more easily picked up: street names delineate a familiar context. However, criticism of the novel often makes the presence of Harlem a much more concrete construction than the text actually provides. As much as the city in *Jazz* is Harlem, it is also something far more abstract, referred to not by its proper name, but instead by the more general term – 'the City' – repeated throughout the novel.

It is this abstraction that closely ties Morrison's urban representations to utopian discourses. Morrison shifts between a specific context – of black Harlem in the 1920s – and a more transcendent use of the city suggesting it may function as a trope. At times, context is foregrounded, and construction of the present seems indissoluble from the past; while at others, history, and indeed time, seem to cease to hold meaning. 'City' creates a construct seemingly demanding metaphorical reading; yet the constant use of simile, where 'daylight slants like a razor' in 'a city like this one' (7) suggests an entity resistant to reduction to other phenomena.

Such movement can be characterised in terms of Walter Benjamin's definitions of empty and messianic time. The former suggests the conception of a 'homogenous' temporality with linear progression through history up to the present, and an unquestionable assumption of positive progress. The latter indicates 'time filled with the presence of the now' (Benjamin 261) so that the past is judged in relation to current events, the present filled with resonance of the past. It is the abstract quality of 'empty-time' in Morrison's city that allows, at particular moments, disassociation from the real in favour of the more magical-real utopia. The familiar is described in such a way as to take on the properties of a folk or fairy-tale: disassociated from history by the removal of 'Harlem', it is possible for the reader to be swept up in *Jazz*'s narrative and come for an instant to believe in an ideal urbanity, a city described as not perfect, but 'better than that' (107). As such temporality abandons the past and exists in a decontextualised freeze-frame, it captures how utopian space denies its nostalgia in favour of suggestions of an unchanging present progressing so that time itself seems no longer to matter: Morris's London, for example, seems to have little interest in progress and nothing positive to remember. Like the utopia, 'history is over' in the city as it denies its longing for the past, the focus instead being on the prospects of the future, the fact that 'everything's ahead' (7). Thus when Joe tries to remember the past 'almost nothing comes to mind' (29). In a telling contrast, Rushdie's critique of the utopia focuses on the opposite temporality of 'messianic time'. History is a crucial part of the present in his novels and, indeed, the past is only constructed through present circumstances, with the need to 'revise and revise, improve and improve' (*Midnight's* 460–61). Such distinction serves to illuminate the way in which such connections between utopia and dead time are not coincidental: for when we examine Rushdie's rejection of the utopia then it is exactly an opposing model of time that emerges.

Approaching its borders, the travellers to Morrison's city exhibit optimism that is resonant with accounts of classical utopia. On arrival, the urban community creates an attractive vision; Morrison cleverly entices the reader to adopt the same heady excitement that Violet and Joe experience as just two in millions of rural-urban African-American migrants. Wandering but essentially coherent narration effectively captures the busy and vibrant, but ultimately culturally cohesive, quality of city life as what Faris refers to as 'communal discourse' ('Cities' 3). The narrator's repetitions echo the incantatory nature of the music consuming its inhabitants, and the heightened reality of its passionate atmosphere.

This feeling does not necessarily abate when 'Harlem' identity and specifics of place and time are reintroduced. Indeed, in an interview for Louisa Joyner's *Toni Morrison: the Essential Guide* (2003) Morrison has suggested that it is precisely in the service of the magical that specifics of place must exist:

> if I'm going to – as I frequently do – impose either the divine, or the dream, or
> the supernatural into the narrative, then the places have to be very realistic. You
> have to anchor them … .So, I try to have streets and towns and neighbourhoods,
> geography exactly the way it is or would be. (17)

Such statement reveals much about Morrison's utopian cities, and the fact that they appear as both abstract and concrete. In these terms, specifics are also integral to the utopian dream: without them the fantasy would lose a coterminous reality, a reality integral to the utopian city as it should suggest possibility, rather than escape.

This utopian possibility *within* the context of Harlem is evident in the way that it is explicitly a black community, offering possibilities for collective movements uncorrupted by the divisive practices of the slave-master. Within such a context, urban enclosure offers welcome protection and a tangible difference to the colonial world: the ability of the slave-master to pursue runaway slaves across boundaries evident in *Beloved* is contrasted here with solid walls offering crucial defence. While the inhabitants of Ohio in *Beloved* – threatened with recapture – find loving too painful, this is a city in which new desires are indulged, and love blossoms. The sense of self in *Beloved* originating in Baby Suggs's education of free blacks as 'flesh that needs to be loved' (88) comes to fruition; for the narrator of *Jazz*, the body itself is transformed in new space, making you 'dream tall' and feel 'strong … top-notch and indestructible' (7). Crucially, this is not presented as a new self. Rather, it is a reclamation of that denied – overwritten – by slavery, grasped as an authentic, if provisional, identity; for 'in a city, they are not so much new as themselves: their stronger, riskier selves' (33). It is this energy for which Joe and Violet are willing to make the anxious journey. They embrace the city's rhythm – the intoxicating passage of thousands of footsteps – and dance their way into its centre, 'dancing … tracks controlling their feet … the City that danced with them, proving already how much it loved them' (32). Imagination – the free expression denied in Plato's ideal city – is not anathema to Morrison's Harlem. It is its very foundation.

The significance of the utopian city as a motif extends, however, beyond the real-world city, to strike at the heart of the postcolonial imaginary. In this vein, a very different utopian urbanity is offered by Harris's *Jonestown*. *Jonestown* takes as its basis events surrounding attempts to realise utopia: the Jonestown Settlement and 1978 Massacre. In reality, Jonestown was home for approximately nine hundred inhabitants, established by cult leader Jim Jones in 1974 as the location for his Peoples' Temple. Jonestown sprang up in the wake of renewed enthusiasm for utopias: the group chose the socialist-led Guyana for settlement and based its community on socialist principles. As has been comprehensively recounted, the settlement ended on November 18, 1978, much to the Guyanese government's embarrassment, when the vast majority of the group committed suicide or were murdered, following the murder of visiting Congressman Leo Ryan a day earlier.

There is no explicit link between the real Jonestown and the city. Yet it is as a city that Harris chooses to represent it in his novel. This fact is of great significance, in that it suggests that when Harris reflects on Jonestown, he reflects explicitly upon the identity not of cult settlements, but of urban locations. In the chapter 'Foundation of Cities' he establishes an alternative identity for the semirural settlement as an urban space, renaming it 'Jonah City' (81). Here Harris's evocation of the city as a motif may be seen to be a strategic choice, powerfully connecting Jonestown to a history of cities and, in particular, their presentation as utopian. Jonestown is linked in the novel to the specifics of Guyanese utopian culture, to the Guyanese Indian cult under the leader Awakaipu who according to Harris, in the 1840s, 'persuaded representatives from many Indian peoples to offer themselves as a sacrifice at the foot of Mount Roraima' (4–5). Moreover, it is also linked to ancient Mayan and Carib civilisations, and to Augustine's city through Harris's invocation of 'City of God' (10). In this usage, Harris characteristically employs a self-referentiality that adds to the significance of such representation. In *The Whole Armour* the same reference is employed; Harris's linguistic juxtaposition and play on words, 'city of God, the city of gold' (367), suggests a spirituality underlying economic motives, where 'his [Ralegh's] narrow expedition is fractured into a prism of far-flung voyages' (Harris, 'New Preface' 55), so that its initial colonial characteristics are subverted in favour of reference to the biblical presentation of Jerusalem as a golden city. When Harris uses the same terminology in *Jonestown*, he points the reader back to this earlier reference and, by implication, to the utopian promise it represents. Such an image is reinforced by Harris's reference to 'Atlantis, Plato's Cave' (81). This link to the Greek *polis* bears important connotations. For the polis was not a 'city' dictated by size. Rather, in Plato's ideal form, it was to be 'a community' (*Republic* 117, 368e). It is to this definition of the city that Jonah City seems closest. In choosing to represent Jonestown as a city, Harris identifies it as sharing the essential features of urban existence, with all its utopian – and colonial – undertones.

Jonestown is no longer an isolated habitat or event. Rather, it forms part of an endless cyclical history in which patterns of behaviour and social transformation come to be repeated across locations, and across timeframes:

> I was obsessed – let me confess – by cities and settlements in the Central and South Americas that are an enigma to many scholars. ... Was Jonestown the latest manifestation of the breakdown of Populations within the hidden flexibilities and inflexibilities of pre-Columbian civilizations? (4)

Here Harris reintroduces the idea of archaeological layering, a multidimensional space accessed through a living earth first presented in *The Guyana Quartet*. Francisco connects himself and Deacon to 'founders' (85), refugees and displaced indigenous peoples of the twenty-first century who will take up the mandate of the founders of epic cities of history and myth. This resonates with the work of many studies of postcolonial cities, such as those by Paul Carter, Leonardo Benevolo, James Donald and Richard Sennett, for all of whom the city consists of layers that may be stripped away to reveal an often violent and power-laden past. For Sennett, in particular, urbanisation is a process of order overwriting chaos: in Chicago the natural environment was overlaid as 'the grids were laid over irregular terrain ... as if what could not be harnessed to this mechanical, tyrannical geometry did not exist' (52). Other critics emphasise this relationship more positively. Bill Schwarz suggests that 'the urban formations of our own times hold together the inchoate traces of many competing historical times, all jumbled together' (269), a blending of time through space echoed by Jacobs in her discussion of Australian Aborigines as representing 'the possibility of sacred space simply appearing, coming from "below ground"' (114), as their settlements are rediscovered, resisting traditional mapping and geographic surveys. In postcolonial fiction, the attraction of this act of mystical archaeology transcends Harris's spiritualised narratives. In *Anil's Ghost*, for example, Michael Ondaatje frames the interrogation of the Sri Lankan Civil War with the desire to recover cities, an action of restoration that offers the possibility of a more hopeful urban landscape:

> Most of what Sarath wished to know was in some way linked to the earth. His desire, he had told her, was to write a book someday about a city in the south of the island that no longer existed. Not a wall of it remained, but he wanted to tell the story of that place. It would emerge out of this dark trade with the earth, his knowledge of the region in chronicles. (29)

Sarath is an archaeologist with an ability that echoes that of Jonestown's narrator: able to 'take one imagined step and be in an earlier century ... eliminate the borders and categories, to find everything in one landscape' (191).

The re-emergence of the cities of the past in such a way not only foregrounds an overwritten space, but also reasserts the unconventional temporality usefully captured in the concept of messianic time already identified as a feature of Rushdie's urban space. The way in which, in *Jonestown*, Francisco's present is filtered through events both past and future – signalling a resonance with the cities of the past and looking forward to their future creation – seems to be captured almost perfectly by Benedict Anderson's definition of messianic time as 'a simultaneity of past and future in an instantaneous present' (24), so that conventional chronologies are disrupted. This application also resonates with the Jungian contexts to which Harris's work is often connected: Jung's definition of a synchronic field of experience in which 'everything is interconnected, and there is no difference between psychological and physical facts, past, present or future' (Salman 54).

Jonestown in many ways retains the ideal city's atmosphere not as ordered utopia, but as an ideal utopia. Harris, whilst essentially conveying the sense of horror felt by outside commentators, continually referring to a 'holocaust' (113 etc), shows in *Jonestown* some sympathy with Jones's aims. He highlights positive aspects of Jonestown overshadowed by its tragic conclusion, the fact that the original intention was that 'sea defences and walls and foundations of villages and cities would be shaken' (84) rather than reinforced. Francisco reflects this when he acknowledges 'I was a South American Utopian in the 1970s [creating ...] a wholly different architecture, a wholly different Imagination from the politics and the institutions of economic fixture and habit' (83). As the *New York Times* at the time of the massacre notes, Jones and his followers did create a new settlement, if not a city, explicitly identified with 'utopian socialist overtones' (Crewdson A20). In the context of cold war politics, newspaper reporting indicates that for the American government it was Jonestown's anti-capitalism that was the source of the massacre. But its establishment was also specifically an anticolonial assertion: Gordon Lewis sees the founding of the Jonestown community as an action that the Guyanese government only agreed to because of problems that were 'the end result of European colonialism in the region' (25). Without colonialism, which drew the Guyanese government into accepting the settlement, there would be no Jonestown.

These texts illustrate how the postcolonial city takes many forms, ranging from distinctly real world urban settlements to metaphorical use of urbanity. Nevertheless, what such representations share is awareness of the resonances that the term 'city' evokes. Tied to a history of the city as utopian fantasy, postcolonial authors create a space that is as much ideal as realised. And as this dreaming is tied to the colonialist's own vision of the function of city planning – Jonestown a 'city' of order connected to Guyanese colonialism, Harlem a city tied to neo-colonial patterns of exploitation – so each city is also a commentary on colonial space.

Nowhere City

Connecting the city to colonial discourse, at the centre of all of these representations is utopian promise undercut with strong awareness of urban space's power inequalities preventing ideals from being realised. The planner's desires are always subject to corruption or inherently prejudicial application. Thus whilst emphasising many of the elements of utopian cities, postcolonial representations ultimately refuse the utopian label. Instead, they illuminate the intensely subjective nature of urbanity: that one person's utopia is another's dystopia. This is not a rejection of the city, but rather suggests a radical re-visioning, questioning the premise that it is possible to construct an ideal, objectified space capable of serving a disparate population. Thus on the urban scale, as with the journey, both colonial ordering and its contemporary legacy are undercut. In illuminating the limits of the utopian urban order – its underlying chaos – so each author also reveals the limits of what may be seen as a parallel colonial ordering.

If Morrison provides the clearest utopian city, then it is Rushdie's fiction that most indubitably delineates the urban space that is from its beginnings explicitly dystopic. Rushdie's cities are the most resistant to abstractions, employing little of the narrative distancing that Morrison and Harris use to give their cities mythical qualities. It is therefore possible that there is a connection between creating a utopian urbanity and magical re-visioning. The alternative reading of this awareness is that there is a distance between the real city and the utopia, which it may be impossible to overcome.

Rushdie's most extreme dystopia is the London of *The Satanic Verses*. In the light of the significance of this text to post-space journeys, as I explored in the previous chapter, this dystopia is particularly significant, providing an often-undermined counterpoint to the novel's postmodern celebration of movement. Ironically, like Jonestown, London is a space that in reality exists within a utopian discourse. Set at the height of Margaret Thatcher's conservative administration, *The Satanic Verses* presents a vision that stands in contrast to the image created for London by dominant individuals in government and international business in the 1980s, so comprehensively outlined by Jon Bird's study 'Dystopia on the Thames' (1993). The Thatcherite image of London echoes previous utopian representations of 'the transforming experience of contemporary London' (R. Williams 272). Yet what emerges in *The Satanic Verses* is the underside of this space, a clear foregrounding of the impossibility of realising a universal ideal.

Rushdie's London also reflects Joseph McLaughlin's view that imaginative writers deploy 'a particular metaphoric discourse … in order to read the increasingly mysterious nature of their metropolitan world' (1). For McLaughlin this metaphor is the urban jungle, but in *The Satanic Verses* the city can be seen to encapsulate what Penelope Reed Doob terms 'labyrinthicity … metaphorical labyrinths … places from which safe exit is difficult or impossible' (2, 48). The novel explicitly defines London in such terms, described as a 'hellish maze' (201). This highlights the confusion faced by the migrant even in a city seemingly ordered and structured, which illuminates the fact that such order is often provisional. As sight is emphasised, 'squeezed lids tightly shut open shut over myopic eyes, replaced glasses, opened eyes' (243), it suggests that the maze viewed from above is very different from the maze seen from within. The former allows panoptic surveillance and manipulation, the latter involves much more limited perspectives, where one is the object of surveillance and is frequently without control. For, as Penelope Reed Doob notes, 'maze-treaders, whose vision ahead and behind is severely constricted and fragmented, suffer confusion, whereas maze-viewers who see the pattern whole, from above or in diagrams, are dazzled by its complex artistry' (1), capturing a space that is both order and disorder. The maze assists containment as it provides a hierarchy of territorial knowledge that firmly divides the cultural insider – the police force or city planner – from those who cannot negotiate an unfamiliar geography.

Such representation by Rushdie draws attention to what has been termed the 'legibility' (Lynch 2) of cities, a view required for meaningful interaction with urban space. This legibility is not available to the migrant who, trapped within a space filled with indecipherable codes and unfamiliar routes, is denied the knowledge available to more permanent citizens. Though Gibreel tries frantically to navigate London, his A–Z of 'lived' space becomes increasingly redundant. He is defeated by a space of twisting and contorting pathways firmly dividing him from the indigenous population. Without belonging and the knowledge this promises – 'he did not have any idea of the true shape' – London makes no sense:

> that most protean and chameleon of cities he grew convinced that it kept changing shape as he ran around beneath it, so that the stations on the Underground changed lines … laws of space and time had ceased to operate. (201)

Chamcha, too, has a similar experience: for him the city is inextricable. Significantly, the notion of sight – so connected to the colonial control of territory – is again emphasised:

> The city thickened around them as a forest; the buildings twined together … 'No light can get in here,' she whispered to him. 'It's black; all black.' (255)

The city itself becomes an enemy, the riddle that must be solved.

Perhaps Rushdie is unaware of the closeness to historical truth in such narrative. For Driver and Gilbert, studying interwar Underground posters, 'the imperial capital was represented through its transport networks … offering the visitor an experience that *could be gained only* through movement between them' (emphasis added, 14). Yet in casting London in such a way, Rushdie succeeds in reversing the stereotypes of magical-realism as the representation of a specifically 'third-world' environment. It is not the former colony that is a land of 'phantom imps' (250), but the imperial centre itself.

Division between the walker of the city and its observers, however, also resonates with more violent images of surveillance. While this undercuts the common perception of utopias as free and suggests Thatcher's idealised presentation of London as fallacious, it also ironically supports utopian discourse in the way it confirms the utopia as walled and hierarchical. In these terms the utopian city becomes a maze that cannot be breached without a link to its dominant forces, a version of Davis's 'Fortress LA' that has been transferred to London by Jacobs in her discussion of the '"re-walling" of the City of London' (67). It is brought to the forefront by Rushdie's evocation of the police force who implement such order as the 'New Empire in Britain', cast as 'that colonising army, those regiments of occupation and control' ('New Empire' 132). Racism exists within a system where, as for colonial control of space, sight is essential. One is judged on physical appearance, and is subject to the defining gaze of other public citizens. Chamcha's experience of the police, and by extension the city they monitor, is one of '"spectating" … "watchfulness" … "surveillance"' (162), a sense of being watched, unsure of what lies ahead and where the controlling forces lie:

> The talk of surveillance techniques had reunited immigration officers and policemen … the faraway voices of his captors speaking eagerly of the need for more video equipment at public events and of the benefits of computerized information. (162)

Yet London is also a twentieth-century labyrinth:

> This is what a television camera sees: … it chooses sides … no slaughters here, no torture, no military coups …. These people are burning their own streets. (454–5)

Surveillance here is supported by what Eugene McLaughlin and John Muncie refer to as 'hyper-panopticism' (130): a voracious media, a mobile eye reminiscent of Mumford's walls of 'instant communication' (*City* 605) and Carter's 'satellite eye' (xx) that views the migrant from the neo-colonial position.

This representation must be seen to extend beyond the postcolonial in its most obvious form, to a more general comment on the insidious control of public space, reinforced by media technology. For Iain Sinclair, for example, writing not from a postcolonial but a postmodern position, London is similarly constructed: it is 'a colony … a surveillance net … . Each time a camera pans to catch you, your life is peeled off another layer' (*Lights* 41). Within this reading, it is more than coincidence that Sinclair's commentaries on London are consumed by a vision of London as colonial city. In Sinclair's *London Orbital* (2002), for example, pubs are described as colonial outposts (229), Wembley Stadium as 'imperialist' (360); new developments are 'colonial estates' (302). What exists is not real, but a geography that resonates with utopian impulses; describing Hessayon's Edwardian novel *Capel Bells* Sinclair notes that 'the gravity of Hessayon's novel pulls towards the notion of Arcadia as an achievable condition' (97). Indeed, the M25 is the embodiment of the utopia or at least the route to it: it 'goes nowhere' (535). It is also resonant with the utopia's empty, abstract time, as Sinclair declares that 'Time has been suspended' (4). Yet – contaminating this vision – there is the opportunity for the past to enter the present as 'part of our task in this circumnavigation of London is to become our fathers, our grandfathers … . Reading Victorian memoirs, we come to believe that these events have not happened yet' (382). What this offers is a direct return to the colonial, as Sinclair reveals his great-grandfather to have been a manager of tea plantations (387).

Fascinated as early as *Lud Heat* (1975) with mythical ley lines, Sinclair, like Rushdie, rejects the utopian myth to expose its silenced, overwritten, dystopian foundations. Focusing in *London Orbital* on the Madhouses at the city's periphery, Sinclair offers an alternative reading of the urban space to its utopian imaginary: what the M25 signifies is not a revolution of communication, but a border that marks the city's exclusion of difference, described complete with pertinent references to Foucault. This is a colonial method of control. Within what are described in terms of the 'prison colony' (337) the inmates/patients must create their own entertainment 'like colonialists in a distant outpost of Empire' (178), whilst the staff are themselves seen as 'colonial administrators' (338). Sinclair continually uses this mode of reference: another hospital is a 'colony-estate' (452); rebuilt in the present such hospitals are still colonies, only now of Barratt homes (489). Quoting Jessie Weston, Sinclair affirms that '"the otherworld is not a myth, but a reality"' (59) and, in doing so, echoes Rushdie's dystopian city.

Equally, in Sinclair's fiction, the same motifs reappear. In his novel *Downriver* (1991), which is framed by a search for rare editions of Conrad novels, the development of London by a Thatcherite government is described in terms of models of division resonant with colonial demarcation of space: chopping the city into fragments, leaving it for Sinclair – like Harris – to strip away the development and reveal an alternative city. In the chapter 'The Isle of Doges (*Vat City plc*)' these parallels are most clearly exposed: the city exists within an 'age of fraudulent dystopias' (268), connected to a 'mental grid ... malign geometry' (269). With its own timelessness revealed in the narrator's comment that 'we have been here forever' (275), distance between dystopia and the utopian planning central to the Thatcherite capitalist vision blurs. And it is here, in the midst of geometry, planning, ordering and utopian/dystopian imagery that Sinclair reveals the urban capitalist developer as colonialist:

> Now serious predators, with multinational connections moved in, grabbed their percentage, and let the place collapse: skins tore from the buildings, radiation-sick lizard flesh. Many were never completed. Only a much-photographed frontage existed: colonies of rats multiplied behind exhibitionist façades. (266)

In Sinclair's literature of linguistic games and interconnectedness, the connection between the colonies of rats and the equally vermin-like previous inhabitants cannot be ignored.

It seems more than coincidental that the form Sinclair employs in the novel, with its fantastic re-creations of history, self-referentiality and mythical reconstructions of place – in this case London – has much in common with magical-realist modes of representation, albeit in their most postmodern form. In exposing what is represented as the neo-colonial forces of Thatcherite England, Sinclair's narrative suggests that postcolonial interrogations of space do not always spring from the most likely of sources. Equally, the realist neo-colonial critique offers a similar picture. For Robert Newman in his anti-globalisation novel *The Fountain at the Centre of the World* (2003), for example, neo-colonial corporations conduct a process of spatial manipulation as they both exploit and facilitate unequal geographical development. Crossing continents as it focuses on Mexico, the United States and England, the novel asks the reader to explore how the urban spaces of the west control local communities in disparate parts of the world. Like Sinclair, these spaces of contemporary global power betray their connection to the spatial ordering of a colonial past, as 'with money and power, it seemed, London shrunk down to its constituent nineteenth-century villages and the city made sense', to form a space of order complete with its own Rushdiesque 'geometrical patterns' (6). Only Evan, the novel's media manipulator and avatar of globalisation, can see the 'true pattern of London' (6–7), aware that 'power was the perspective from which a confusing urban layout became legible' (6). For those in the novel without this power – the displaced figures of Chano and Daniel caught in the Seattle riots of 1999 – the western city offers a different perspective: confusion, alienation and a police presence that bears comparison with Rushdie's own imperialising force.

Here dystopia is not in the future, it is in the present, and is real: like utopia, it reveals its inherent connection to the reality of cities. Rushdie creates a palimpsest city that is not a magical underworld but a hellish one, in which the immigrant community is supervised and yet, paradoxically, is denied recognition by political administrations, and also by the majority of society. Ironically, this negative vision is the only way the postcolonial novel presents utopia in the traditional sense: the representations of cities it offers truly are 'nowheres' that form the denied undersides of the real. For within this community, 'another … was also right there, visible but unseen' (Rushdie, *Satanic* 351), reflecting Jacobs's argument that 'First World cities have their Third World neighbourhoods, global cities have their parochial underbellies, colonial cities have their postcolonial fantasies' (158). Rushdie finds multiple Londons, exposing the versions so frequently denied space by the Thatcher administration. Sinclair reaffirms this vision of the city: it is London's poorest boroughs that are at the centre of his own dystopian representation: Hackney, with its run-down estates, is being rebuilt in miniature, redesigned for the future. What such models offer are 'ghosts of soon-to-be-demolished Utopian experiments' (*London Orbital* 526).

As Sinclair emphasises, these perspectives are not only tied to the outlooks of particular racial groups, they are also gendered, classed and generational. Rushdie, too, does not deny this complex reality in *The Satanic Verses*. As Hind mourns a language, in 'translation … lost' (249), making her 'merely one-of-the-women-like-her' (250), her children exist in a world that is as different from their parents' existence as it is from the official London they exist beneath, 'growing up refusing to speak their mother-tongue' (250) and rejecting '"Bungleditch"' (259). The poverty that encircles Gibreel as he walks through East London is a damning indictment not only of racism, but of the class inequalities that lie beneath the City of London's prosperity:

> Low-cost high-rise housing enfolds him. *Nigger eat white man's shit*, suggest
> the unoriginal walls ... . The towers stand up on stilts, and in the concrete
> formlessness beneath and between them is the howling of a perpetual wind, and
> the eddying of debris: derelict kitchen units, deflated bicycle tyres, shards of
> broken glass, dolls' legs, vegetable refuse extracted from plastic disposal bags
> by hungry cats and dogs, fast-food packets, rolling cans, shattered job prospects,
> abandoned hopes, lost illusions, expended angers, accumulated bitterness,
> vomited fear, and a rusting bath. (461)

Rushdie follows one short line of racism, nine words long, with one over seventy
words long on the decay and decline that has allowed it to emerge on the estate
walls. Thus while the council estate's racist graffiti suggests Rushdie is well
aware of the poor urban community's tendency to turn to racism as an answer
to its problems, this is situated within the context of a broader sense of London's
inequalities and harshness. As for Sinclair, so for Rushdie it is clear that London's
colonial control affects more inhabitants that just the ethnic minority or migrant.

   Rushdie's London here captures heterotopia through discontinuous,
multiperspective reality, a space where 'I see myself there where I am not'
(Foucault, 'Of Other Spaces' 24). Yet, it is also the opposite – Foucault's
panopticon – as Bentham's design reflects the labyrinth, maintaining the chaos
and containment, the inextricability and impenetrability, which are the dangers
inherent in the maze: the disciplinary structure of a 'segmented, immobile, frozen,
space. Each individual is fixed in his place' (Foucault, *Discipline* 195). Here it is
worth remembering that, for Mumford, the panopticon is a utopia (*Story* 252).
Both panopticon and heterotopia, order and disorder, the distance between utopia
and dystopia is increasingly narrowed. The fact that Gibreel lives in a magical-
realist extension of messianic time – as he literally survives within two divergent
historical periods through the spaces of London and Jahilia – is of great assistance
in allowing us to clarify the role of temporality in the migrant's existence. If utopia
relies on empty time, it is clear that the complications of postcolonial space rely
upon its opposite.

   Such distinction is illustrated by the fact that Rushdie's New York quickly
features the same complications as London. In *Fury*, New York is initially cast by
Rushdie in more utopian terms, described as representing the possibility of 'living
in a golden age' (3). And yet before the novel's pages even reach double figures,
New York comes to serve as both colonial city of the past and imperial city of the
present. If London has its labyrinth builders, New York has its 'Puppet Kings'
(161) that invoke the philosopher kings of Plato's ideal city. Its utopian aspects are
quite clearly reliant on its neo-colonial form, its order stemming from international
capitalism, from neo-colonial profit, that means the city 'boiled with money' (3).
One cannot get further away from the socialist ethos underlying the utopias of
Morris, yet at the same time one could not be closer to the power and exploitation
upon which the nations at the centre of such dreams were so often built:

> Such plundering and jumbling of the storehouse of yesterday's empires, this melting
> pot or *métissage* of past power, was the true indicator of present might. (43)

In the light of such representation it is impossible not to agree completely with
Sharon Zukin's view that New York is 'a dismembered imperial space ... whose
utopian joining of freedom and power looks like a dystopia of dirt, violence and
anarchy. Simultaneously utopia and dystopia' (50). Indeed, there is a particular
relationship between the utopia and its failure that will be further developed in
Jonestown. As Jones gradually corrupts his own ideal with his thirst for power,
so Rushdie's narrator reflects a similar corruption of ideals in his comment that
'Rome did not fall because her armies weakened but because Romans forgot what
being a Roman meant' (86). Attached to a lament at New York's lack of community
and divisive 'electric fences' (86), Rushdie's critique of both classical and modern
cities focuses on their relationship to order and control.

This construction of New York reflects the fact that American planners were
not exempt from temptations to use the grid to formulate social hierarchies: for
Sennett such use of the grid is clearly a neo-colonial usage of planning as it forms
for Americans the way to 'erasure of the presence of an alien Other rather than by
colonization' (62), its control of public space used to demarcate exclusion zones
denying the diversity of its population. The Harlem of *Jazz*, too, reinforces this
reading. For 'if you pay attention to the street plans, all laid out, the City can't
hurt you ... . All you have to do is heed the design' (8, 9) as there is a track you
'can't get off' (120). Reflecting such control, Morrison's city is unwelcoming of
outsiders and does not tolerate difference. The fact that there is 'one building ...
full of rich West Indians who kept pretty much to themselves' (43) exposes Harlem
as a city of 'racial exclusion' (Pile, 'Heterogeneity' 24).

Such reversal in *Jazz* of the utopian promise of Harlem as a free black city
is deeply ironic. Despite more freedom, movement is more limited; with the
security of the neighbourhood comes stagnation as 'you don't please to go many
places because everything you want is right where you are' (10). What results
is an increasingly narrowed existence. This reflects the fact that a strong black
presence in the city was a relatively new, post-1900, phenomenon. Although the
national picture was one of greater integration, black migrants were increasingly
located within particular cities, and, indeed, isolated in particular areas within
them. Morrison's urban space is not New York, but Harlem: a city-within-a-city
that announces its exclusion from the wider locale. Hence Malvonne is only
interested in 'neighborhood people' (41), while Alice Manfred finds herself 'first
... frightened of Illinois, then of Springfield, Massachusetts, then Eleventh Avenue,
Third Avenue, Park Avenue. Recently she had begun to feel safe nowhere south
of 110th Street' (54). As 'Fifth Avenue was for her the most fearful of all. That
was where whitemen leaned out of motor cars with folded dollar bills' (54), class
difference is implicitly connected to these limitations. Here Morrison captures the
essence of Harlem's social history, reflecting Steve Pile's argument that 'class and

racial relations interact to produce Harlem as a doubly marginalized urban space' ('Heterogeneity' 21).

Morrison's Harlem is explicitly a post-slavery space: the narrator acknowledges the erased history that is so much a part of its inhabitants' movement, in the same way that the utopian ideal always comes in the wake of perceived hardship or political unrest (E. Barker xiii.). So 'part of why they loved it was the specter they left behind … . The wave of black people running from want and violence crested in the 1870s; the '80s; the '90s but was a steady stream in 1906 when Joe and Violet joined it' (33), as black Americans aim to remake their lives through post-slavery migration. Such awareness means the illusion of the empty-time of utopia cannot be maintained; ironically, it is in descending into the 'messianic time' of a fluid past and present that we are back in the real. Within this resisted remembrance newness as a retrieval of the self is transfigured into a loss of the community that pre-existed individualism. Joe reminds those he visits of this distinction in the form of rural and urban divisions, with a voice 'they heard only when they visited stubborn old folks who would not budge from their front yards and overworked fields to come to the City' (71).

Were it not for Morrison's awareness of the horrors her characters are fleeing from she would be in danger here of opposing artificially city and countryside, replacing urban idealisation with a rural parallel. However, Morrison's presentation suggests not negative nostalgia indicating a rejection of improvement, but instead rather the genuine threat of a cultural void. Morrison reflects the fact that Harlem allowed black Americans to believe 'they too could be modern and lead city lives', asserting 'their *right* to participate in city life and the production of the New – to be creative' (Pile 21). But she also notes the flipside of cultural loss, that 'many felt the loss of older (and for some, distinctly African) identities' (Pile 24). There is a new capacity for love in the city, but Morrison's contrast of the nature of this passion with the security of rural courtship suggests not only celebration of freedom, but also mourning for less aggressive times and places, the fact that the inhabitant 'forgets little pebbly creeks and apple trees … forgets a sun that used to slide up like the yolk of a good country egg … doesn't look up to see what happened to it or to stars made irrelevant by the light of thrilling, wasteful street lamps' (34).

The city's music embodies this distinction; the flipside of its freedom is a quick-paced and sensual abandon directly connected to Joe's infidelity. Here Morrison suggests that such behaviour would be unlikely had Joe and Violet remained in the rural south. In contrast with Rushdie's nostalgic migrants and Harris's nonlinear fluidity, it is clear that for Morrison rapid change to urbanisation has had a strong corrosive effect. The forgetting of history is, as De Man recognises in his reading of Nietzsche, a return to the sensual (here represented by jazz itself), as 'Moments of genuine humanity thus are moments at which all anteriority vanishes, annihilated by the power of an absolute forgetting' (147). Yet it is also a dangerous and impossible task; for 'in severing itself from the past, it [modernity] has at the same time severed itself from the present' (De Man 149). Violet, in particular, is increasingly aware of the strength she has lost, as 'twenty years doing hair in the City had softened her arms and melted the shield that once covered her palms and fingers' (92). Without such a shield, you are more vulnerable, as urban space offers its own dangers for which you are unprepared. Described through geographical metaphors, 'alleyways, crevices one steps across all the time' (23), Violet's city life ends in increasing mental deterioration and a split identity.

For Morrison, there is a complex negotiation to be made: between freedom and security, love and pain. History tells a story of enslavement, but also the security of a common belief system where there is no room to love, and where the resulting pain is not only this but also physical and brutal. Yet the future, seemingly full of freedom, contains its own imprisonments, more mental than physical, and with the freedom to love comes a new kind of pain. Morrison's use of the divided city may also be seen as a metaphor for this tension: between those seeing clearly from above and those confused by the limited horizons of the pedestrian, 'the watchers on the pavement and those in the windows above' (58). Upstairs there are 'looking faces', below there is 'shadow where any blasé thing takes place' (7): those dreaming in the city's windows and those walking on its streets.

That the utopia can be complicated like this may explain Harris's use of the city and its utopian associations. Revisiting the plethora of settlements Harris engages with, it is clear they are not only utopian cities in the sense of being based on ideals of freedom and harmony, but that in most cases they are also cities that declined in the wake of similar forces, ultimately diverging from their original ideals. The Mayan and Carib civilisations and the Guyanese Indian cult Harris references all suffered due to an assertion of power. Thus as Harris connects the utopian city as it is transferred to reality with a violent end, so Jones becomes an echo of both Awakaipu and the Spanish colonists, Jonestown an echo of the cities they destroyed. Like Awakaipu, Jones's charismatic personality ultimately evolved into authoritarianism. Like the Spanish colonists, he also destroyed a population in the name of settlement. Ironically, this means that despite its initial motivation, what Jonestown ultimately becomes is the model not of the anticolonial city, but – in its ordering and ultimate imprisonment of its inhabitants – of the colonial city. Rather than opposing the ordering on which the utopian city is ultimately built, Jonestown comes to mirror it: the negative aspects of the western civilisations Harris invokes encapsulate not only what Jonestown is initially against, but also what it eventually becomes.

In this sense Harris must be seen, like Rushdie and Sinclair, to utilise the ideal city to illuminate its failings. Connecting to a history of urban settlement offers connection to a history of oppression, exposing the inherent contradiction in trying to realise the 'nowhere' of utopia and to form from it a real space. Using Jonestown is a pertinent choice. The nature of the Jonestown settlement did in reality show an affinity for colonial models and their ancient precursors. As Plato's ideal city abolishes the family, so Jim Jones would abolish family rights in favour of the group: it was the removal of individuals, particularly children, by concerned family that was a strong motivation behind the massacre. Cast by newspaper and magazine reports as a king on a makeshift 'throne' (Steele 34), Jones invoked the philosopher-kings of Plato's utopia. As he was seen as someone forming a 'colony' (Neff 6), despite the support of the Guyanese government, so Harris's Jonah Jones *is* a colonialist, referred to as a 'conquistador' (*Jonestown* 123). The sexually charged atmosphere of the Greek city was echoed in the real Jonestown's sexual promiscuity. This allows Harris to suggest in his own text that Jonah's colonialism extends to his preoccupation with women, who are described as 'a collective map of place to be conquered' (120), as they take on the properties of territory.

That it is Plato's cave that Harris uses to introduce his continuity of settlements particularly illustrates this intention. Referring to 'The Simile of the Cave' in Plato's *The Republic* reinforces the flawed nature of those who establish settlements, caught in an illusory condition where 'they would believe that the shadows ... were the whole truth' (Plato, *Republic* 318, 515c). Atlantis, while it points to Harris's interest in hidden fragments of the past, also immediately invokes loss; it is a settlement destroyed by ecological disaster, which, for Harris, is frequently attributed to the abuse of the environment by man:

> I glimpsed the rape of Atlantis, Plato's Atlantis, far beneath me. Rape of Virgin Atlantis. It encompassed Jonestown, nameless Jonestown, in the belly of the flood. In that flood lay the lineaments of the drowned, pre-Columbian New World, since the European Conquest, in every mutilated landscape and catchment and lake. (135–6)

It is to this dystopic reading of the city that the name 'Jonah City' itself directs us, suggesting a correlation between the biblical figure of Jonah – represented as a man whose personal feelings overrode the fates of those within the city he was supposed to care about, and who, despite being God's messenger, held desires that were in fact in conflict with this role – and Jim Jones. It also draws comparisons between Jonestown and Nineveh, a city of unruly individuals worshipping false gods. Once again, distinction between utopia and dystopia is not a matter of empiricism, but perspective.

The harsh nature of the postcolonial city is reinforced by how even those writers who seem most disposed towards magical narratives find it difficult to engage the city in such representation. An author such as the African magical-realist Ben Okri, for example, is seen by some critics as presenting a marvellous world 'untroubled by hard reality' (Hattersley 5), obscuring social commentary with magical descriptions. Whilst *The Famished Road* (1991), Okri's Booker Prize triumph, has been praised (Gates Jnr. 3), its sequel *Songs of Enchantment* (1993) has been described as full of 'purple passages' that make it 'less convincing' (Robinson 10). Michael Gorra's review complains about a lack of logic in the novel (24) while, symptomatically, discussing it without reference to Africa. Similarly, reviewing *Infinite Riches* (1999), the final part of the Famished Road trilogy, Fiona Pitt-Ketley wants 'fewer spirits and more reality' (4), and Andrea Henry 'yearns for solid ground' and feels the need to remind the author that 'African is magical, but it is also real' (15). In terms of spatial politics the result of such readings of Okri's most famous work is that they tend to emphasis the central character of Azaro's 'physical and sensory engagement with immediate surroundings' (Cezair-Thompson 39) rather than on any sense of spatial alienation. If any author, therefore, should be able to present the postcolonial city positively, one might think it would be Okri. Yet Okri's engagement with the city in the trilogy defies this reading. Rather, in common with the depressing and dystopian visions of the city I have outlined, the urban space is the most problematic to successfully re-vision.

It is only in the third book of his trilogy, *Infinite Riches*, that Okri makes the political, and explicitly imperial, nature of the setting explicit. Azaro, a spirit *abiku* child, lives in an unnamed locale that is a reflection of Nigeria's troubled history, displaced on to a mythical space. The Governor-General is the ultimate maze-creator, a figure who can alter the very nature of reality. Here, chaos is not that of chaos theory, but instead a representation of the destructive forces of imperial rule:

> He rewrote our nightspaces, made them weirder, peopled them with monsters and stupid fetishes; he rewrote our daylight, made it cruder, made things manifest in the light of dawn seem unfinished and even unbegun … . The alternation created new spirits which fed the bottomless appetite of the great god of chaos. (127–8)

Here we see not the reinstallation of chaos by postcolonial citizens, but instead that original chaos that the imperial force utilises to justify expansion, only to then overwrite with order.

Such a view means that the postcolonial critique is never as explicit as in Rushdie's narratives, for example. Yet, while Azaro, as spirit child, is able to fly unhindered above the city, those inside it, such as Mum, face an experience that is not in fact dissimilar to that of Rushdie's panoptic and police-controlled London. There is a force whose advantage lies in its ability to monitor her, and in its imperial knowledge of the maze. Not only does the maze-like city turn into the winding pathways of the Cretan labyrinth, but it also assumes the heat of a labyrinth of fire; it is the maze as conceived by Dante; maze as dystopia, as hell:

> Bottles cracked on the street. The road became a boiling river … . Cracks appeared on people's faces. Children playing in the street collapsed suddenly. The air was still … . There were inexplicable fires in the market place. (137–8)

While Mum would like to liberate the city's prisons, she is prevented from doing so by the 'ears' of the city (24). The 'hidden view of the Governor-General' (38) baffles the women on their mission:

> Together, all eight of them – hard-headed women ... spent the whole day
> tramping the labyrinthine streets of the heated city. ... But at the first precinct
> they came upon the policemen were *patiently waiting* for them. (40–41)

Okri's choice of language suggests that there is no coincidence in such an
occurrence: the police are waiting, and waiting with the composure that only
comes with the arrogance of prior knowledge – the women are defeated by a power
privileged with a vision that they are themselves denied. What is important about
such a chaotic city is that here, in the urban space, transformation of that chaos to
possibility does not seem to be available. Whilst the death of the mystical villain
Madame Koto at the end of *Infinite Riches* means that 'a pestilence had been lifted'
(392), the city is still policed and the confusion remains. So tied to wider political
structures (and in this case undoubtedly reflective of Nigeria's continued troubles),
even a mythical narrative such as Okri's cannot help but acknowledge the limits
of the chaotic city.

Carnival City

I want to suggest, however, that such complication need not be entirely pessimistic.
The problematised city offers its own possibilities. In particular, an imperial city
such as London does not signify uni-directional influence; to study it is not simply
to acknowledge oppressions caused by colonisation, but also to subvert the colonial
discourse of progress as the colonised city is seen to have actively influenced its
imperial counterpart. Within this reading, as the site of anti-imperialist politics, the
oppressive city is also the most politically powerful: within it, there are avenues
for resistance and subversion. Two strategies, I would argue, are central to such
re-visioning and need particular consideration, strategies which can be referred to
as *carnivalisation* and *displacement*.

In Chapter Two, I indicated the possibilities of examining spaces smaller than
as well as larger than the nation-space. It is to further development of this need
that the strategy of displacement is invoked, where the city gradually shifts out of
focus in deference to its microstructures. Here, the belonging that ethnic minorities
aim to produce does not mean taking over an entire city, but rather involves
celebrating difference at the level of the public buildings and certain open spaces
which construct the city. For Nestor Garcia Canclini, these spaces have particular
importance as 'violence and public insecurity, the incomprehensibility of the city
... lead us to search for selective forms of sociability in domestic intimacy and
in trusting encounters' (208). The displacement of the city in favour of smaller
spaces thus offers the possibility for an alternative location of resistance, a pocket
of safety within the city-proper.

It is this strategy of displacement that Morrison uses in *Jazz*. More personal
relationships indicate that the city is still a space of possibility compared to what

preceded it.[3] Outside of public view, 'under the covers' where 'they don't have to look at themselves anymore', Joe and Violet continue to survive, 'inward toward the other' (228). Here the intimacy between two people holds significant meaning. It might be argued that such moments are dependent on the freedom the city represents for their continuation. Yet it might also be speculated that they have always been stolen: thinking in *Beloved* of Halle and Sethe, 'scrunched down among the stalks' (26), or Sethe and Paul D., 'his holding fingers are holding hers' (273), reminds us that such quiet, unseen assertions of individual agency have always found a way to survive. Nevertheless, they do offer a particular relief within the city's oppressive structure, a relief that, ironically, ultimately means that actions of defiance at the level of the city proper seem ever more distanced by statements of individual pride and identity captured in more personal moments. Morrison is not alone in such construction – in Adichie's *Half of a Yellow Sun*, the central characters find relief from the turmoil of civil war in the actions of cooking, and of physical contact. Whilst around them the tragic legacy of British rule is ever-evident, in their homes and in the personal connection between individuals they find the relationships which are obscured in the urban squalor into which they are increasingly absorbed.

Harris may be seen to take a different approach. Invoking in *Jonestown* what he calls the 'Mathematics of Chaos' (5), the function of chaos not as endless disorder but rather as meaning within multiplicity becomes explicit within the narration:

> Chaos is misconceived as an anarchic phenomenon. Whereas it may be visualized as portraying an 'open' universe. Continuities running out of the mystery of the past into the unknown future yield proportions of originality, proportions of the 'genuinely new'. (5–6)

Such an emphasis echoes Schwarz's argument that 'the post-colonial city is hybrid: but it is neither random nor indecipherable' (269), chaos that must be seen not as never-ending free play of tumult but rather chaotic disruption of norms suggesting the potential for new meaning. In such chaos emerges the possibility that, as continuity is traced between seemingly disconnected locations, so – in what is almost a process of natural selection – the ideal will ultimately be achieved.

For a moment, Harris here seems to echo Morrison's strategy of displacement. As in *Jonestown* 'fractions and circles are profoundest mathematics that one needs to weigh and reassess with the greatest care in returning to the foundations of lost cities' (81), Harris mimics the scientist's treatment of a fractal. He takes a seemingly chaotic series of events and magnifies their constituent parts until an underlying structure is revealed, choosing fractions and circles to represent the partiality and cyclical nature of settlements and their history, defying the geometric construction of the ideal cities of the past. Traced through to the novel's conclusion, however, this

---

[3]   For negative reading, see Paquet-Deyris; for a counter to this see Yeldho and Neelakantan.

chaos suggests more than a strategy of displacement. It is a re-visioning that results in what I term carnivalisation of city space, where hybrid, chaotic performance of identity undermines official discourses of power within public space. Discussing the grid, Carter states that 'it reconciles all viewpoints to one unifying cause-and-effect perspective' (204). In its Bakhtinian invocations, carnival is the absolute opposite of this process, 'a weakening of ... one-sided rhetorical seriousness, its rationality, its singular meaning, its dogmatism' (Bakhtin 107). Moreover, this carnivalisation also fits well with the idea of post-space I began with, in which the central, defining premise is that it is precisely through the re-visioning of an oppressive force that empowerment is achieved. For carnival 'ironically began as the annual entertainment of slave masters in eighteenth century Trinidad', only later 'appropriated by ex-slaves and the common people who made it into a ritual symbolic of their freedom and their uninhibited expression of themselves' (Dabydeen and Wilson-Tagoe 64, 66).

Such a reading of *Jonestown* is supported by Bundy. For him, the circle, Jung, complex temporality, and carnival are all intimately related (Bundy 38n). This can be seen in *Jonestown* as, filled with 'bustling throngs' (110), the city is acknowledged as a space invoked, 'to explore overlapping layers and environments and *theatres* of legend and history' (emphasis added, 3) and it is through 'Memory theatre' (82 etc.) that Francisco attempts to make sense of the nonlinear presentation of his experience. This is a facet of the 'Body of Carnival' (175) allied not only to carnival as Caribbean heritage and performance, but also to Bakhtin's presentation – linked explicitly to the city – of carnival as a cross-cultural discourse that brings different worldviews together in 'carnivalistic contacts and combinations' (123).[4] Equally, it resonates with Quentin Stevens's representation of the 'ludic city' as a space of radical play that 'transgresses norms of bodily action and perception and the body's relation to space' (3). What results from this is a locale acknowledging a polyphonic and cross-cultural space; pre-colonial cultures of the Americas fuse with traditions of Anancy and Legba, mediated through a classical culture that Harris also claims. In one passage, World War Two, Jonestown, Bosnia, Rwanda and Ethiopia are brought together with 'Carnival mirroring blood in feature and mask' (86), while such 'giants of chaos ... masked players' (156) also represent 'all parties across the generations of colonial and post-colonial histories' (156). Integral to such theatre is the play of trickster; for the frequent referencing of Anancy signifies both layering and carnival, as the limbo dance is a ritual performed with 'spider-anancy masks' (Harris, 'History' 159).

Harris is not alone in such a strategy. If we return to Sinclair's *London Orbital*, for example, we see that amongst the discussion of the chaotic London landscape, the reader is offered a characteristically tangential discussion that in fact suggests the possibility of pattern within such disorder:

---

4   For the connection of carnival to the city see Bakhtin 160–69.

The scientists Gaze and Keating established that 'nerve fibres arising from the back of the eye form a pathway that sends an image of the world to the brain. The image fits with what we expect.' But what happens if expectations are confounded? Gaze showed that the brain is capable of configuring chaos, re-establishing order. (114)

Declaring, 'we need to explore total alienation and move beyond' (269), Sinclair, too, looks to London's chaos as something to be challenged and transformed. Against the official line of roads as 'an architecture of "managed" space' (328), they reveal instead a history of the unmanaged. Tellingly, at the centre of this meaningful chaos is the racially marginalised. Made more significant by the fact that he rarely discussed race, Sinclair connects the city's current unacknowledged immigrant inhabitants with an interrogation that parallels magical anti-imperialist subversion:

Yesterday's Undead are today's asylum seekers … . The Gothic imagination invading – and undoing – imperial certainties of trade, law, class. (487)

Yet as Morrison's displacement inevitably distances acts of resistance from the city, so carnivalisation, too, has inevitable consequences that indicate the limits of citywide resistance. Harris cannot avoid restrictions that suggest the ability to remake real cities is very different from the endeavours of the writer-as-artist. The re-visioning of Jonestown exists *only* within the carnival-dream; its conclusion seems to differ from original events only in terms of emphasis, rather than actual substance. The most obvious example of this is the fact that re-visioning the city cannot prevent the Jonestown Massacre. Equally, in the novel's final re-visioning, Francisco may find personal awakening but, ultimately, Deacon (played in memory theatre by Francisco) still faces the same fate. As Deacon proper his life ends 'perpetually falling to his death yet suspended above his death in a net' (190). Played by Francisco the same fate awaits him as he 'fell into a net' (233). All that has changed is the interpretation. In Jungian terms, this re-visioning allows Francisco to attain knowledge of the *unus mundus* that encapsulates all spaces and times and provides an overarching unity in which resolution is offered. Yet as a message of postcolonial resistance, such an action relies too heavily on individual changes in perception, rather than physical change. In this way, the text returns to the utopian cities from which it springs: positing only a *potential* reality.

Indeed, against carnivalisation, there is a more realist strain of postcolonial literature that suggests it is in fact a repetition of colonial order that offers the security so desired by the alienated postcolonial subject. Whilst Chamcha and Gibreel may celebrate chaos as a challenge to London's surveillance and control, alternative renderings of the city suggest that its chaos may in fact be the problem, and that an ordered space is in fact the solution. Nowhere is this more evident than in Leila Aboulela's *Minaret* (2005). Centred around the story of a rich Sudanese Muslim woman, Najwa, who is abandoned in London after her family are exiled during a government coup, *Minaret* offers not chaos but structure as a solution to migrant alienation. For Muslims in the wake of 9/11 the city is a space of danger, as Najwa proclaims 'it is safe for us in playgrounds, safe among children. There are other places in London that aren't safe, where our presence irks people' (111). Najwa's relief from this is not in chaos, however, but in the unchanging certainty and structure of the mosque. Her statement that 'We never get lost because we can see the minaret and head home towards it' (208) is not just a matter of geographical positioning, but also a metaphor for the centring and comforting role of Islam in Najwa's troubled existence. Here, the distinction is not between order and chaos, but between two alternative modes of order – that which is chosen, and that which is enforced. The former is, it seems, paradoxically a route not to lack of agency, but a newfound sense of liberation. This is drawn into stark relief by the contrast presented by Aboulela between Najwa's life in the mosque, and her brother Omar's confinement in a British prison. Only two pages apart, these two spaces are described in ways which offer alternative modes of containment. There is a lack of physical space in the mosque, but this is thrown into counterpoint by its spiritual largesse:

> I nod and in the pause that follows say, 'Tell me about your seclusion at the mosque. What was it like?'

> 'I found the first two days hard but at the end I didn't want to leave.' (191)

Against this, the prison order has the alternative effect:

> I try and take the feeling of Eid to Omar but the prison puts me in my place. It shrinks me like it shrinks him. I wish it would purify him, wring him and bring him back to me restored. Instead, it contains, habilitates. (193)

Such a discourse challenges unproblematic dismissal of strict control mechanisms as restrictive; there is a distinction between a community of principles, and the imposition of those principles. Interestingly, the mosque's central position in the novel offers confirmation of the deferral to microstructures I have outlined. Yet, against carnivalisation, it is order – singular identity rather than hybrid heterogeneity – that for Najwa allows her to find a place in the city.

Ultimately, however, the ambiguous ending of *Minaret*, in which Najwa finds herself again alone, means that her turn to order offers no more a complete resolution than carnivalisation. Realist or magical-realist, the bleak result is surprisingly similar. It is in recognition of these limits that, as I began with Rushdie's spaces, so I end with them. It is here that the strategies that I outline come together in one city. Rushdie's London is both carnivalised and displaced, illustrating a power, perhaps, that is not evident in more singularly focused strategies.

In terms of displacement, the unseen London Chamcha and Gibreel exist within has another layer below it, another palimpsest world: a world of reduction.

The Shaandaar Café and Bed and Breakfast directly resonates with Canclini's construction of 'microsocial structures of urbanism – the club, the café, the neighbourhood society, the political committee' (209) – where we find initially unseen, but ultimately powerful, resistance. In the Bed and Breakfast Chamcha can exist in his difference, his mutations accepted with 'pluralistic openness of mind' (245). Yet Rushdie does not stop at this level of reduction; he further increases concentration of hybrid elements by overwhelming the personal and intimate. A perfect example of this is evident in Hind's cooking. One facet of Sufyan's personality and his Café – acceptance of difference – becomes intensified at the more personal level of the food Hind serves as she 'struggled, in her kitchen, towards a parallel eclecticism, learning to cook the dosas and uttapams of South India as well as the soft meatballs of Kashmir' (245–6). This intensification through the act of cooking has been a theme in Rushdie's fiction: the chutney jars of history in *Midnight's Children* where '"things – even people – have a way of leaking into each other ... like flavours when you cook"' (38), or *The Moor's Last Sigh* in which the cooking of Ezekiel puts, for Moraes, 'yesterday in my tummy' (273). It is also a theme for Indian postcolonial novelists more generally, taken up famously by both Arundhati Roy in *The God of Small Things* and Vikram Chandra in *Red Earth and Pouring Rain* but also in less well-known texts such as Vijay Singh's *Whirlpool of Shadows* (1992). Tellingly, it is in this space that Chamcha makes his only act of resistance. In standing up to the racists at the Café Chamcha makes an important acknowledgment of both his solidarity with his own community and his difference from the English ideal he originally aspires to. In this space the power relations of the world, and their subjectivity, are made clear:

> 'Objectively,' he said, with a small self-deprecating smile, 'what has happened here? A: Wrongful arrest, intimidation, violence. Two: Illegal detention, unknown medical experimentation in hospital,' – murmurs of assent here, as memories of intra-vaginal inspections, Depo-Provera scandals, unauthorized post-partum sterilizations, and, further back, the knowledge of Third World drug-dumping arose in every person ... because what you believe depends on what you've seen, – not only what is visible, but what you are prepared to look in the face. (252)

The Café is not the only such space. In the Brickhall Friends Meeting House 'every conceivable sort of person' (413) comes together. This reflects what Peter Marcuse has expressed as the difference between ghettos and enclaves, the former reflecting regulation, and the latter 'voluntary clusters ... in which solidarity provides strength (277). Significantly, however, such people are not defined by ethnicity as Marcuse suggests. Instead, their cooperation offers a cross-cultural alternative resonant with Soja's expression of the desire for urbanity to be constructed around a space where 'the *right to be different* is asserted as the foundation of the new cultural politics' (*Postmetropolis* 280). Such celebration of a cross-cultural margin stands against the destructive power of the narrow communities of *Jazz*, and also against the authoritarian individualism – the denial of diversity – at the heart of Jones's construction of himself as idol. When the Brickhall community erupts into rioting, the possibility for larger change that Harris cannot realise in his conclusion is in this space achieved, born initially in a space out of the sight of those who police the city's public spaces.

It should be noted, however, that such displacement is not always in the service of positive revelation. It is also through such a strategy that the most depressing political speculations become concrete, as the Shaandaar Bed and Breakfast also explains how the unseen remains so, full of 'five-person families in single rooms' (264). Rather, it is the fact that the carnival is here too, capturing London as a space of 'variegated, transient and particoloured inhabitants' (243) which produces possibilities absent from other postcolonial urban spaces. In the same way that carnival celebrates the city's ambiguity – 'a carnivalistic fusion of praise and abuse' (Bakhtin 161) – Rushdie, like a mythological Ariadne, weaves a narrative thread that re-visions the contradictions of the city into positive events. In these terms, the city's labyrinth is not a simple geometric construction; its complexity reflects a space that, while on the surface planned, on another level is a twisting structure capable of revealing the chaos undermining all absolutes, what is seen as the maze's characteristic as a space 'linear ... becoming "complex"' (Hillis Miller 68–9). Thus, following this lesson, we must read in between Rushdie's geometric forms. It is through his carnivalesque mutations and the confusion of these pathways that Chamcha is forced to explore the palimpsest London of ghettos and migrant communities that he would otherwise avoid. Encountering other migrants, Chamcha discovers how to refuse defeat. It is also in reading between these forms that London is paralleled with other forms of fundamentalism. In an architectural metaphor, the chaos of the maze unravels geometric space. But this space is not an absolute London, but rather an equally absolute interpretation of Islam:

> In the old days he wanted to protect the baby daughters of Jahilia; why shouldn't he take the daughters of Allah under his wing as well? But after asking herself this question she shakes her head and leans heavily on the cool wall beside her stone-screened window. While below her, her husband walks in pentagons, parallelograms, six-pointed stars, and then in abstract and increasingly labyrinthine patterns for which there are no names, as though unable to find a simple line. When she looks into the courtyard some moments later, however, he has gone. (119)

Echoing the colonial city-planner's practice of obscuring fluidity with order, Mahound recognises that his singularity is an illusion.

Yet carnivalisation too is limited. Like Chamcha, Gibreel becomes increasingly immersed in carnivalesque London. For Gibreel, however, this only leads to a repetition of colonial forms: flying above the city Gibreel obtains 'the view from without' (Doob 32) of the maze-builder for himself. Alone and refusing the communal aspect so necessary for carnival's success, Gibreel cannot face the might of so large a construct as the imperial city, and he soon becomes another authoritarian figure, another Jim Jones whose ideal turns into totalitarianism. Obsessed by the need for a true 'Geographers' London', Simon Gikandi notes in acknowledgment of this that Gibreel's 'conquest of the city depends on his adversary's maps' (222). It is this politically realist, depressing message of Rushdie's conclusion – its city and the failure of its inhabitants to achieve political recognition – that is often subsumed by postmodern agendas: its fluid, celebratory journeys. This is particularly significant given the fact that Rushdie's representation of London in *The Satanic Verses* is *not* an exception. Ultimately, the New York of *Fury*, for example, presents a similar story. Here there is literal carnival, playing 'the true satirical music of the Jamaican troubadour-polemicists' (7), and the play of identities so attractive to Harris is present. Yet Malik must ultimately leave New York to improve his life. In both cases, the reality of the city is far less a simple version of postmodernism than Rushdie's critics would cast it: positive urbanity is no more possible in the seat of empire or neo-colonialism that it is in colony or postcolony.

To attempt some resolution, I would suggest that only a fusion of carnival *and* displacement fosters real postcolonial resistance within the city, regardless of the specifics of location. Such fusion is exemplified in *The Satanic Verses* by Chamcha's experience at Shepperton studios. A film set recreates London in line with Chamcha's desires: the London of Dickens on a smaller scale. The purpose of such space is not, however, to present order but rather atemporal chaos, always present in a Dickensian 'city crazed into fragments' (Poole xiii). Here Rushdie's choice of intertextual reference, as with Harris's deference to Conrad in relation to the journey, again betrays the way in which writers, even at the heart of Empire, were beginning to employ strategies to challenge the concept of an ordered, authoritarian space. As Chamcha is directed to 'behold the dustman's mounds of Boffin's Bower, supposedly in the near vicinity of Holloway, looming in this abridged metropolis over Fascination Fledgeby's rooms in the Albany, the West End's very heart ... rearranged' (422) he proves the order of the colonial city a fallacy. In making such disorder a revelatory experience, Rushdie successfully undermines the imperial discourse that connects well-functioning space with order. Similarly, in the city-enclave that is the Club Hot Wax carnivalesque mannequins become 'History' (292), a history that cannot be defeated on the outside, but that, here, melts with the call of '*Maggie, maggie, maggie* ... crumpling into formlessness' (293). It is a postmodern carnival space with new masked figures that nevertheless reflect Garcia Canclini's belief that 'when we do not succeed in changing whoever governs, we satirize him or her in Carnival dances' (261).

It is only, *The Satanic Verses* is clear, with more personal interaction that the labyrinth loses its grip and the city surpasses its initial status as a 'dream of childhood' (55). It is not in the public city-space but in Chamcha's return to the smaller space of his Bombay home that the carnivalesque erupts and promotes real lasting change. No longer needing to search for healing chaos in the diaphanous spaces of the sky, Chamcha finds it instead on solid ground:

> When his father fell asleep again ... with his open, dreaming eyes, which could
> see into three worlds at once, the actual world of his study, the visionary world
> of dreams, and the approaching after-life as well (or so Salahuddin, in a fanciful
> moment, found himself imagining). (524)

Such three worlds express not only an element of performance in their fusion of
dreams and reality, they also capture the concept of third space that inspires post-
space. Out of trauma develops awakening, as the postcolonial citizen rises to the
challenges raised by the continued legacy of an imperial past, tentatively emerging
with a positive development from what might easily have been defined merely
negatively.

Such spaces must be developed, Rushdie suggests, before we take on political
administrations or large organisations; we must find resources for survival in our
own lives before looking outside. In *Fury*, Malik's departure from New York is not
to another scene of international negotiations; instead, it is to Kenwood Heath, to
foster the strength of his son:

> But grand and high was his bouncing; and he was damned if he was going to
> stop leaping or desist from yelling until that little boy looked around, until he
> made Asmaan Solanka hear him in spite of the enormous woman and gathering
> crowd and the mouthing mother and the man holding the boy's hand and above
> all the lack of a golden hat, until Asmaan turned and saw his father up there, his
> only true father flying against the sky, *asmaan*, the sky, conjuring up all his lost
> love and hurling it high up into the sky like a white bird plucked from his
> sleeve ... . 'Look at me!' shrieked Professor Malik Solanka, his leather coattails
> flapping like wings. 'Look at me, Asmaan! I'm bouncing very well! I'm bouncing
> higher and higher!' (259)

It is only here that Malik literally finds his wings, resistance against those who
would denigrate his race – 'lack of a golden hat' (259) – in what is, in the flight of
an individual body, crucially a carnival performance of small things.

The city provides postcolonial authors with a catalyst which stimulates
movement to other spatial locations, and offers the promise – if not the realisation
– of an alternative to colonial models of spatial ordering. Within this, the chaos that
blurs simple distinctions between utopian and dystopian cities is not something
that must be cathartically exorcised. To do this would be only to repeat the
colonial implementation of an order that – whether its initial intentions are good
or bad – eventually proves both false and destructive. Rather, the postcolonial
novel seizes the mixture of positivity and negativity that results: a seizure that is a
defining feature of a post-space where chaos is negotiated and re-visioned, rather
than feared, forming more anti-utopia than dystopia. Unlike Murray Bookchin,
postcolonial authors do not seem to promote the idea that the city is 'the locus of
our most intimate social and personal concerns beyond the family circle or the
workplace' (48), but instead point to a displacement of this location on to ever-

smaller scales. The fact that the city is challenged is testament to the political realism of magical-realism, and its desire to question public space. Yet the fact that the city cannot be, ultimately, altered, is also perhaps testament to the limits of magical-realism's 'magic', and to the inevitable connection between public space and national policy. In such a way what the construction of city-space indicates is a beginning: a bridge between the unspoken nation or global journey, and the personal resistances of individuals caught up in smaller spaces. It is to these more intimate spaces, rather than the geographies of nation, journey and city, that potential is deferred, and to which this book now turns: acknowledging the lesson from this chapter that what is really needed is to 'look within cities' (Byrne 56), once more, displacing the large: reducing the scales.

Chapter 4
Reversals of Representation: Postcolonial Homes

> Imperialism cannot be understood without a theory of domestic space.
>
> (McClintock 17)

Neither city, nor nation, nor journey provides a complete alternative to nationalist scales of resistance. In its celebration of the nomad the journey only reinforces a relationship with fixed location, in its absence of a locality only pointing more strongly to the need for postcolonial identity to also be rooted in a tangible space. Yet the urban space is ultimately too public to provide this alternative, suffering at times the same imposition of institutional forces as the nation, and failing thus to sever the relationship to colonial models of ordering and their legacy. Indeed, what journey and city both gesture towards is the need for a more intimate experience of space. With its centrality for lived experience, it is the domestic space – the home as physical location, rather than metaphor – that may provide this function.

I begin here by outlining what I believe to be the essential use of the home in the service of colonialism: a construct fulfilling a political role in the reinforcement of colonial values and yet, because of the nature of that political role, presented – paradoxically – as an idealised and apolitical location. In the dwellings represented by the postcolonial novel, this 'colonial home' is an unspoken intertext. The postcolonial home stands in relation to its colonial forebear and interrogates its values. At the centre of the postcolonial literary treatment of domesticity, therefore, is a reversal of representation, in which the home is no longer presented in denial of its political status to construct a colonial ideal, but is instead explicitly political. This reversal has implications not only for colonial discourse, but also for associated concepts of colonial and postcolonial gender politics. Through a reading of the home's personal spaces, it is evident that it is in fact the domestic space that embodies the subversion of colonial order.

The Colonial Metaphor

Focusing on the physical space of the house acts to correct the lack of prominence of this location in spatial discourses. In their major studies on space, Marcus Doel and David Harvey find no room for the home, while Edward Soja's discussion is limited to acknowledgement of bell hooks's focus on 'life's intimate human spatiality' (*Thirdspace* 104). These studies therefore continue an anthropological tradition, treating the house as self-contained, the globe split between an inside of emotional dialogues and an outside of political negotiations. In these readings, the home is isolated from political repression, a space seemingly outside the influence of the administrative structures of public space.

Colonial discourse analysis challenges such readings of the home by focusing frequently on how it forms a site of power contestation. For Bill Ashcroft, 'the idea of enclosure, or property, has dominated colonizers' views of place' (*Transformation* 162). Such readings make the physical structure of the home central to colonial settlement, and to subsequent political control. Following from this awareness, postcolonial critics also explicitly connect the home to political struggle; for hooks the domestic space is 'a site of resistance' with 'a radical political dimension' (*Yearning* 41–2). Not only is such a politicised home distanced from representations in geography, spatial theory and conventional anthropology, it is at the same time distinguished from colonial representations of the home. In such a distinction are two opposing representations of domestic space: the dwelling of the postcolonial novel, and the home as a force of colonisation.

What then is meant by the colonial home? Paradoxically, it is a structure both prominent and overlooked. It is prominent because of ideological investment in both fiction and nonfiction at the height of colonialism that saw it given a central place in political and literary discourse. Yet it is overlooked precisely because of the motivation behind this prevalence, meaning the house never really is taken simply for what it is – a site of intimate power contestation – but rather must act metaphorically for the colonial project itself: an exemplification of Homi Bhabha's argument that the nation is maintained by metaphorical and metonymic strategies ('DissemiNation' 292–4). Such appropriation in the service of metaphor is supported by postcolonial readings of the colonial use of domesticity. For Alison Blunt, domestic imagery was a crucial factor in encouraging outcry against Indian mutiny, where 'the domestic images of "houses", "wardrobes" and "cravats" appear to stand for British rule in India' ('Embodying' 406). For R.M. George, writing on similar themes, 'the tales and tasks of homemaking ... are not very different from the tales and tasks of housekeeping on the national or imperial scale' (5). This is reflected in the work of Sara Mills, for whom the colonial home has an ideological function, the colonial bungalow evidence of how 'private life was lived as if always in public' (114). Similarly, for Anne McClintock domestic middle-class values were precisely those required for aggressive imperial expansion, so that the home becomes a microcosm of the colony as 'the cult of domesticity became a crucial arena for rationalizing emergent middle-class identity and its presiding values' (169). Even increased usage of particular household items is intimately entwined with colonial expansion, revealing 'the mass marketing of empire as an organized system of images and attitudes' (McClintock 209).

Both the cult of domesticity and the new imperialism found in soap an exemplary mediating form. The emergent middle class values – monogamy ('clean' sex, which has value), industrial capital ('clean' money, which has value), Christianity ('being washed in the blood of the lamb'), class control ('cleansing the great unwashed') and the imperial civilizing mission ('washing and clothing the savage') – could all be marvelously embodied in a single household commodity (McClintock 208).

This use of the house exemplifies the colonial strategy of overwriting previously identified. Presented as 'fixed, rooted, stable – the very antithesis of travel' (George 2), the fluidity of the home is obscured. In this sense, the home forms a microcosm of the colonial tabulation of space. Acquisition of territory, and its association with violence, is replaced with the establishment of home, and – rather than violence – an association with the natural and timeless processes of settlement. Creation is substituted for destruction. In keeping with this, the metaphorical role of the home – though ever present – is obscured. A harmonious ideal is invoked, as 'the values and behaviour inculcated in the home were considered crucial to the formation and maintenance of national identity, a necessary protection against less predictable social and economic changes' (Bryden and Floyd 2). Using the home to stand for the colony, the colonial nation's discourse of naturalness is propagated.

Yet as Sigmund Freud in his writing on 'The Uncanny' (1919) would capture – as what is homely is always unhomely to emphasise the repression of damaging domestic experience, exploding in 'uncanny' events both frightening and disturbing – such an ideal is all part of the fiction, part of the desire to present a vision of natural order: nineteenth-century metropolitan homes that were already 'fluid spaces' (Marcus 3) despite seemingly solid boundaries. This is the home that Charlotte Bronte, herself obscured under the pseudonym Currer Bell, would reinforce in *Jane Eyre* (1847). As Jean Rhys' *Wide Sargasso Sea* (1966) so powerfully exposes, the denied inhabitant of Bertha Mason represents the colonial exploitation the home is built upon, treated according to colonial attitudes as a chaotic presence that must be denied. Such domestic order was, in the colonies themselves, rigorously enforced. Observation of indigenous citizen's homes via their employers and indoctrination into normalised domestic practices through a discourse of moral concern was commonplace, as is evident in the fact that, in colonial settlement, 'the dwellings are to be constructed in a specific way, because they are to be used in a specific way … a strategy of surveillance and classification' (Noyes 274). The fact that such a statement is part of J.K. Noyes's argument for his colonial, tabular space only reaffirms the connection between domesticity and wider colonial practice.

Here what happens inside homes plays its part: orderly, clean and well-kept dwellings serve to maintain the colony's order on the scale of the individual family. The domestic ideal of the nineteenth century was an illusion but, as Antoinette Burton emphasises, it was nevertheless – indeed perhaps even more so because of this – a powerful force, and one inherently tied to colonies. At least in English colonies and neo-colonial America, the home followed Victorian trends in domestic practice. Not only was the colony described in household terms, but the household, in all its grandeur, was a microcosm for the wealth of empire and its maintenance – echoing the city also – by surveillance. The Victorian home 'became a space for the display of imperial spectacle … while the colonies … became a theater for exhibiting the Victorian cult of domesticity that needed constant and scrupulous policing' (McClintock 34). The spatialised hierarchies of the colonial home seem to enforce such suggestions, 'domestic space ... mapped as a hierarchy of specialized and distinct boundaries' (McClintock 168) in the same way that the colony is divided into territories; both divisions are heavily enforced, the boundaries of both naturalised by documents: architectural plans or national maps. This reflects a wider pattern of colonial ordering of domestic settlements. Thus for Mills the Civil Lines of the British colonial settlements in India were laid out on precisely the same grid that would typify their overall use of space, contrasting to indigenous British town planning, and representing 'a strict segregation between indigenous peoples and the British (107). Yet, as for colonial space in general, such ordering was clearly a myth: in reality the divisions set up by the British obscured a constant crossing of their borders (Mills 108).

One result of this division and idealisation is the production of an explicitly gendered space, placing women at the heart of the imperial project. The idealized domesticity of Victorian society not only constructed gender roles, it did so partly to serve colonial needs. Nineteenth-century fiction and conduct books emphasise both this gendered division of space and the desire to order it, where open domestic space – less hierarchical and with no division of male and female spheres – is 'in need of spatial and narrative closure' (Marcus 53). As males are responsible for maintaining political and public order – to overwrite chaos – so females are responsible for echoing this in the home, providing refuge from the perceived struggles of the marketplace in a space of harmony and rigid organisation. Firmly establishing the metaphorical connection, in the colonies 'competent home management was part of a wife's "'civilising mission'" (Brownfoot 195); as the coloniser battles with territorial expansion, so his wife engages in her own struggle against unfamiliar domestic conditions.

Such practice is evident in the domestic manuals read by Englishwomen in India. Mrs R. Temple Wright, an author of several such manuals at the fin de siècle, gives advice on how to be a good English 'hostess' in India. She informs us '*never to eat Bazaar bread*' (5), to improve the nation 'through the improvement of the nation's *homes*' (7), to buy pots from 'any large European shop' (41) and 'buy and keep cows' because of poor local standards of herd raising (202). Temple Wright is vehement on the division of the household:

> Things you must never, under any circumstances, allow in your kitchen are – a *hookah*, a *bed*, and the *personal apparel* of the cook and his mate. (42)

It is not a relationship that is consigned to the past, but instead one that fully embodies the notion of postcolony: as Elleke Boehmer's *Stories of Women* powerfully argues, the home continues in the postcolonial period to be intimately connected to nationalist discourses, and to play a significant role in how power is constructed in the contemporary nation-state.

It is precisely the order and metaphorical function of this home that is called into question by postcolonial representations. For whilst colonial representation of the home obscures disorder and separates the home from the public sphere of politics, postcolonial representation foregrounds this disorder, and the home's intrinsically political status. This extends beyond a role in nationalist or colonial ideals, to recognition of the home as a space with its own internal politics. Such re-visioning is a twofold strategy. Firstly, there is reclamation of the home from colonial metaphor to establish the 'house as house' rather than in the service of something larger such as nation or colony. Secondly, there is a reinvestment of the home with chaos. An awareness of such chaos will illuminate the perpetuation of colonial models due to factors such as servitude and slavery, highlighting the hierarchies and violence which many postcolonial citizens must negotiate that are obscured in the vision of domestic normality. The second process of reinvestment is inextricably connected to the first process of reclamation: it is in altering the mode of representation that diversity is reinstilled in the varied form of the house structure. This gives the home its own identity where it no longer conforms to ideals tied to colonial ideology. Moreover, it means that the home may also question the prejudices of patriarchy and class differentiation that are equally prevalent in the home.

Magical-realism, however, adds a third term to this process. Opened up, the home becomes as an explicitly political space by an acknowledgement of its trauma; through magical-realism this trauma may be transformed into resistance. Released from its metaphorical function, the home is open to diverse meanings encompassing the fluid and subversive: not closed down into order, but – like the larger space of the journey and the more public urban space – rather opened up to marvellous possibility. This transformation moves beyond anything suggested by Freud. It exceeds his violence, transcends his lack of reference to larger power structures, and also surpasses his association of magic with the primitive. Yet in coming from tension, rather than acting in denial of it, the home's positive potential also does not return to an ideal. Politicised, the split between public and private space is corrupted, and the fluid boundaries established by postcolonial fiction instead offer the opportunity for a reassertion of influence by both the female inhabitants whose lives are related to domestic discourse but also, more widely, all its inhabitants.

What is also significant about postcolonial representations of the home is that they reject assumptions that domesticity is wholly the sphere of women and, moreover, that control of the home affects men only indirectly through its impact on the public sphere. The gender implications of the colonial home do not only affect women and, more significantly, the influence of colonialism is felt by all the home's inhabitants. For all, the home becomes tied to colonial power relations, and the subversion of these interests is a shared aim, whether that subversion would ultimately lead to a concomitant dissolution of domestic patriarchy or, ironically, even a reinforcement of patriarchy in a new nationalist form. Notably, however, whilst emphasising nationalist patriarchy, postcolonial fiction seems to indicate ultimately that the former result is one shared by both female and male indigenous challenges to colonial domestic discourse. With patriarchy indissolubly linked to the colonial project, a reversal of the latter is also a reversal of the former. This may be at odds with analyses which emphasise a nationalist patriarchy with equally restrictive gender politics centred upon the home; however, it may be seen as a powerful component in the postcolonial novel's use of domesticity as an anti-imperial setting. Whilst gender differences are indicated, remaking the home – reinstilling its political status as a challenge to the colonial discourse of domesticity – largely takes precedence over representing the complexities of gender relations outside the colonial dynamic.

The power of this contamination of the colonial vision should not be underestimated. Following Nancy Armstrong's argument that nineteenth-century fiction's representation of domesticity was not only a reflection of social forces but also had a role in history as that which 'helped to formulate the *ordered* space we now recognize as the household' (emphasis added, 23–4), the postcolonial novel's strategic *disordering* of this space may be seen to hold the same potential now: a force not only reflecting the *status quo* but also offering pathways towards new experience.

The Representational Shift

To some extent postcolonial novels do retain the home as metaphor for the colony, undoubtedly making connections between domestic oppressions and colonial regimes. In Dambudzo Marechera's *House of Hunger* (1978), for example, this connection is made explicit as the suffering in the domestic space is a mirror of the tensions and violence at the centre of Zimbabwe's neo-colonial political corruption and instability. Not only is the narrator's literal domestic space one of deprivation, this is explicitly acknowledged as representative of a wider state of affairs:

> Life stretched out like a series of hunger-scoured hovels stretching endlessly towards the horizon. One's mind became the grimy rooms, the dusty cobwebs in which the minute skeletons of one's childhood were forever in the spidery grip that stretched out to include not only the very stones upon which one walked but also the stars which glittered vaguely upon the stench of our lives. (3–4)

The narrator referring to himself in the second and third-person, personal experience is transcended to suggest a nation as postcolony caught in decay of which intimate personal circumstances are only a reflection.

Equally, novels such as Morrison's *Tar Baby* (1981) can be read as presenting a world of masters and servants that may be read as a metaphor for the treatment of individuals within a wider colonial world. Yet I have suggested that central to the postcolonial novel's re-visioning of the home is a shift in representation. This is centred on the fact that, due to the critique involved, postcolonial use of metaphor is for a distinctly different purpose: acting not to uphold, but to dismantle by revealing the inequalities colonial structure is based upon. This is metaphor used not to serve an ideal, but rather to reveal inconsistencies and the fact that the discourse of order is both inherently false and – from a postcolonial point of view – immensely damaging. Such usage supports Nathaniel Mackey's discussion of imagery in relation to Wilson Harris:

> Such recourse to metaphor betrays an estrangement, a distance, that the metaphor – the word is derived from a verb meaning 'to carry over' – seeks to overcome. The use of metaphor is then a 'confession of weakness,' the recognition of a chasm one wishes to cross, to be carried across. (176)

In such usage there is always a recognised gap between the house and the colony. Metaphorical associations continually attempt to bridge this gap and yet, in failing to do so, only draw into clearer relief a representational chasm. Even as house and colony are brought together, so the house is freed from the colony, revealing it as an independent form. The metaphor of the home as colony is no longer the mirage of a perfect colonial construction; rather all metaphor is grappling for the unspeakable and lost. Such connections transcend the colonial novel's desire to parallel the historically coterminous. For as a text such as *Beloved* proves, when the postcolonial home is not a metaphor for the limits and hierarchies of the colony, it is instead a powerful connection to a fragmented past, not the calling up of the familial that so interests Freud in his haunted houses, but instead a complex layering of meaning that reflects magical-realism's 'slippage from the individual to the collective to the cosmic' (Zamora 501).

Interestingly, this strategy is often described not in terms of metaphor, but metonym, a substitution that appears as a conscious choice by the postcolonial critic. Stephen Slemon, for example, describes magical-realism as a genre of 'transformational regionalism so that the site of the text, though described in familiar and local terms, is metonymic of the postcolonial culture as a whole' (411). Both in expression and practice, however, this 'metonym' shares many qualities with metaphor. In relation to Morrison's *Beloved* these terms have been recognised to be both privileged and interchangeable (B. Bell 11, Keenan 61). This seems to be true of representation of houses more that elsewhere. 124 Bluestone Road may be read as metaphor for the slave ship: the two spaces are seemingly unconnected, fulfilling Roman Jakobson's description of metaphor as dealing with the similar rather than the directly associated (106), at times presenting 'no deliberate transfer of meaning': '*Spyglass* for *microscope* or *fire* for *gaslight*' (107). Yet the relationship is also metonymic, because there is in fact an explicit connection between the house's meaning and the slave community. As 'the implied history of the house covers the same time-span as Beloved's ancestral memories' (Schmudde 411), so the house also fulfils the definition of metonymy as 'a figure of speech which consists in substituting for the name of a thing the name of an attribute of it or *something closely related*' (emphasis added, *OED*). This is what Jakobson terms contiguity, where 'knife', for example, becomes '*pencil-sharpener, apple-parer, bread-knife, knife-and-fork*' (102). It is particularly significant when contiguity may be seen as defining 'proximity of ideas or impressions in place or time' (*OED*), so that the postcolonial critic's use of metonym, rather than metaphor, facilitates the fusing of historically divided spaces. In postcolonial magical-realism's nonlinear framework, the calling up of the past is not in contradiction to metonym but, in fact, is an integral part of an alternative spatial model of representation: such spaces are not divided either geographically or historically, but are in fact contiguous as a result of this nonlinear imagination.

In a similar way, homes in Rushdie's *Midnight's Children* appear to function metaphorically as microcosms of the nation, where the greatest home is the 'noble mansion of free India' (118). Yet the intimate connection means they are in fact metonymic, as the small and the large are interrelated, even interchangeable, Saleem's 'destinies indissolubly chained to those of my country' (9). This use of metonym defines what might also be referred to as 'postcolonial metaphor'. Such metaphor no longer serves to uphold ideals or discourses of power, but instead dissolves them; it connects to that which is always fragmentary and provisional, and – because in contrast to the colonial metaphor, metonymy 'is context bound and therefore exposes specific cultural values, prejudices, and limitations' (Keenan 61) – counters the colonial metaphor of a universal ideal.

Yet in the service of this difference, authors evoke strategies beyond the supplementation of metaphor with metonym. For Harris, for example, the home echoes his representation of other spaces. Metonym is not supplemented by other figurative techniques, but is accompanied by dissolution at the level of language itself. Words related to dwelling come to lose their signified meaning, as the gap between the literal and figurative subject of metaphor is mirrored in a similar distance between the common connotations of words and their meaning in the text. Echoing his representation of the journey, Harris juxtaposes words, throwing them out of common contexts, as the reader strives to make connections between seemingly incongruous pairings of words. The home is represented in terms of 'vague outlines of mutual egg, sea, silence, sound … fossil fire, deep-seated sun, crystal music, rain, glass' (Harris, *Silva* 4). The accumulation of nine nouns overloads the image, preventing the construction of a solid picture of the surroundings, as we struggle to reconcile opposites such as 'sea' and 'fire' in one sentence, one representation.

Such choice of words is not arbitrary. Rather, it is part of a complex transformation of nouns, adjectives and verbs that transfigures the domestic space away from conventional description, replacing its colonial certainties with postcolonial fluidity. Again Mackey highlights such a process in both postcolonial art as a whole and in Harris's work. For Mackey, postcolonial artists reverse a process of 'verb to noun' associated with colonisation of black identity, where the move towards nouns is a 'containment of black mobility' (266), and the verb signifies fluidity and movement. This postcolonial reversal may be enacted not only by a focus on verbs, but also by a change in the use of the noun, so that it becomes verblike, signifying movement, as Mackey notes in the writing of Harris. Harris's domestic images epitomise this. Nouns proliferate, but are given movement, becoming verblike; in the example discussed above such properties are evident in words such as 'fire' and 'music' as they suggest action rather than static concepts. Adjectives are heavily used, not to fix the meaning of nouns, but to destabilise them: music is 'crystal', the sun 'deep-seated' so as to throw common terms out of common contexts.[1] Such a process is akin to what Erickson terms 'antilogical discourse' (*Islam* 139), where language is used to promote contradictory ideas, so that 'no one truth or order prevails' (*Islam* 153). Importantly, this means that in the same way that metaphor is proved fallible and must be replaced with more specific metonymy, so at the level of words there is no longer domestication: these words neither normalise the home in an abstract ideal, nor curtail its fluidity.

For Morrison metaphor-metonym transference is supplemented by frequent rejection of metaphor in favour of alternative figurative strategies. As with the city in *Jazz*, personification and simile are used to construct dwellings. Such a strategy develops the gaps between abstract metaphor and context-bound metonym. Personification of houses in *Tar Baby* and *Beloved* establishes spaces with specific identities, difficult to reduce to allegorical function. This is a common feature of postcolonial narratives: the Ayemenem House in *The God of Small Things*, for example, that is personified with an identity of its own, a house that 'wore its steep, gabled roof pulled over its ears like a low hat' (1). Simile reinforces such resistance, establishing that – while the house may be *like* or *as* something else – it is never a simple cipher, the house in *Tar Baby* that '*like* an ear ... resists easy penetration but cannot brace for attack' (emphasis added, 40), a place where 'fog came ... in wisps sometimes, *like* the hair of maiden aunts' (emphasis added, 60). Unlike Harris's more pervasive strategy, Morrison appears to restrict this technique to description of the city or home: a conscious choice of representation and not one extended easily to other spaces.

Providing further contrast, Rushdie's strategies cannot be defined in terms of particular uses of imagery, or in the transformation of grammatical structures. Rather, use of metaphor to reveal the limits of figurative association feeds into exuberant representation, a continual fluidity in terms of content, language and structure that suggests a refusal to be hemmed in by any absolute metaphorical identification. This is a strategy Rushdie shares with writers such as Okri and Chandra. Here, more than elsewhere, magical-realism is crucial: dwellings seem to reflect traditional nostalgic construction, seem to act as simple metaphors for the nation, but they are quickly imbued with a fantastic life which complicates such connections, full of open doors, rushing water and unlocked chests that suggest a refusal to be hemmed in by reductive meanings. In all its forms, such shift in representation – away from the service of colonial discourse – means that chaos and hierarchies in the home are no longer overwritten with either harmony or order.

---

[1]   This is similar to Harris's Conrad-inspired use of the adjective in relation to the journey: see Chapter 3.

Reversing the Overwriting: Hierarchies and Chaos

Thus as harmony and order are removed from the home, the overwriting of its political nature is stripped away to reveal a space of power negotiations, hierarchies, and tensions. In removing the codes and patterns signifying conventional domestic space, favouring instead the turmoil and tensions that the colonial ideal obscures, the postcolonial home functions differently to its colonial predecessor. Filled with disorder and chaos, the postcolonial representation of the home challenges the colonial ideal of domestic space, and powerfully interrogates its status as haven, or location of order. Repoliticised, the home in the postcolonial novel explicitly becomes a space where negotiations of power are played out, illustrating colonial hierarchies as clearly as the nation or city, and where critique of colonialism is clearly possible.

In Harris's twenty-three novels spanning over forty years as a writer, it is unusual to uncover a focus on the home. While Harris's Guyana novels express environment almost entirely in terms of natural landscape, it is Harris's migrant novels – those that autobiographically follow his own emigration to London in the 1950s – that focus upon built structures. This is an important substitution, a focus on the landscape to discuss indigenous experience of colonial patterns of exploitation replaced with a focus upon houses to express interaction between migrants and colonial power. As we read the colonial legacy in Harris's Guyana landscapes, so we see its transference to the migrant's home.

The history of Guyanese housing during colonialism indicates underdevelopment and neglect clearly illustrating the control of colonial space reflected in domestic structures. This includes attempts to overwrite local Guyanese patterns with those of the British Empire. Town planning legislation in Guyana was developed directly from the 1932 Town and Country Planning Act for England and Wales.[2] Moreover, this application of planning regulations can be seen as an extension of colonial tabulation of space: Robert Home interprets the colonial planning project in Guyana as focused largely on what he describes as 'control of land by zoning' and 'regulating layout' (406). Additionally, the reported shift in Guyana from granting freeholds until 1938 to the establishment of leasehold – again echoing English property law – also supports the impact of colonisation on Guyanese housing rights.[3] The legacy of the losses of dwellings caused by this, Mohammed Rauf suggests, leads to a culture in many rural areas of Guyana where 'house construction is not looked upon with favor and is perceived as a superficial display of wealth' (58). Thus da Silva – travelling to England, flying over the Andes – witnesses a change in domestic structures from the air that is both the migrant's move to a new country but also, as the first two lines of the paragraph suggest, representative of the impact that colonialism has on housing over time:

---

[2] See Home 397.

[3] See Meek 226–7.

> The wheel of the seasons ran. Houses vanished. New mansions appeared woven
> from a sheep's underbelly of cloud against the mountains. (7)

There is thus a shift from ordinary dwellings to those that signify status and the move to a colonial mentality.

Following from the premise that the 'house as house' – rather than the house as national metaphor – is an explicitly political structure in its own right, even Harris's poetic narratives illustrate unequal access. In *Cultivated Wilderness* hierarchies exist not only within houses but also between them; Manya's life 'in a deprived area in his mural of a city' (16) makes da Silva aware it was 'unlike the rich masts and tides da Silva had painted within the new houses in Addison Road' (16). Indeed, the colonial discourse of domesticity is often clearly present. When da Silva is reminded of a colonial past, his home fulfils the myth of domesticity, a scene of 'tea, raspberry sponge, cherry cake … . The great Liberal spokesman Charles James Fox had once lived here … . Empire builders, da Silva thought' (56). The fact that some homes were built on the profits of empire is no longer hidden in dark corners; it is visible in the home's very architecture, emphasised in the acknowledgment that there is 'deprivation in those rotting beams or walls that belonged to a past economic code or day' (63).

Harris's detail only substantiates the foregrounding of colonial influence, as it introduces historical figures to create a text with multiple layers of interpretation connecting with colonialism. For example, the history book on the house that da Silva reads – *Chronicles of Holland House* (1937) – was written by the sixth Earl of Ilchester, Giles Stephen Holland Fox-Strangways. The cousin of the second Earl of Ilchester was Charles James Fox, the eighteenth-century politician who once lived in the house and appears in the text as da Silva's representative of empire. Henry Rich, who also appears in the text, was the first Earl of Holland who did much to develop the house in its early years. The death of Sir Giles's wife is echoed in the real death of the first Earl of Holland's daughter, who 'met with her own Apparition' and 'about a Month after, she died of the Smallpox' (Aubrey, qtd. in Fox-Strangways 499), a connection that Harris reinforces by quoting directly from Fox-Strangeway's account (*Silva* 31). Such characters are connected in ways not immediately obvious. Yet they create the sense in which houses contain the remnants of colonial events and figures, and refuse to deny their colonial pasts. Indeed, the 'wildernesse' of the title itself refers to this process. Taken from *Chronicles of Holland House* where it describes the land surrounding the house, '"the Wildernesse"' (Fox-Strangways 486) had disappeared by 1734 when 'order seems to have replaced disorder' (Fox-Strangways 486). The importance of this cannot be underestimated: Harris is renewing that which was lost in the eighteenth century, lost during the imperial creation of order and its transference to its own imperial homeland – the removal of nature as 'few trees have survived' (Fox-Strangways 486) – and is reinstilling its chaos, reinstilling the fluidity of the lost wilderness, in the houses of contemporary Kensington. What is obscured in the colonial representation of the home can no longer be denied.

While Morrison's *Beloved* might seem to present a more obvious construction of a house, it is in *Tar Baby* that representations of the home are most suited to examination of postcolonial space. The opulent house on Isle de Chevaliers is a 1970s house existing in the shadow of French colonial administration identified by 'French colonial taxes' (51) and 'administration buildings' (296), owned by a family still influenced by the legacy of colonial America and its perpetuation of slavery in independence. Yet it also presents a perfect example of the 'house as house' rather than metaphor. Tensions are no longer overwritten, but are rather starkly evident, and the ideal 'house as nation' is no longer maintained.

Tar Baby clearly illustrates the impact that nineteenth-century imperial images of the domestic ideal had on the rest of the world. Perhaps more than anywhere else nineteenth-century America adopted nineteenth-century English domestic discourse. This was architectural through 'abstract arrangements such as the rigid grid' (Chandler 13), but also ideological as 'strategies of domestication would be turned into a broad-reaching – and inherently colonial – policy in the States' (N. Armstrong 91). Despite her opposition to slavery, this is evident in the nonfiction writings of nineteenth-century author Harriet Beecher Stowe. For Stowe the apartments in Paris are rejected because of their lack of permanency. Instead, there is an '*ideal* home' (Stowe, 'What is' 491), a space of 'order and beauty' (Stowe, 'What is' 492), specifically related to the separation of public and private space as it is constructed to ease 'the man of business' (Stowe, 'What is' 491).

What is interesting about the house in *Tar Baby* at the novel's opening is that it has moved little from these constructions. It differs considerably from the definition of the 1970s American home as a place where women assert increased freedom, and rather reflects Phyllis Palmer's argument that the image of service transcended slave emancipation, and was itself 'nothing less than slavery' (72). Sydney and Ondine, the long-serving servants of the privileged American Street family at the centre of the novel, reflect the loyalty of favoured house slaves, and in Ondine's work to benefit not herself but her niece Jadine we find a woman reminiscent of those who returned to domestic service in the continued inequality of the Reconstruction era. The nature of their employment in many ways also suggests a colonial model. While Sara Dickey in her reading of the role of servants within the home suggests that the kitchen is a space shut off from modern servants, like the bedroom 'most pure and most private' (477), it is for Sydney and Ondine the locus of their activities. This makes them more akin to house slaves of wealthy families than the other workers employed at the house who, fitting this modern image, remain outside. In this respect the inhabitants of L'Arbe de la Croix have not even moved to the 'industrial relations with domestic help' (Hedrick 494) it is suggested Stowe was moving towards in 1864. Rather, what remains is still a pre-Civil War familial relationship that masks the home's hierarchies.

Geographically dislocated from the homeland, the Street family are the new colonialists. Hierarchy places the *Tar Baby* home squarely within the sphere of politics, as it illuminates racial and class difference. This extends from the 'frightened houses of the whites' (296), to the simple difference that a 'shower had curtains, not sliding doors' (131), to the servant's designation of living 'down below' (58) where the 'difference between this room and the rest of the house was marked' (161). A layer below even this we find Therese 'not having access to a toilet (she felt unwelcome even in the kitchen) … shacks and cement-block houses' (104, 296). Such representation is a strong social critique that exposes the undemocratic nature of houses, and the levels of different access to space that reflect the home's divisions and hierarchies. Yet such division still has explicit resonance with the homes of the nineteenth-century middle class, where 'space was divided … and only some of the inhabitants had the freedom to cross over these boundaries' (M. Donald 107). In foregrounding such tensions, and such a connection to the colonial past, the postcolonial home exposes those elements obscured in the colonial ideal.

Within this context, Son's invasion into a house that is described as 'cool and civilized' (134) makes his position as outsider quite clear, not simply in terms of race but also class, evident in Ondine's reluctance to serve him. He is no longer, as in the nineteenth-century novel, a shadowy figure lurking on the outskirts of the narrative; Morrison focuses on the household's reaction to his invasion in order to illustrate the house as a place of stereotypical judgements and exclusions. Son's burglary, though he steals only food, does not only promote anger and fear, but also stands as a threat to domestic order and cohesion. This reflects what Perla Korosec-Serfaty highlights as the sense of 'being defiled' (77) central to reactions to the invasion of personal space by outside forces. The association of burglary with '*rape, a violation of privacy*' (Korosec-Serfaty 77) is reflected both in Morrison's emphasis on Son being 'in their *things*' (113) and in his comment that 'you little white girls always think somebody's trying to rape you' (121). Son's awareness of the rape issue and its presentation of him as an animal with 'smell' (121) typifies the construction of the black male as a threat to the domestic ideal and to white middle-class society. As I shall explore in Chapter 5, this construction of the body has its own spatial politics. Yet within the context of the home, it has a particular resonance worth noting here. The threat of the indigenous male as domestic invader was a common theme in colonial discourses.[4]

What is in the closet in *Tar Baby* is not a person; rather what is in the closet is 'Black' (77). In these terms, it is not the dirt created by burglary that fulfils the disorder that Korosec-Serfaty argues is required for theft to reach 'the dweller's secrecy and identity' (78). Rather, it is Son himself who in this case provides the 'soilage' (Korosec-Serfaty 78). Therefore while Son is not literally a servant, he nevertheless represents this force in the novel. He is 'the dirt, disease and "rubbish" … of a disorderly outside world' (Dickey 462), unsocialised unlike Ondine and Sydney. Indeed, when Son washes, smoothes out his hair and changes his clothes the implication is clear. He comes to prove that, as Sara Dickey has emphasised, 'cleanliness is a crucial marker of the privileged home' (475) as the inhabitants

---

[4]   This is evident if we return to Blunt's discussion in which the indigenous male was associated with 'discourses of defilement' (422).

respond to his washing by noting 'he was so beautiful they forgot all about their plans' (Morrison, *Tar Baby* 130). Son's actions may also be heavily identified with the employer's rules, a breaching of the fact that ordered domesticity prescribes that wardrobes remain closed spaces, locked to prevent outside access, and sex between employer and servant is a 'form of mixing that is intensely feared' (Dickey 479). Yet they also have a colonial context, the association of indigenous dwellers – and by extension in particular those of African descent – as the chaotic antithesis of home which reflects Noyes's awareness that the writing on 'the destruction resulting from rampaging natives and their traces on the settlers' farms' (248) is part of the colonial project to control space.

Morrison, however, does not simplify such hierarchies. Largely overlooked in readings of *Tar Baby*, the character of Margaret Street encompasses the postcolonial novel's foregrounding of the inherent tensions that the colonial ideal of domesticity is built upon. Margaret is expected to fulfil a domestic image she has no ability for, unable to order the servants as expected. The fact that she cannot hide violence against her child marks the gaps in the house's privacy, but also the threat felt by masters from their servants, 'living in the same house with your own witness' (242). Her resulting claustrophobia reflects the limits for a woman who, in terms of both gender and class, is viewed as incapable of fulfilling the colonial ideal.

Equally, African-Americans are not only victims of ideal homes, they also perpetuate them: Son's own domestic ideal of an all-black Eloe is heavily criticised even as we sympathise with his desire for authentic familial experience. Indeed, part of what Jadine must escape is Son's own patriarchal extension of a colonial ideal of womanhood: trying 'to press his dreams of icehouses into hers' (119). Early readings of *Tar Baby* such as Eleanor Traylor's that proclaim 'Jadinese is the disease of disconnection' (146) are thus too simplistic. For accepting Son's vision of the past also means advocating his inherently gendered encouragement of domesticity. This is not so far from the ordered control of Ondine and Sydney that Son, at L'Arbe de la Croix, interrogates. The politics that emerges, therefore, is not straightforward, but it is nevertheless a reflection of the inherent power hierarchies at work within the domestic structure.

With an explicitly political setting, the tensions of the home are foregrounded. Echoing Harris's narrative, *Midnight's Children* may be read as a reconstruction of home by the migrant. Saleem's attempts to create firm meaning reflect the colonial need to order domestic spaces and their histories, and the chaos he faces the impossibility of this task, foregrounding the fluidity which the colonial discourse of the home overwrites in spaces of 'violent disorder' (21) and 'gloomy spidery corridors' (22). Social realities invade, water rushing in so 'there were towels wedged against the doors and windows of the house' (59) because 'things ... have a way of leaking into each other' (38). There is a strong awareness of exclusions and divisions, homes with 'repeatedly-slammed doors' (250). Such acknowledgment of the social role of housing extends to differentiation between dwellings as Tai lives in 'the insanitary bowels of the old wooden-house quarter' (14) that are the

Indian equivalent of *Tar Baby's* lower-class Caribbean cement houses. Saleem is clearly aware of his own privilege where 'the brutalizing effect of servant status' is defined by 'a servants' room behind a blackstove kitchen' (144), 'his grandfather's house containing 'the low outhouse rented cheaply to the family of old Hamard and his son Rashid the rickshaw boy' (49), the new 'ugly concrete blocks' where 'we looked down on them all, on white and brown alike' (180), the magician's ghetto of 'higgledy shacks' (386).

Echoing Margaret's experience in *Tar Baby* – and reflecting the connection between the discourse of domesticity and patriarchy – such exclusions particularly affect women, for whom the home may become a prison. This is ironically often a self-enforced attempt to block out the outside world, yet is also part of an Indian nationalism that echoes the colonial, establishing order in the home as an effort to protect it from colonial influence. Here Indian nationalism is set up against western influence, but nevertheless forms its own version of patriarchal domesticity in a fusion of indigenous patriarchy and western values, a transference of ideals that resonates with wider nationalist processes. Mumtaz 'saw very little in those days of the father whom she loved' (59) because of her marriage to a fugitive, Amina is 'immobilized in a room in a tower' (101), the often-ignored Padma is consigned to sitting in the narrator's 'enchanted shadows' (121) and Toxy Catrack, echoed in *Shame* in Sufiya Zinobia, waits at 'a barred top-floor window' (130) because of mental illness. For Reverend Mother the security of the home is so hyperbolic that it becomes imprisonment, 'an invisible fortress of her own making', complete with the colonially resonant 'traditions and certainties' (40). The sense of familiarity that the home provides, its provision of assuredness in the wake of anxiety, is ironically the feature transformed from comfort to trauma, the sense of walking a tightrope across a precipice that is made clear by Rushdie through his linguistic subversion:

> the domestic rules she established were a system of self-defence ... leaving her, like a smug spider, to rule her chosen domain. (Perhaps, too, it wasn't a system of self-defence at all, but a means of defence against her self.) (40–41)

Colonial infiltration of the home cannot be denied; it is personified in Major Zulfikar entering 'with a force of fifteen men' (62) to expose Nadir. In line with Noyes's theory, this is the classic colonial utilisation of openness – here potentially damaging as it makes the house a space that cannot be separate – that is then tabulated, controlled and denied. Nowhere is this more evident than in Methwold's sale of his home to the Sinai family. Methwold's Estate echoes colonial tabulation of the journey and the city, the same geometry and symmetry in 'four identical houses ... conqueror's houses ... red gabled roofs and turret towers in each corner' (94), the same attempt to overwrite indigenous identity through language as the houses are named after 'the palaces of Europe' (95) in order to transfer the west to India, reflecting Blunt's picture of the British 'reproducing an empire within as well as beyond the home' (*Domicile* 1).

The use of geometry, as for colonial space in general, is here again particularly significant. This is because, in alternative contexts, the geometrical construction of houses is connected to order and control, with specific colonial implications. For Ross Jamieson Spanish colonisation can be seen in part as the process of 'nonsymmetrical houses with large multifunctional spaces ... replaced by closed, symmetrical forms with barriers restricting access to small interior compartments for separate activities' (17). Equally, for Henry Glassie the nineteenth-century American designer's geometric tendency is connected to a lack of imagination and traditionalism. Glassie connects this shift in American practice with colonial England, the division of space based on 'partitioning ... closure over openness' (27, 157) in a pattern common throughout many areas of empire. The potential result made clear by Glassie is an echo of the impact of geometric ordering as exposed in the postcolonial novel:

> Personal energies are removed from the immediate community and invested in abstract ideals, such as racial superiority, nationalism or artificial, symmetrical order. (190)

This abstract ordering can be seen to be what Methwold's own geometry in *Midnight's Children* represents. His 'little game' (95) of selling the houses as they are left, complete with all their contents, marks the continued dominance of colonial ideas of domesticity, 'transferring power, too' (96) but doing so in such a way that his patterns become part of Saleem's own family as they adopt 'talking budgies ... imitation Oxford drawls' (98, 99). Here Rushdie is undoubtedly laughing at the Anglo-Indian. Yet he is also constructing a postcolonial metaphor that raises explicitly the realisation of the colonial metaphor's fallibility. Now when the home stands for the colony, it does so only to make such a connection self-consciously constructed, to prove its impossibility, and to signal a need for the return to a home *qua* home.

In the novel's last words we find the hopelessness caused by the invasion of domestic space, but also the reality of the home. It is a space that will never be private, when the reality is instead 'to forsake privacy and be sucked into the annihilating whirlpool of the multitudes, and to be unable to live or die in peace' (463). Here the colonial ideal of home, and the fluidity that it would obscure, gradually fades into the distance. Such representation of the home, as with all the texts discussed here, identifies an intensely political structure; tension and tumult is no longer hidden or overwhelmed by the need to act metaphorically in the service of a colonial ideal, instead proving George's belief that 'imagining a home is as political an act as imagining a nation' (6).

The Postcolonial Re-visioning: Home as Space

So does the postcolonial home reveal only a space of trauma? While rejection of the colonial ideal may be one element of the postcolonial writing of home, it is not its whole. Politicisation of the home is not only a negative factor prompting lament for a lost ideal, but also the potential for new interruptions. The multiple meanings repressed in the colonial writing of homes are now released; no longer forced to serve as colonial metaphor, homes come to serve other purposes undermining discourses of power. Whilst the colonial or nationalist domestic ideology may utilise chaos, only in the postcolonial home is this presence acknowledged and its subsuming refused, opening up the potential for alternative meanings, and ways of living that corrupt – on the small, personal scale – public ideologies.

Although Gilles Deleuze and Felix Guattari do not discuss the home explicitly, their concept of deterritorialisation – signifying removal of fixed boundaries and the renewal of the abstract – offers the possibility for a positive disorder that opens up the domestic space to new significations. The house is not rejected for its complexity, but reclaimed so that its politics can be turned around and used decisively in the service of the postcolonial cause, rather than its colonial predecessor. Such multiplicity is prevented from evolving into postmodern free play, however, as deterritorialisation may contain a 'reterritorialization; we re-inhabit a world of our making' (Kaplan, 'Deterritorializations' 195). This first-step reterritorialisation may also be seen in terms of what Perla Korosec-Serfaty designates '*appropriation*' (74), where the status of the home as contested space leaves it able to be claimed through various activities including 'Ornamentation, maintenance, and housework' (75). This may appear at odds with the postcolonial endeavour to create fluidity; yet it is also the necessary first step towards such liberty. For here I would question Caren Kaplan's reading of deterritorialisation as a strategy that is always an 'imperialization' (*Questions* 89) because it includes a subsequent reterritorialisation. Such patterns are not permanent but often momentary, providing the necessary security that precedes even more deterritorialisations. The postcolonial home is deterritorialised away from its colonial implications. The necessary appropriation which follows this process is only the first step to a further – and final – removal of hierarchies.

What is important here is that the politicisation of the home should not obscure its positive potential, but must instead be seen as intimately connected to it. In readings of Roy's *The God of Small Things*, for example, the home's reflection of wider political concerns is often noted (Lane 100); but what is neglected is the *positive potential* of the invasion of politics into the home: the way in which domesticity displaces the nation from centre-stage and allows alternative sites of identification (Boehmer, *Stories* 193). Whilst the Ayemenem House offers one model, it is in counterpoint to another home at the centre of the novel: the History House. As these spaces are reversed 'what becomes uncanny – the haunted History House – becomes instead a refuge; what should be a refuge – Ayemenem House – becomes a house of correction and a prison house' (Lane 102) and, at the same time, usual orders of state and community alike become subverted. Thus although the History House is a space of 'moral corruption and spiritual degeneration' (Barnabas 299), a 'symbol of colonial authority' (Chanda 42) that is also reflective of India's communal conflicts, it also provides opportunities for the reversal of these against its colonial past. The status of the History House in the world of the postcolony announces a refusal to be indeterminately defined by this relationship. Chacko says that the house is locked, and therefore that the past is no longer available to the autochthonous citizens who would try and enter. But Estha, Rahel, Ammu and Velutha *do* enter, giving Chako's metaphor physical form. As Simon Barnabas notes, it is outside the History House, in defiance of its official connotations, that Velutha and Ammu find 'some of the most precious moments of their togetherness' (299): the linkage between caste development and increased control over sexual relations, so present in the Ayemenem House, becomes unravelled in this alternative domestic space. Such subversion is undoubtedly temporary, and the novel's ending, in which the house returns to it negative signification, further entrenched as it is bought by an international hotel chain, suggests a limited impact. And yet the fact that such an interruption does take place suggests the hope of further disruptions, and asserts the power of individuals to make changes to their circumstances, however limited.

A biographical example may elucidate this distinction further. In *Reading Lolita in Tehran* (2003), Azar Nafisi documents her organisation of secret underground reading groups in 1990's Iran, directly engaging with the nation-state as postcolony through her representation of state order and control. Nafisi exposes the political status of the home underlying the Iranian construction of a sacred domestic sphere, a state which, to her, 'invaded all private spaces' (77) meaning she could not 'separate the most personal and private aspects of our existence from the gaze of the blind censor' (273). Yet against this denied politicisation, Nafisi seizes the contamination of private and public to create the home as a space of fluid potential. In this space, revolutionary comments are aired that would be impermissible in the universities and eating establishments. Just as significantly, different cultural standpoints are negotiated, and the ideal of a universal Iranian womanhood is deconstructed. What makes such a disorder positive against the disorder implemented by the Iranian authorities is its acknowledged and permanent status, allowing the home to be used as a site of counter-discourse, a 'place of transgression' (8). Chaos is no longer something to be resolved, rather it is celebrated by Nafisi and her women as offering the potential of alternative points of view which seem impossible in more official discourses.

Harris's construction of domestic space embodies the consequences of this re-visionary process. Though Harris's postcolonial home reveals chaos, such new vision also provides opportunities to subvert social expectations. At the forefront of this in *Da Silva da Silva's Cultivated Wilderness* is the interesting gendering of the apartment. It is Jen who gives da Silva 'the money he needs to buy bread, to buy food' (6), and who spends her time not in a domestic home but rather an aptly named 'publishing house' (8). This reflects in domesticity Harris's often unconventional casting of women: Emma in *The Carnival Trilogy* who is a 'female priest' ('Introduction' x), and another Jen, the woman in *Black Marsden* who chooses to shun marriage and raise a child alone. From its opening, therefore, Harris's representation of domesticity transcends the conventional.

Harris's choice of an apartment here is also particularly pertinent, a space more open than traditional homes, where, as Marcus argues, in the nineteenth century a different urban geography in opposition to clear divisions of public and private space was already being produced. In this way, da Silva's presence in the apartment reflects the most politically radical site of nineteenth-century housing. This develops the critique from Marcus's own position, which illustrates how the apartments of nineteenth-century London and Paris challenged the creation of a separate sphere for women – a subversion of 'patriarchal power' (5) – in such a location, but does not recognise it would also be a subversion of colonial imperatives as they relate to this gendered discourse.

What the choice of the apartment reveals is how the architectural construction of a home, as much as its contents, may represent a challenge to conventional spatial ordering. If Rushdie employs geometric motifs to suggest colonial patterns of order, then alternative structures may interrogate this. In Keri Hulme's *The Bone People* (1985), for example, the socially isolated central character of Kerewin reflects her isolation in the home she builds for herself: a linear tower, 'a prison' that leaves her 'encompassed by a wall, high and hard and stone' (7). Such a home is a literal manifestation of her marginal position, as an independent woman, but also as a mixed race individual whose whiteness alienates her from the Maori culture she longs to be a part of. It is a space of control, a space that denies community, as Kerewin admits she builds it because she likes 'to be able to do most things for myself' (107). Yet even in this imprisoning structure, there is the possibility of an alternative for Kerewin. The home's spiral staircase interrogates order with the promise that 'you can't see more that a step and a half in front' (Hulme 32), symbolic of a Maori conceptualisation of time as 'past, present and future' that defies the linearity of Western concepts (Keown 123).[5] In the wake of the transformation facilitated by the alliance between Kerewin, Joe (a troubled local Maori man) and Simon (his equally troubled foster son), the tower is destroyed and, at the novel's conclusion, Kerewin builds a very different sort of home. This home will provide an alternative not only to her own fixed structure, but also to the equally austere home of Joe and Simon. The spiral is no longer overwritten by order in the way that Kerewin's own cultural identity has been obscured:

> Sunflowers and seashells and logarithmic spirals (said Kerewin); sweep of galaxies and the singing curve of the universe (said Kerewin); the oscillating wave thrumming in the nothingness of every atom's heart (said Kerewin); did you think I could build a square house? So the round shell house holds them

---

5   See also Najita, 100.

all in its spiralling embrace. Noise and riot, peace and quiet, all is music in this
sphere. (442–3)

The spirals that for Kerewin 'wind and flow together, like eddies of smoke, eddies
of water ... make more sense than crosses, joys more than sorrow' (273) become
the centre of the new building, challenging the violence, and the social and racial
exclusion, that precede it. As connection to both music and the land, the house
is intimately connected to Joe and Kerewin's Maori past. Here, the alteration of
domestic structures is even more profound: not only an insertion of chaos into
an existing structure, but in fact the replacement of the very architecture that
embodies it with a new form.

What distinguishes Harris's subversion, however, is the combination of
imaginative exterior geography – like that offered by *The Bone People* – with
an equally imaginative interior. Harris undermines the common presentation
of indigenous homes. Written in 1977, his novel casts the migrant home very
differently to the stereotypes of ethnic minority domestic practice in wide
circulation at that time.[6] Here the immigrant home is presented by Harris as the
height of creativity and sophistication. While this may seem now like cultural
mimicry, it is in fact a far more complex act that is better understood by Bhabha's
utilisation of the term. Da Silva's home *does* fuel nostalgia for the home of
Marsden-Prince, yet it is also a location that represents a cross-cultural fusion
that disrupts an uncomplicated repetition. Da Silva's cultivated wilderness is not
only the Holland Park he attempts to capture – a 'wildernesse' (33) – but also
the apartment, a space inextricably linked to the outside. The home is no longer
a metaphor for a national ideal, denied in order to secure its strategic function.
Rather, it is now an acknowledged metaphor for a fluid frame of mind that intends
to dissolve solid notions. This is precisely the distanced and provisional metaphor
– the postcolonial metaphor – that I have outlined.

The breaking down of boundaries makes the house into a liminal space where
the collective histories of the past leak through its walls with restorative results.
Windows proliferate to represent the transition between inside and outside, the
passing of light through the glass creating a permeable membrane of 'vulnerable
thresholds' (Dickey 479); hence 'windows were invaded by bright lakes of sky.
The interior of the houses really swam then, each elegant spar vanished into the
reflection of trees upheld in the middle of the water' (14). As the sterility of the
home is overcome by the power of nature it creates a 'new architecture' (63) of light,
translucent and never lost to the history that underlies it. Such nonlinear fusing of
different timeframes, the contiguity that I outlined as so important to postcolonial
metaphor, cements the importance of the home as a social and political space, with
an acknowledged history beyond the private and familial. This significance also
allows a reappraisal of the criticism of apartments as lacking the history of houses,
criticised at the height of colonialism as spaces that 'maintained insufficient ties to

---

[6]   See Webster.

both the past and the future' (Marcus 162). Rereading such criticism, it indicates that apartments were unacceptable not because they had no past, but because they did not serve the nineteenth century's false ideal of that past. The house divided into flats on Holland Park certainly holds a historical connection, an 'old house' that, as it is moved through, creates a 'whispered dialogue' (11), but it is a real social history:

> Faint thuds and tremors arose from an underground train perhaps as it ran from Holland Park to Shepherd's Bush. Then there was silence. But sounds soon arose from another quarter like a ghost swishing a racket. There was an underground stream somewhere hereabouts, a tributary perhaps to a buried river called Counter Creek. He had seen it on an old map. (11)

In these terms any house can be a gateway to the past; the watery houses of London in *Cultivated Wilderness* draw da Silva back to 'his lake antecedents' (15), and open the doorway to 'Legba Cuffey' (10). This is a figure whose name suggests both the revolutionary power of Guyanese hero Kofi, but also the God of crossroads who 'presides over gateways' and is connected to Harris's frequent invocation of the 'phantom limb' as a signifier of what Mackey has referred to as not 'deformity but multiformity' (244) which is precisely post-space re-visioning. Such refusal to cast the home as a space of absolute privacy is clear in one passage from *Cultivated Wilderness*. It is worth quoting at length:

> From the bed on which they lay they could see through the window, through an opening in the curtains there, into the trees and the sky outside. The sun painted a variety of features in space, hollow spaces like lips, curved/slanted spaces like brows and eyes in the leafy mask of space. Da Silva and Jen were secure in their privacy, secure box, secure mask, yet haunted by apparent anonymity, apparent uniformity, at the heart of a great city. Under the floor beneath them were other floors, other beds, tables, chairs; other bodies that sat, moved, ate, like features of space to match those out there against the sky, implicit shapes hidden from each other yet witnessing to a universal statement or proof or self-survival; frame within frame of the genealogy of a house, flat built over flat, varieties of unstated collaboration mirrored in unfathomable person and non-person. Mirrored in hollow spaces painted into the tree at their window, hollow beaches, hollow oceans in the sky that sailed over them and around them. (47)

Here the metaphorical removal of physical stability is an important subversion of the home's status as a place of hierarchies. This is facilitated by the destabilisation of language. Space is at once 'curved' and 'slanted', embodying opposing properties at the same time in a way that produces paradoxical meanings. As each floor is ripped away, the dwelling is defined not by geometry, but by a fluid sense of endless layers both seen and unseen, not order but ambiguity, as Jen and da Silva experience at once both disorientation and revelation. Such buildings are not in conflict with nature or history as it remains as a latent force within the earth, rather – as they expose a corporeal space of 'lips', 'brows' and 'eyes', connected to the 'sky' – they are a powerful gateway and continuum.[7]

As mark of the inherent positivity of such experience, such a home not only gestures backwards, but also forwards. It offers not only a way to understand the past but – through this – a route to understanding the present. For while the daemon who visits da Silva at the end of *Cultivated Wilderness* suggests 'I'm never quite sure where home is' (43), the protagonist is always sure of his, rejecting any sense of a 'back home' (52) to end the novel with the capitalised reassertion: 'Home' (77). Despite its hierarchies the home is therefore a space of hope, re-visioned by the postcolonial novelist away from the domestic ideal towards something quite different.

Linking the narratives of Morrison and Harris, *Tar Baby* also utilises shifts away from conventional representation of the home in order to rewrite gendered domesticity. For Morrison this does not mean removing women from the home, but rather reclaiming the domestic space as a site of female strength. This places Morrison within a tradition of African-American women's commentaries on the home, where 'houses belonged to women, were their special domain' (hooks, *Yearning* 41). Yet it is also a corruption of the domestic ideal as a haven from public concerns. Here Son's burglary is itself an act of deterritorialisation: fragmenting the home, awakening it from its ideal status, and providing new opportunities for its inhabitants. What Son enacts with his burglary is a 'rupture of the boundary between the inside and the outside' (Korosec-Serfaty 77) when, in the case of L'Arbe de la Croix, this is exactly the chaos needed to move its inhabitants beyond the domestic stasis consuming them. Here Son's status as 'soilage', and as lower class, may take on more radical dimensions, signifying him as Other in the sense of Julia Kristeva's 'abject' – 'these bodily fluids, this defilement' (*Powers* 3) – which is capable of altering individuals, as Son does, and is related to a breakdown of boundaries and totalisations:

> It is thus not lack of cleanliness or health that causes abjection but what disturbs identity, systems, order. What does not respect borders, positions, rules. The in-between, the ambiguous, the composite.' (*Powers* 4)

While Margaret and Valerian have normalised Ondine and Sydney into the inside, Son on the other hand represents an inassimilable outside, illustrating Dickey's sense that the servant who is not a member of the household marks 'the introduction of a dangerous outside into an orderly and protected inside' (462). The fact that it is Son who begins this process illustrates how in *Tar Baby* such a challenge is not limited to women, but instead unites the marginalised. Complex interactions constantly reflect upon a triptych of race, gender and class issues.

---

[7]   There is a similar passage in Harris'ss companion novel, *Genesis of the Clowns* (1977) (92).

What emerges in this reassessment of domestic roles is indeed an appropriation. In the wake of Son's invasion, Ondine and Sydney finally assert themselves outside their own sphere, in the very public space of the family dining room. They take their lead from Son's own usage of the twofold process I outline: Son's deterritorialisation – his insertion of disorder – is followed by an appropriation of the space as he 'grew to know the house well' until 'it became his, sort of. A nighttime possession' (138–9). Subtle language usage confirms a shift in the home's power dynamic: Ondine's comment 'to meddle in my kitchen, fooling around with pies. And *my* help gets fired' (208) reflects a newfound confidence in the servants, and a movement away from a past still characterised by slave models. The outcome confirms Dickey's assertion that 'too much closeness makes employers vulnerable to their servants' (480). Yet, from a postcolonial point of view, this powerful subversion represents an important movement, a crossing of social boundaries that undermines the home's 'hermetically sealed walls' (Marcus 2) as the servant's place in the house is revised.

Once this model of chaotic domesticity has been introduced, it leaks, via individuals, into other domestic spaces. At the house in Eloe, a magical haunting reminds Jadine of the community of strong women she belongs to. Marilyn Chandler has emphasised this aspect of the house in *Beloved* as it suggests 'an escape from domestic life into magical or spiritual time is possible … moments when contact with things invisible and too subtle to penetrate the walls of houses restores the energy, vision, and sense of purpose that give the women the strength they need' (293). Here *Tar Baby* foreshadows techniques used in the later novel, where the haunting of a house is necessary in order to allow its inhabitants to move on. Yet such movements by Jadine in relation to her sense of home also epitomise the constant postcolonial journey between deterritorialisation and a reactionary reterritorialisation. It is a continual oscillation between marking identity on space to create place, and then travelling beyond this to new space, and new chaotic constructions: between the migrant, who must reterritorialise, and the nomad for whom 'there is no reterritorialization *afterward*' (Deleuze and Guattari, *Plateaus* 381).

Rushdie, too, does not reject domestic chaos, but rather seizes it as a window to magical awakenings, houses in *Midnight's Children* that are full of possibility with 'potential mothers and possible fathers' (51). Just as much as for Harris and Morrison, however, the house also provides opportunity for a reappraisal of postcolonial interactions with gender. Indeed, Rushdie appears to combine the techniques of different writers, again uniting differing postcolonial responses. Like Harris, he enacts deterritorialisations or reversals, removing the female from the centre of the home so that Aadam Aziz's mother 'had suddenly found enormous strength and gone out to run the small gemstone business … while his father sat hidden behind the veil' (12). Yet more often, as Rushdie's women are imprisoned in their homes, so they become its most powerful figures. A strategy such as this is more evocative of Morrison's appropriation. Women seem almost magically to take their place at the centre of the narrative, moving to its core as they overwhelm the boundaries delimited for them. While Reverend Mother is imprisoned in the home, it is also her 'inalienable territory' (41) at a time when perhaps, in terms of both patriarchy and colonial rule, it is the only territory available, a space where the domestic is used to gain a sense of empowerment so that 'at the dinner table, imperiously, she continued to rule' (41). There is a particular colonial connotation here, where use of 'imperiously' – 'supreme or absolute rule, imperially' (*OED*) – means it is Reverend Mother's own personal appropriation of political agency. Reverend Mother cannot reject her role as Jen does; instead she appropriates the house and uses her assigned role to her advantage. In this way, it must be remembered that Rushdie's chaotic home presents not only an answer to colonialism or a metaphor for migration, but also a subversion of Indian patriarchy. The chaos that was the impact of Indian nationalism on the home is neither only negative, nor only a factor that foregrounds the hierarchies of the home and its connection to social forces, but rather represents the sense that the '"new woman" emerged in the liminal space between colonial subjection and an incipient nationalism' (Ray 6). Though Reverend Mother may seem a long way from this 'new woman', her negotiation of chaos, and her utilisation of such forces, nevertheless stands as metaphor for an emerging female agency.

Here the postcolonial form of narration enacts a crucial intervention: Rushdie's focus on fragmented, chaotic presentation is not the mark of the migrant's trauma alone. Coterminously, it provides an effective deterritorialisation of the colonial totalisation of space, as a complex interweaving of secret spaces undermines the projected simplicity of colonial architectural construction. For when containment is combined with this chaotic setting – containment acting to subvert official forces rather than reinforce them – it may be turned to serve radical ideals rather than domesticity, as is evident in Nadir Khan's concealment that acts against the Indian establishment because 'things seemed permissible underground that would seem absurd or even wrong in the clear light of day' (56). Similarly, while the 1947 house may reflect colonialism, its description also continually marks resistance to imperialism. The assertion that 'this is still India' (100) indicates possibility for appropriation. This is enacted by the Brass Monkey, whose burning of shoes and items 'broken accidentally-on-purpose' (151) obliterates the last remnants of the mirage of colonial domesticity, and by cleaning that, in common with the association of appropriation with housework that Korosec-Serfaty identifies, means 'his successors emptied his palaces of their abandoned contents' (128), so that Methwold's empire passes simultaneously with its British parallel.

As personal narratives replace colonial writing of official history with a postcolonial narration, the home for the postcolonial author is a politicised space functioning metonymically as it is strongly connected to public space, and is also a site of resistance in its own right. Representing unseen pockets of space still available as places of subversion, homes contain the power to both reflect and subvert colonial discourse, but also its postcolonial reincarnations. At the centre of this is an important reversal, a reversal not of the domestic whole, but of its interior.

Postscript: Inside as Outside; the Whole in the World

The importance of the home illustrates a central tenet of this book. It substantiates the fact that the scales constructed when judging political importance are inverted by the postcolonial novel's presentation. As a postscript to this argument, I want to suggest that such a reversal can be taken even further, to the individual rooms that construct a home, and also the spaces within even these spaces. This deferral extends the displacement of the city to more personal structures. Enter through an undescribed doorway to an undescribed room, to a Bombay bathroom, to a heavily described white washing-chest of slatted wood, and it is here that you find the real power of the post-space house, the miniscule spaces where resistance is ultimately and most securely held.

Such a suggestion means that the postcolonial domestic is not a space of the home as a complete structure, but rather is a space of its deconstruction, its turning around and inside out that is reflected in the fact that the house may be seen as 'simultaneously huge and tidy ... with all its infinite possibilities' (Marc 23–4). This strategy is the ultimate confusion of public and private, as the most private of spaces – the spaces of the house which visitors never enter – paradoxically become the most contested sites: the most private containers, wardrobes, chests, and boxes – as well as individual rooms – which are the secret spaces, even more obscured than the house proper itself. It is not the small discussed here, but what Frances Armstrong has referred to as *miniaturization* which enriches 'by condensation' (405), magnifying meaning and power by creating a 'magical condensed domain' (413).

The implied action here is at the centre of repoliticising the home from its colonial ideal. Marcus makes exactly such a point in her deconstruction of the nineteenth-century novel, as she explains that 'interiorization cannot be sustained because the very activities and attributes associated with perfect interiorization – containment, enclosure, covering, wrapping, repression, silence, sequestration – produce diametrically opposite effects of explosion, discharge, excess, escape, and overflow' (180), so that 'total internalization collapses in on itself' (198). Rewriting the political as personal foregrounds the fact that there are some spaces the establishment cannot enter, though its influence is always found within them: spaces where resistance operates for the individual. It is in these pockets that dreams of changing the outside flourish: the neglected by the establishment – and therefore protected – spaces of the domestic interior.

If we take Rushdie, Morrison and Harris as potential models of postcolonial domesticity, then they all reflect this reframing. It is the interior of Harris's homes that begin a re-visioning of domestic space. In da Silva's apartment all rooms lead to the studio and it is this space, rather than the conventional images of domesticity, that is the focus of the narrative. This plays an integral part in Harris's rejection of the heavily gendered domestic ideal, as the home is represented not primarily as a space of nurture (there are no children) but rather a space of art. It is an idea already foreshadowed by representation of the home in *Black Marsden*, where characters draw on the walls of their Edinburgh home in an act of self-expression (43–4). Yet in

Cultivated Wilderness the image is extended so that the apartment itself becomes da Silva's art; as he is reluctant 'to move along the corridor in his own canvas towards the front door' (9) the studio space allows him to 'look back' (32), and to reject what he calls the *'fixed, immovable'* (55).

The layering witnessed in the house proper is magnified at this level, as the studio door leads to 'the sap of lost gardens ... invisible lakes and rivers ... the corridor (that shook almost imperceptibly to another corridor of earth or passage of underground trains)' (75). Painting the Commonwealth Institute from his studio, da Silva remembers the invasion of the outside as the floor 'shone like water' (65), resonating with the coastal regions of Guyana and the rivers of Brazil. Charlotte Williams has written in a similar way of the Guyanese writer Pauline Melville, where she describes a character who 'slips through the plaster of the wall of her London flat' into Jamaica as the 'wonderful confluence of connections with other worlds' (183). Williams is unaware, however, of the rich tradition of Harris's limbo gateway from which Melville borrows when she represents a 'frail spider's thread suspended sixty feet above the Atlantic attached to Big Ben at the one end and St. George's Cathedral, Demerara, at the other' (Melville 149, qtd. in C. Williams 190). It is this process of magical remembrance that allows da Silva to find 'approaches to his second alternative stage or painting of *the exhibition*' (65), to re-vision the institute.

Significantly, what da Silva now paints is a rejection of empire, 'a comedy of empire, a dying empire, a newborn commonwealth' (65). When the repainted institute is translated into writing, its description as both 'violated bodies of history and the beauty of freedom' (69) captures the ambivalence of post-space. Cementing limbo, the studio returns da Silva not only to the Caribbean but also to Africa, to the deck of a 'metamorphosed ship' (72). Such an image translates to the Middle Passage, and exposes the legacy of slavery that continues inexorably to haunt the present. This transformation through the everyday may be seen as a common strategy uniting Harris with the Caribbean poetry of writers such as Grace Nichols and Kamau Brathwaite, poems such as 'Hurricane Hits England' and 'Ogun' where nature and physical space merge to create aspects of Africa in other locations. Here, the individual structures within homes are deeply connected to the disruption of linear time, and the recovering of the past: spaces as conduits to different historical timeframes and experiences.

Yet for Harris the dominant space within the domestic is not the studio but the television, a seemingly strange choice for a writer so often preoccupied with the natural environment. Harris does not critique the television as we might expect. Rather, he returns its to its etymology, the 'tele' that is communication 'operating over long distances', the magical 'vision' that is 'otherwise than by ordinary sight', so that what emerges is 'the vision of distant objects' (*OED*). This presents in *Cultivated Wilderness* something more akin to a folding of space and messianic time – a route to history and other places – a modern means of capturing the layering of the house and its memories which, like the natural environment, is always latent in the space though often obscured, an oxymoronic 'ancient television box' (46).

That it is contained within the studio offers multiple layering. The television is a microcosm of the studio, 'another canvas' (46), yet it is also an amplification of its significance. For itself, it contains all of da Silva's art and inspiration, the space from which his memories emanate and to which he returns as it forms an internal window where the outside is what da Silva envisages. Being 'vacant' (25) and yet personified, its projections are his own, as 'paradise paintings began with an unlighted television set … . It stared across time and around the globe at him' (24–5). As the object that tells da Silva of the death of his English benefactor it becomes, because of this, his link to the past: it is his most important post-space of trauma turned into positivity. Reminding da Silva of 'other mornings, other evenings' (26), the television brings da Silva back to Brazil, to his past as a traveller and his childhood migration. He hears 'voices buried within tides of the globe' (32), sees the world in its pinpoint of light as the narrator of *The Palace of the Peacock* would in the natural landscape. From Holland House we can still hear 'the cry of a peacock' (33): the environment may have changed but the magical connection to the past, the potential for resistance to the colonial obscuring of indigenous beliefs, is still available.

Tar Baby, too, contains such spaces. They may begin sinisterly: Son's use of the wardrobe as a space of surveillance, the synecdochical trunk that never arrives. However, in Valerian's greenhouse a space is identified that provides protection, and an exemplification of the domestic's significance. This use of the glasshouse is not surprising, a space associated with 'escape into fantasy' (Hix 89) and, in common with the sense of spaces within spaces, in modern terms often seen as '"houses within a house"' (Hix 170). For Valerian, it is a space to contemplate privately. Ironically, however, the fact that the glasshouse is most associated with 'Victorian geometry' (Hix 93) and its popularity ascribed to its provision of a 'unique moral contribution … in a changing society' (Hix 89) means it is also a space that reaffirms Valerian's affinity for the colonial model of domesticity.

Yet as a surprisingly spiritual place the greenhouse in *Tar Baby* also leads Valerian to 'imagining what was not so' to the point where he can see 'the back yard of the house of his childhood in Philadelphia' (140–41), a shifting of space that may again draw from African concepts of limbo and nonlinear time in its fusing of two separate locations. In this way, Morrison's sense of re-memory space so associated with *Beloved* is also evident here. Valerian builds another small space intentionally to keep this space of the past alive, a separate washhouse 'for the remembrance of having once done something difficult and important' (142). This sentence only reaffirms the connection between *Tar Baby* and *Beloved* in terms of re-memory in its similarity to Morrison's later line in *Beloved* referring to the actions of Amy and Sethe, who 'did something together appropriately and well' (84). The significance of the smallness of such spaces, their inversely proportional significance and positive value, is nowhere more evident than in the fact that, despite much social climbing, Margaret ultimately prefers the trailer of her youth (55). Michael hides from his mother's violence in a similar space, in the sink cupboard, while Son has a comparable experience when he finds a sense of belonging at Therese's home that he never finds in the mansion. For Ondine it is the kitchen, the only space with 'permanence' (10). Indeed, the kitchen is also the only space in the house in which Margaret has ever felt happy, sharing jokes with Ondine.

In all cases this is where resistance to violence and social hierarchies begins. Ondine and Sydney begin their appropriation of the house by finding a space that, significantly, becomes '*Ondine's* kitchen' (emphasis added, 165). 'Closed to outsiders' (161), where the servants can express their dislike of Margaret's behaviour and assert themselves, it is a space Ondine calls 'her own territory' (95), reflecting African-American stress on the need to find a 'private space where we do not directly encounter white racist aggression' (hooks, *Yearning* 47) to enact 'subversion and resistance' (hooks, *Yearning* 48). Only when negotiations of social hierarchies are in these spaces complete can the appropriation of the house as a whole begin: the final confrontation in the dining room – the space of public reception – is only the culmination, the overflowing, of debates in seemingly less significant, less noticed, structures. Here isolation is turned around: spaces of hierarchy are made into a post-space as they form the beginnings of resistance precisely because they exist outside the dominant spaces of the structure, precisely because they are spaces of marginality. For Morrison such reduction may be seen as a defining pattern in her novels. Taken even further in *Sula* (1980) and *Beloved*, the private, smallest spaces – a bathroom and a closet of 'emerald light' (*Beloved* 28) – become the greatest refuge: in the former 'a place to be … . Small enough to contain her grief. Bright enough to throw into relief the dark things that cluttered her' (*Sula* 98), in the latter a 'secret place' (Chandler 293). Such spaces facilitate powerful acts of self-assertion in the wake of tragedy.

It is the bathroom that began this discussion, and will form its conclusion. For it is this bathroom, among other of Rushdie's spaces, that provides greatest evidence of resistance focused upon the small and contained in the postcolonial text: the homes within houses. *Midnight's Children* immediately foregrounds the positive importance of such spaces, with an opening chapter that introduces us to 'an empty pickle jar … an old tin trunk' (19), where an 'old brass spittoon' (44) is a 'lost receptacle of memories' (449) which allows Saleem to assert his own identity as it has been gradually stripped from him by armed combat. Just as each section of the novel begins with a remembrance of a house, so each of these remembrances leads to an even smaller and more personal contained space. Spaces are layered, getting ever more smaller yet more significant, like Russian dolls, so that Saleem's grandparents' house in Agra leads to 'an old trunk', which itself leads to 'this leather bag inside this trunk' (31) in which is contained the perforated sheet of the novel's opening; the house on Cornwallis Road leads to a cellar, which itself leads to a 'gemstone-crusted silver spittoon' (58) that itself will also later be placed within the same tin trunk. The structure that emerges is reminiscent of Stewart's dollhouses that are 'center within center, within within within' (61).

Like Michael's trunk, such spaces in *Midnight's Children* are also synecdochical, reflecting what may be seen as an extension of the metaphor-metonym transference.

Aadam Aziz's bag, for example, 'to the ferryman ... represents Abroad' (21). They are the markers of meaning, Doctor Aziz not simply that but rather 'Doctor Aziz, leather bag in hand' (34), Amina not simply travelling, but travelling 'with her feet on the green tin trunk' (66), the narrator literally swallowing such spaces as his way to 'swallow the world' (109) as he is 'fattening up on washing-chests' (108). Yet they are also open spaces, open both to the narrator's privileging of them, but also to multiple meanings, evident in Saleem's surprise when going to the trunk to find 'it had not been locked in the first place' (31).

Most magical of these spaces are the pickle jars which allow the 'chutnification of history' (459), contained within the home of the frame story itself: the factory-home that is both public and private space so that Saleem may write 'above present and past' (194), a home which holds both the history of India and, as Marquez style denouement, Saleem's own story. The jars are the novel itself, a metaphor for the creative act of filling empty spaces, 'chutneys and kasaundies ... connected to my nocturnal scribblings ... the great work of preserving' (38). The transformation within the pickle jars is, on a smaller scale, the same transformation from negative chaos to positive space, of incongruous significance and capacity, which typifies the domestic structure. Yet the fact that it is represented as the origins of Saleem's whole story, indeed contains the whole of the transformations within its pages, makes it in fact a larger space than any building that could contain it.

What is approached here is an extension of Proustian memory with a postcolonial provenance, in which objects come to capture a vast history, and contact with these objects brings such history – complete with all its tensions and exploitations – to life. What is experienced might also be read, however, through what Jacques Derrida terms *invagination*, where 'the boundary of the set comes to form ... an internal pocket *larger than the whole*' (emphasis added, 'Law' 59). Derrida is discussing precisely the technique that Rushdie invokes, how the novel *La Folie du Jour* proclaims its beginning in the story's conclusion in the same way that Rushdie's jars hold the potential of the story from the very first line we read, so that we find 'the first line of a book, is forming a pocket inside the corpus' ('Law' 70) just as Derrida outlines. Yet Rushdie takes this invagination further, gives it physical form. The story is not contained merely within the promise of language, as *La Folie du Jour* captures 'an account' or Gabriel Garcia Marquez writes of the history of a family constructed so events in the book 'one hundred years ahead of time ... coexisted in one instant' (421). It is caught within a physical structure, itself contained: the jars. In this way the 'one jar [that] stands empty' in *Midnight's Children* (460) must be seen as hope as well as the novel's resignation: marking the 'questions ... dreams' (461) that remain. Such containers, be they a line of narrative or jars, have undeniable possibility as they suggest life 'without beginning or end ... without boundary' (Derrida, 'Law' 70). The filling of such spaces is a renewal of optimism, and an act of resistance against those who would seek to empty other significant spaces, where 'testicles were removed from sacs, and wombs vanished for ever ... and they drained us of more than that: hope, too, was excised' (Rushdie, *Midnight's Children* 439). Even when resistance against such state violence may seem impossible, there are always other scales, other spaces, where survival can occur. In *The Bone People*, a central part of Kerewin's survival is a logbook which contains a multitude of different expressive forms, but also the absences which, like the jars, offer continued hope:

> The pages are mainly blank, because there are 1000 pages. There are no headings, dates, day names. She has filled in some pages at random with doodles and sequences of hatching. Small precise drawings and linked haiku. Some days a solitary word. 'Hinatore' says one, 'Nautilids!' another. (36)

As for Rushdie, such a logbook is a space within space, contained on the bottom shelf of a 'grog cupboard' (36), itself contained within Kerewin's tower. Like the spiral staircase, it is a mark of the possibility latent in Kerewin's life – obscured and only to be revealed with the disruption offered by Simon's entry into her life. Like Saleem's jars, it is full of concoctions of influences, rather than a unified meaning. It denies the colonial use of language as definition, refusing authority in its rejection of headings, dates and names. Maori language challenges the authority of classical Latin.

So I finish with Saleem's washing-chest as the final example of such spaces. Lingering, still visible to Amina in her blindness, the chest is foregrounded early in *Midnight's Children* by Nadir Khan's use of it as a space of 'sanctuary ... muffled by linen, dirty underwear and old shirts' (52) that establishes it as a space of security, echoed in other bathrooms where 'we emerged ... with the illusory optimism of freshly-soaped cleanliness' (283). Nowhere is this space of shelter seen more clearly than in Saleem's reminiscence: the sanctuary of the bathroom where you can be anything because 'there are no mirrors' (156) and because – bringing us back to Son's role as the abject – it is at times an 'unclean' (160) space that demands none of the usual deference to domestic cleanliness or purity. It is a level of intimacy that creates a place that cruelty, even if it permeates through the rest of the house, can never enter. Hence in the washing-chest in the bathroom of Buckingham Villa 'servants are excluded ... school buses, too, are absent' (153), leading Saleem to the powerful proclamation:

> Banned from washing-chests: cries of 'Pinocchio! Cucumber-nose! Goo-face!' Concealed in my hiding-place, I was safe ... I could forget, for a time, my ugliness. (154)

The power of such a secure space is not simply to remove personal anxiety but also public danger, engendering resistance by providing a site in which identity can be safely asserted, and secret plans made. It is a space outside the tumult of society that is, under transition from empire to freedom, in political crisis:

> A washing-chest is a hole in the world, a place which civilisation has put outside
> itself, beyond the pale ... safe from all pressures, concealed from the demands
> of parents and history. (156)

Here the basket takes on a more homely significance than the actual dwelling,
its status as a breach in the normal spatial order giving it a capacity far beyond
its linear measurements. As abstract space, this is absence as positivity: a silence
of the currents of time passing and of political change, stillness, a pause, a gasp
for breath that facilitates survival. What emerges is the deterritorialisation that
leads to the appropriation before the further deterritorialisation of leaving the
home behind. A new politics appears in this private space, where what matters is
the possibility outside of an official public history that has been revealed to bear
only limited truth. This is confirmed by the fact that it is the space of Saleem's
awakening – his transformation into an 'untuned radio' (163) for the children of
midnight – and a chance at democracy.

The house becomes the outside, the public. With the 'basket of invisibility'
(380) not only is space transformed into a fluid 'cloudy nowhere' (381), but the
body within it is also reconfigured as Saleem 'vanished instantly into thin air ... in
the basket, but also not in the basket' (380–81). As post-space it is both liberating
but also dangerous: giving Saleem 'the characteristics of ghosts' but also placing
him in 'mortal danger' (381). Ironically, what returns Saleem is another container:
the silver spittoon that serves as the final repository of memories required to
jolt him back into reality. The ability of the spittoon allies Rushdie to the other
postcolonial authors discussed here through the capacity to seemingly merge past
and present, even when the past has been deleted. In one passage the importance
of such spaces is encapsulated:

> No – there was more to it than spittoons: for, as we all know by now, our hero
> is greatly affected by being shut up in confined spaces. Transformations spring
> upon him in the enclosed dark ... . In a cramped wash-room ... Alone in a
> washing-chest ... Squashed, in a small abandoned hut. (382)

Constructing, like Harris, a cross-novel strategy of representation, Rushdie's use of
domestic spaces in *Shame* only reinforces this picture, where 'eighteen shawls of
memory ... Locked in their trunk ... said unspeakable things' (191). It is a wooden
chest that, like Saleem's jars, seems capable of holding the whole of history within
its now fluid boundaries.

In their reversals and inversions – their replacement of depoliticised order
with politicised chaos, the inversion of large and small scales so that the home
itself ultimately becomes the public of a smaller structure – postcolonial authors
engage with a magical-realist mode of representation that allows domestic space
to transcend the colonial model. Through motifs of movement and fluidity,
layering and invasion, flowing and leaking, a new vision of the home emerges. Its
architecture refuses to succumb to norms and ideals. Its layers and complexity – the

very nature of its confusion – make it a space of important protection: outside the linear narrative of history and all that represents in colonial and patriarchal terms, and instead within magical space. Unlike the ideal home of Gaston Bachelard, in which 'the outside has no more meaning' (85), the postcolonial home is always in tension with this outside, both echoing and challenging its prejudices as it is intensely involved in their construction. Invaded by public space, the gender politics of the home is foregrounded. Yet, at the same time, politicisation creates the home as a site of resistance for all its postcolonial inhabitants, regardless of gender. Renewed by chaos and possibility, the postcolonial home reverses the colonial ideal, and, with it, the assumptions and stereotypes on which such a home was so evidently based. The productive chaos at the centre of such movement is refused naming by Freud. Acknowledging it, such chaos, I suggest, might be productively termed post-space.

Chapter 5
Last Scale:
Postcolonial Bodies

The body is not open to *all* the whims, wishes, and hopes of the subject …
On the other hand, while there must be some kinds of biological limit or constraint,
these constraints are perpetually capable of being superseded, overcome, through
the human body's capacity to open itself up to prosthetic synthesis, to transform
or rewrite its environment, to continually augment its powers and capacities …
surpassing the body, not 'beyond' nature but in collusion with a 'nature' that never
really lived up to its name, that represents always the most blatant cultural anxieties
and projections.

(Grosz, *Volatile* 187–8)

The climax of Toni Morrison's novel *Paradise* sees the convent women seemingly
killed, only to magically re-emerge unscathed. Central to their survival is the
suggestion that they have transcended violence against the body and limits on
its form. Arrival at the crime-scene uncovers 'No Bodies. Nothing' (292). There
are 'no dead to report, transport or bury … unnatural deaths in a house with no
bodies' (298). Such conclusion to what is largely a realist novel, certainly more
conventional than *Beloved*, is problematic for readers, a response epitomised
in Christine Bold's reaction, for whom the ending is 'a too easy retreat into the
supernatural, escaping the details of everyday struggle' (22).[1] Yet, contrary to this,
Morrison's ending can also be taken to reveal an important concern. Centred on
survival implying the ability to transcend fatal violence, the ending of *Paradise*
raises key questions about the nature of bodily absolutes and the imposition of
body image by neo-colonial and patriarchal culture. Beginning from *Paradise* as
exemplifying such a position, and recognising the corporeal as an often-unspoken
element in so many of the transformations already discussed, I suggest in this
final chapter that postcolonial texts aim to magically reconfigure the body's
significance in a way that marks the ultimate reduction of spatial scales, as the
site of greatest colonisation becomes a resource facilitating the most powerful
statements of resistance. Because of their exemplary status, Morrison's texts are
used here as foundation. Yet as a concluding chapter, I also draw together texts
already discussed and provide new examples, weaving in and out of narratives in

---

[1]   For reader reviews, see '*Paradise*: Customer Reviews' at Amazon.com: <http://
www.amazon.com/exec/obidos/tg/detail/-/0452280397/ref=cm_cr_dp_2_1/002-6638068
6019259?v=glance&s=books&vi=customer-reviews>. For critical reviews echoing Bold
see, for example, Heller.

a way that allows the form of this investigation – as well as its discussions – to support the productivity of a positively chaotic post-space.

Definitive Space

Neither the concept that experience is ultimately encapsulated in the body, nor that the body is a spatial form, is unique to postcolonial thought. Both concepts may be traced back to phenomenology, captured in Maurice Merleau-Ponty's view that we are conscious of the world through our bodies, and where particular attention must be paid to 'spatiality' (98). Frequently in both literature and theory, other spatial scales are read through their impact upon the body and, conversely, on the body's role in their construction. In this way, the reduction to smaller scales that I identify in the experience of both domestic and urban space, displaced onto buildings and even rooms and containers, has a missing final stage, in which even these structures are deferred to a more intimate and personal space: that of the body.

Too numerous to list, in the texts already focused upon such deferral is *always* evident: one need only reconsider the role of Sethe's body in her journey in *Beloved* – enduring childbirth, feet bleeding and worn – or the very corporeal transformations of Chamcha in the city of *The Satanic Verses* which emphasise a ludic city of bodily performance. Such deferral is most pronounced in a text such as Wilson Harris's *The Dark Jester* (2001); here all spaces are ultimately connected to bodily forms: amongst many images we encounter 'arteries of space and time' (11), the 'body of the precipice' (81), a 'mouth of space' (65), the 'belly of a slave-ship' (99), a calendar which has a 'face' (61) and a tree that grows from an 'eye in the soil' (63). These interactions are not only metaphoric or metonymic: other spaces are not simply figurative representations of the body, and, conversely, the body is not simply the metaphor of choice for exhibiting other experiences. Rather, these are complex connections, spaces indicating a particular experience at their own scale inherently interwoven with experiences at other scales, of which the body is often the end (or beginning) point. Yet are there distinct reasons why the body as space holds such particular significance in the postcolonial text?

Ultimate Territory

Perhaps more than in human experience in general, colonisation has been a project centred upon manipulation and appropriation of bodies as both a territory and the key to maintaining successful control of land: equally classified through vision, recorded and defined to the extent of classifying particular racial mixes and types. As Michel Foucault has shown, power relations are invested in the body. His famous statement that 'it is always the body that is at issue – the body and its forces, their utility and their docility, their distribution and their submission' (Foucault, *Discipline* 25) is particularly relevant to postcolonial contexts: his emphasis on the control of bodies not only through violence, but also more subtle means of regulation, reflects a colonial discourse of the body which is not simply a story of beatings, rape and slavery. Though these undoubtedly demand attention, the colonial maintenance of bodies is also a story of the propagation of bodily norms through writing, education and administrative practice. As Achille Mbembe (2003) has thus persuasively argued, to study colonial power is to engage directly with the maintenance and manipulation of bodies in diverse and complex ways. Such knowledge enforces the view that the postcolonial body is not an autonomous entity, but one already marked by the colonial past.

The histories of the United States and Guyana which Morrison and Harris reflect are pertinent examples of the more obvious, physical abuse of bodies under colonialism. If colonialism is the seizure of territory, then slavery is the colonial seizure of the body as that territory, in which the person is construed as property. The Middle Passage was inherently a bodily experience. Violence took horrific and multiple forms: temperatures in the hold of a slave-ship rose to unbearable levels, and massive overcrowding, combined with the use of chains, meant the body was physically contained. Ship captains practised malicious and cruel treatment with a high level of physical abuse, as Ronald Segal's account illustrates:

> In 1764, for instance, a certain Captain Marshall flogged a nine-month-old child because it would not eat; treated its swollen feet by putting them in water so hot that the skin and nails came off; and, when it died, battered its mother until she threw the body overboard herself. A certain Captain Williams delighted in flogging slaves who would not eat. (35)

On the slave holding, abuse of the body did not abate. The hard physical work of slavery is, in itself, abuse of a body owned as just another colonial resource. Floggings and beatings were as common as on the slave-ship, and physical containment – chains and inhospitable living conditions – only compounded the containment already signified by ownership. Yet if slavery was the extreme, it was not the exception. The atrocities perpetrated under colonialism are too numerous to note; attempting to capture the scale of such violence through a few examples would only undervalue the reality of such aggression.

What must therefore be emphasised is the pervasiveness of bodily abuse, something which collections such as Simon Ryan and Leigh Dale's *The Body in the Library* (1998) highlight, as they draw attention to a colonial discourse of the body with subtleties that resonate with Foucault's arguments. In the introduction to their collection, Dale and Ryan outline empire as a bodily process, where the seizure of territory must also be seen as a capture of bodies, and the maintenance of power can be read as a mastery of these bodies as much as of physical landscape. As the colonised body was made abject, so efforts at assimilation into colonial standards led to ever-increasing control of the indigenous body. For example, in his discussion of early missionary work in Papua New Guinea, Christopher Fife illustrates increasing colonial concern for the cleanliness and control of the bodies of the autochthonous population, a dirty or undisciplined body signifying the impossibility of being 'civilised' (259). Rejecting the possibility that culturally specific processes of bodily discipline might already be in place, working the body and military training such as drill was implemented to promote an ordered, obedient subject. Ever more subtle, as 'the earlier preoccupation with fencing in stations and encapsulating children ... changed into a more concentrated attempt to control individual bodies through the institution of moral hygiene' (Fife 262), the regime employed follows closely Foucault's history of bodily discipline. Equally, printed texts, education, and public health programs all propagated the stereotypes of the unruly colonised body. As Robert Young argues, such texts meant that the relationship between race and cultural difference 'did not have to be sustained by any form of empirical evidence' (140): it simply passed into 'truth'. The accuracy of such interpretation is affirmed by a text such as Frantz Fanon's *Black Skin, White Masks* (1952). The power of this text, and its continued contemporary relevance, lies in its expression of the subtle and hegemonic perpetuation of stereotypes in late colonial rule. Fanon's account of how such feeling is internalised, as the black man's consciousness of his body is 'a solely negating activity' (110), shows the traumatic impact of such bodily definition. His often-quoted discussion with the refrain 'Look, a Negro' (109, 111, 112) illustrates in personal terms how the discourse of the black body constructed by white society regulates and ultimately destroys positive black identity.

As one body (the colonial body) is extended, so the other (the colonised body) is increasingly narrowed, its meanings and possibilities reduced. Yet this relationship, like the relationship to space in general, obscures a more complicated story. The paradoxical relationship of the coloniser to the colonised body has been heavily explored. Both Robert Young and Homi Bhabha argue that the colonised body is paradoxically a site of attraction and abjection, a location 'always simultaneously inscribed in both the economy of pleasure and desire and the economy of discourse, domination and power' (Bhabha, 'Other' 150): desired and yet feared as racially hybrid bodies were associated with 'threatening forms of perversion and degeneration' (R. Young 5). In this way, the colonial treatment of the body can be seen to echo the treatment of all space. Chaos and desire are overwritten with rigid, linear systems, doubt and difference are obscured by homogeneity. Colonial order is presented as natural and unquestionable. Uncovering this obscured diversity reveals how bodily purity is impossible: how the body of the coloniser, as well as the colonised, is characterised by hybridity. The body is subject to the same ordering employed in the appropriation of homes, journeys, nations and cities. Indeed, connection to Euclidean space is here explicit: the colonial body was the body as defined by René Descartes, relying upon the same mathematical principles – the same geometry – that defined the Euclidean gridded space used for mapping territory, making the body as 'whatever has a determinable shape and a definable location' (17). It was measured by colonial science which accepted Descartes's construction of it as a discrete entity. Indeed, examining Elizabeth Grosz's outline of the three lines of investigation of the body following from Descartes which made the body an object, a tool, and a passive form (*Volatile* 8–9), then all of these seem integral to colonial representation of the body, and of space in general. Descartes's construction allowed for representation of the body as a passive form that could be seized and appropriated, described by Descartes as opposite to the fluid mind that was representative of the creative and transcendent. Such basic form meant the body could be defined absolutely, used as a defining principle of an individual. Yet, paradoxically, as it was without agency it could also be endlessly redefined. Colonial discourse of the body relies upon this contradiction, a body at once intensely visible, but at the same time unrecognised: nothing because it has only one form but also, for this very same reason, strongly defined.

In order to maintain superiority, colonists introduced increasingly hegemonic structures to separate different bodies in often-elaborate hierarchies, using a discourse of inferior bodies to justify conquest. Associating the colonised body with animal rather than human characteristics sees the stereotype of the animalistic and savage black male as only part of a larger discourse, in which indigenous males of all races were frequently cast as rapists who defiled the bodies of white women.[2] Interestingly placed together, knowledge of the colonial and criminal body could now be produced: personality traits seemingly capable of being determined by skin colour or bone structure.[3] Robert Young's account of colonial practices of classification to identify these 'flaws' illustrates the colonial obsession with bodily purity, Joseph Arthur Comte de Gobineau's splitting of the global population into ever more multiple classifications with accompanying personalities, strengths and weaknesses, and J.J. Von Tscudi's division of the Peruvian population into twenty-three different racial groups, each with its own name (104, 176). Such studies were used in nineteenth-century anthropological accounts, such as those produced by *Anthropological Review*, encouraging the development of tests for hidden blackness that would explain negative behaviour or predict its future possibility. Their motivations cannot be seen as objective; Gobineau's *Types of Mankind* that Young refers to, for example, was edited by a figure, J.C. Nott, who was, according to Anthony Synnott and David Howes, 'a convinced racist' (151).

The postcolonial novel can therefore on one level be seen to reflect the centrality of the body to colonial power, the fact that the body is an imperial target and, indeed, bears a legacy of bodies marked and defined by outside forces. Moreover, they are testaments, equally, to the continued maintenance of bodies in the postcolonial world stemming from the continued legacy of colonialism, evidence of the Foucauldian disciplining of bodies in the postcolony that Mbembe has made much of (*Postcolony* 113), with its 'intimate rituals' (*Postcolony* 128) that reaffirm tyranny and bear little difference to their colonial forebears, at times even surpassing colonial violence in a 'necropolitics' of death.[4] Of the three

---

2   See Blunt, 'Embodying' 406–9.

3   See Dale and Ryan 7.

4   Mbembe's discussion of the colonial use of bodies, and the extension of this practice in the postcolony, echoes much of the discussion on the ordering of bodies presented by the

authors considered in detail in this book, it is Morrison who may be seen to have most closely explored the continuation and explosion of defined bodies, and the violence against these bodies in all her texts. One text in particular, however, can be seen to encapsulate Morrison's awareness of the body, bringing together earlier concerns with bodily form in novels such as *The Bluest Eye* (1970) and *Beloved*. Centred around an isolated and outcast community of women living in a disused convent, *Paradise* is constructed through a series of individual female stories, each of which is to some extent consumed not simply by tales of bodily violence, but by experiences of bodily judgement. Mavis's status with her husband is passive and objectified, Gigi is driven to the convent by the trauma of seeing 'body bags ... little boys splitting blood' (68). At the hands of a high-class woman, Seneca submits to experience ranging from 'peacock feathers ... abject humiliation ... coddling to playful abuse ... caviar tartlets to filth' (137). We learn later of this worthlessness, a result of sexual abuse by her foster brother which means Seneca physically damages what she sees as a worthless body, trying to cut out what makes her the target of unwanted sexual attention, but also attempting to take back control of her body in what is an essentially spatialised relationship. She literally makes her body into a map, cutting 'streets, lanes, alleys' (261) after the deaths of Martin Luther King and Robert Kennedy, echoing Susan Bordo's argument in *Unbearable Weight* that self-harm is also an attempt to be accepted into social norms, and to reclaim power via the body. Our first image of Pallas is of a woman threatened by male sexuality, hiding in the lake while the call of 'here, pussy' (163) reverberates across the water from the bank, though what has actually happened she cannot repeat. She cannot understand, however, why Carlos, who loved her when she was a 'butterball' (178), abandons her when she is thin – she sees her attractiveness as directly related to American standards of beauty. Finally, there is Consolata. She suffers for more than herself; in a 'space tight enough for a coffin' (221), echoing *Beloved*. She waits to die in a place where 'her voice was one among many that packed the cellar from rafter to stone floor' (221). Yet Consolata also has her own pain, 'the dirty pokings her ninth year subjected her to' (228).

In an attempt to counteract this negative attention the convent women have only one mirror that is not covered with chalky paint to discourage critical appraisal of their physical appearances. However, when the women expose themselves to the wider community of Ruby, they find the return of the judgments that previously haunted them. Judged by the Ruby men as abhorrent because they 'don't need men and they don't need God' (276), the convent women threaten the men of Ruby in their refusal to succumb to a stable, ordered image of black femininity. The men have a classificatory system to which they subject the convent women – they are objectified as 'detritus' (4) and, upon arrival at the wedding of a Ruby woman, Arnette, are judged entirely by their outward appearances. Their clothes and jewellery from 'Jezebel's storehouse' mark them out as immoral: the fact that

---

other critics discussed here. See also pp. 187–96. In relation to the black male body more specifically see Rodriguez, and also Gilroy's *Between Camps*.

Gigi shows her navel, her breasts refuse to be 'hushed' (54), and that she walks provocatively, identify her immediately as a sexual target for the Ruby men.

What emerges in such representation is in fact not so different from the colonial man's mixture of desire for, and repulsion of, the both racial and sexual Other. As 'golden-skinned' (279) Consolata is the subject of Deacon's attention but later she is also 'ravenous … a travesty of what a woman should be' (280). As the men punish what they are ultimately also attracted to, the novel reflects the suggestion that it is our own excesses for which the abjected Other is ultimately punished; the novel is clear that what the men ultimately destroy are their own bodily 'transgressions' – their own sexual desires and fear of hybridity – displaced onto the women.

While the founding males' concern for women and children on the journey to Ruby – their refusal to let them work in white kitchens where sexual assault is seen as possible – is admirable, it sets in motion nevertheless a social hierarchy. What a female body, as well as a black body, should be is defined from outside as the colonised takes up the values of the colonist. Ruby women do not know their own bodies, only what they have been told they are. For Arnette, 'everything she knew of her body was connected to' (148) her boyfriend K.D., while the connotations a female body carries are laid down unambiguously: the women do not powder their faces and wear 'no harlot's perfume' (143). K.D. believes himself not to be responsible for Arnette's pregnancy because she willingly gave her body to him, making her – in his eyes – a woman of low morals who has no right to demand male responsibility. In traditional nineteenth-century terms, she must now be responsible not only for her own 'impurity', but also for his. This echoes a theme first presented by Morrison in *The Bluest Eye* in which Pecola is initially blamed for her own rape.

In the same way as the discourse surrounding domestic space, what this relationship reveals is the explicit connections between race and gender. And, once again, there is colonial precedent for such association. Anthropological representations of the body in the nineteenth century did support interweaving notions of white and male supremacy, where British anthropologist Edward Taylor and American anthropologist Samuel Taylor Morton used craniology to support the former and French anthropologist Gustave le Bon in 1895 used the same methods to support the latter (Synnott and Howes 151–2). Gender stereotypes developed alongside racial ones, in opposition to perceived indigenous weakness and a female body placed centrally in its role as reproductive source. Forced inspection of even some white women in India outlines how female bodies, regardless of colour, became victims of obsessive colonial concern for purity, made responsible for virtuousness, while at the same time being used sexually through endorsed prostitution.[5] In this way, as Grosz has noted, the subtle control

---

[5]   See, for example, Jo-Ann Wallace's essay on the control of both white and indigenous female bodies in nineteenth-century colonies.

outlined by Foucault may be extended to discussion of specifically female – as well as colonised – bodies.

Paradise keys into this particular colonial concern with the black female body, from which, arguably, the Ruby men can be seen to draw their violent reaction. Cast as 'grotesque' (Peterson xi) and as possessing a dangerous and deviant sexuality, black female bodies were excluded from nineteenth-century ideals of femininity. Rape of female slaves was eroticised and unpunished as criminal law failed to recognise such crimes. This destroyed not only female rights over their own bodies, but also male slaves' sense of worth as unions between slaves were not honoured. Realist postcolonial novels such as *Nervous Conditions* (1988) show how, even outside slavery, the female body in particular suffers from the impact of colonial discourse. In Tsitsi Dangarembga's novel, the two central female characters of Nyasha and Tambudzai represent how the alienated body that Fanon so powerfully presents translates to the female colonial subject, correcting an acknowledged lack in Fanon's own study. Nyasha descends into anorexia, an expression of her feelings of worthlessness. Raised in England, she proclaims herself a 'hybrid' and argues 'I can't help having been there and grown into the me that has been there' (79). This latter statement illuminates how her exposure to English values is seen to have a direct result on her body image. Whilst Tambudzai admires herself in the mirror, Nyasha criticises her cousin's backside (92). Here Dangarembga explicitly reflects upon the stereotypes of and judgments against the black body that extend back to the Black Venus, but are still seen in contemporary culture through advertising and screen representations. Like the convent women, Nyasha is judged on the basis of her body, marked not only as a traitor to her race, but also as sexually deviant because of her way of dressing (95). Against this is cast Tambudzai's delight in nourishing her body, her pleasure in the school walk where 'you could run off the road into more wooded areas to look for matamba and matunduru. Sweet and sour. Delicious' (2–3). Colonialism's role in this change is emphasised by its contrast with our first understanding of Tambudzai's ease with her physical form:

> Nevertheless, when I was feeling brave, which was before my breasts grew too large, I would listen from the top of the ravine and, when I was sure I had felt no one coming, run down to the river, slip off my frock, which was usually all that I was wearing, and swim blissfully for as long as I dared in the old deep places. (4)

As the quotation suggests, adolescence certainly plays a role in the erosion of this image. But it is also more than this. After leaving Zimbabwe for England, Nyasha is represented as alienated from her own black body in a way that directly echoes Fanon's commentary. Returning to the village from England, she is marked by a change in not only the physicality of her own body, but also her awareness of it:

Maiguru entered last and alone, except for her two children, smiling quietly and inconspicuously. ... she did not look as though she had been to England. My cousin Nyasha, pretty bright Nyasha, on the other hand, obviously had. There was no other explanation for the tiny little dress she wore, hardly enough of it to cover her thighs. She was self-conscious though, constantly clasping her hands behind her buttocks to prevent her dress from riding up, and observing everybody through veiled vigilant eyes to see what we were thinking. (37)

Back in Zimbabwe, Nyasha now views her body from the position of the African gaze, 'silent and watchful, observing us all' (52), and is ashamed. Yet, coming from England, her dress reflects her desire to fulfil the alternative white gaze through which she also now judges her physical appearance. Her gradual decline is that of a subject alienated, slowly descending into judgement of herself and division from her surroundings. Imbued with the western belief that 'angles were more attractive than curves' (137), Nyasha's developing breasts and clearly female form (133) are at clear odds with the white ideals of beauty into which she has been socialised in England. With colonialism comes a new ideal body image, creating conflict for the individual caught between indigenous and colonial practice. As Kwame Anthony Appiah notes in his introduction to the novel, Nyasha's search for the perfect body is 'conceived of in a most un-Shona way in terms of an ideal thinness' (ix).

In contrast to Nyasha's decline, Tambudzai's education offers a transformation of her physical self. In being educated and challenging the patriarchal conventions of her society, Tambudzai sees her very body altered, leaving behind the shabbily dressed, unwashed and malnourished (58). Against a society that denigrates female bodily process, foreshadowing *Paradise* as Tambudzai declares that 'menstruation was a shamefully unclean secret' (71), Tambudzai celebrates her form: her menstruation and increasing plumpness is associated with how her 'mind and body relaxed' (96). Equally, against Nyasha's anorexia, the novel affirms the value of black beauty: Lucia, who is described as both 'dark' and 'plump' and is noted for her beauty (127, 129). Yet what is significant is that, despite her seeming success, Tambudzai too has not escaped this construction of self. The *Bildungsroman* form of *Nervous Conditions* offers Tambudzai the narrator as a very different voice to Tambudzai the adolescent. It is this older voice which uses terms such as 'lightening of diverse darkness' (105), and which proclaims in relation to the whites that 'it did not take long for me to learn that they were in fact more beautiful and then I was able to love them' (106). Whilst Tambudzai as an adolescent is less psychologically damaged than her cousin, we can speculate that the narrator's experience has been less different than such childhood divisions suggest. At its conclusion, only the first part of Tambudzai's story has been told: its continuance (Dangarembga in 2006 released an eagerly anticipated sequel) promises a very different narrative. As for Morrison, it is clear that although exposure to racial and cultural difference is here the significant defining feature distinguishing Tambudzai and Nyasha, there is an overarching gendered aspect to their treatment. This, regardless of race, can explain the reasons for the continuity between Nyasha's voice and the voice of the narrator:

> The victimisation, I saw, was universal. It didn't depend on poverty, on lack of education or on tradition. It didn't depend on any of the things I had thought it depended on. Men took it everywhere with them. ... all the conflicts came back to this question of femaleness. Femaleness as opposed and inferior to maleness. (118)

It is a point her aunt confirms, that 'it wasn't a question of associating with this race or that race at that time. People were prejudiced against educated women. Prejudiced' (184) as does her mother, who experiences her own anorexic crisis not because of the 'Englishness' she blames for Nyasha's problems, but because of her domestic circumstances (187). As for the convent women, it is the combination of these features that causes female inequality. Nyasha's statement that 'I was comfortable in England but now I'm a whore with dirty habits' (119), and that her alienation is a result not just of 'her language' but also the fact that 'I beat the boys at maths!' (200) exemplifies the interaction of racial and gendered definition of the body. She is not simply a cultural hybrid, but also 'not a good girl' (201): an explicitly female hybrid. It is neither her mistreatment by her patriarchal father and academic pressures, nor her changing body against western ideals, that condemns Nyasha to an eating disorder, but the powerful combination of these two factors together.

In contemporary discourse, this representation has continued in dominant images of black females. As bell hooks notes:

> black women are seen and depicted as down to earth, practical, creatures of the mundane. Within sexist racist iconography, black females are most often represented as mammies, whores, or sluts. Caretakers whose bodies and beings are empty vessels to be filled with the needs of others. This imagery tells the world that the black female is born to serve – a servant maid – made to order. She is not herself but always what someone else wants her to be. (hooks, *Art* 97)

What both *Paradise* and *Nervous Conditions* reveal – *a la* Fanon – is the incorporation of such values into black male thinking about black female sensuality, whether in the colonial or postcolonial period. Their outside definition of the women's bodies may be seen as both a gendered and colonial practise, a practise that continues in the postcolonial age as the colour and sex of bodies still determines an individual's place in society.

In *Paradise*, however, the endemic nature of bodily prejudice is asserted not only through expression of the impact of gender norms, but also through consideration of what bodily 'norms' really mean in terms of racial identity. The closed African-American community of Ruby has reversed dominant American body images and replaced them with their own. After being constructed as animals and experiencing a 'Disallowing' – turned away from towns after leaving Haven by fairer skinned black men – the founders transcend colour prejudice by implementing a new 'colorism' (Gutmann 45). There is great comfort for the community in this position, reflecting Fanon's belief that 'as long as the black man is among his own, he will have no occasion, except in minor internal conflicts, to experience his being through others' (*Black Skin* 109). Yet it induces a damaging system of hierarchies as destructive as that it replaces. Instead of resisting oppositions that construct a body as weak or strong, here the ex-slave, as representative of the still-colonised, simply replaces the coloniser in its role as ideal body, assuming its values and creating a new inferior body below its own. Elleke Boehmer notes celebration of the body within colonial resistance as 'a totality with which to subsume the denial' ('Transfiguring' 273) under colonialism. Yet in the terms represented here it is clear that it is also the subsuming of a totality with a totality, with another ordered, easily understood body. This is Patricia's awakening in the novel: that the treatment of the community is not equal, but is based on who qualifies as 'eight-rock', a division 'light-skinned against black' (194) that means Menus must give up his sandy-haired girlfriend and that Patricia is never accepted because of her light skin. Such inversion is an ironic awareness of 'passing', as individuals try to prove their 'blackness'. But it is also a warning of replacing old definitions with new ones, changing the rules governing treatment of an individual in relation to the body, but refusing to question the validity of the existence of such rules in the first place.

If white racist values are rejected, then they are dismissed via an alternative elevation of black supremacy, but also through patriarchal bodily norms. This connects with what Bill Ashcroft, in his discussion of male bodies, terms construction of the '*national* body' ('Constructing' 209), where imperial discourse on corporeality is simply replaced with an equally hegemonic representation. Both Fanon's and, more recently, Richard Rodriguez's narratives, seem to offer this alternative. Fanon's male-centred text sees the desirable alternative to being recognised as black as being recognised as a male body: to be 'nothing but a man' (*Black Skin* 113). Rodriguez does not mind being 'darker than I ever was a boy' (277) because he has pride in his athletic form (277). In *Paradise* a return to a dominant male body signifies reclamation of that stolen by slavery, where the black body was emasculated in its powerlessness.[6] Ruby men are 'coal black, athletic' (160); they go shooting and are surrounded by discourses of war that promote their masculine status. Even Reverend Misner has a body that calls attention to it, making him almost 'too handsome' (58) for his occupation. This may challenge colonial definition, the sort of stereotypes with which Son in *Tar Baby* is associated. Yet it is at the expense of previously colonised women's bodies.

What is significant is the way in which racial and gendered bodily definition is brought together in the narrative, so that it is the interaction of these two factors,

---

[6]   For the connection between patriarchy and colonial resistance see Boehmer, *Transfiguring* 273.

together, that produces the tragedy at the novel's centre. As Patricia realises, the colorism at the centre of the community means that it is women who represent the threat, producing new generations who might not meet eight-rock standards. For Ashcroft, ideal male bodies are inherently linked to colonial discourses of purity, with hybridity evidence of weak bodies.[7] The Ruby men seem to bear out this connection: Billie Delia's sexual reputation is connected to her light skin (93). It is these two interacting forces – sensuality and its casting as deviant in relation to race – that the convent women epitomise as they interrogate Ruby values. None of them are eight-rock; Consolata and at least one other woman are white.[8] As for Billie Delia, race is the visible marker. Yet, as for Arnette, it is for subversion of an ideal female body that the women of the convent are ultimately punished. The judgment on the women is blurred, punishing them for both sexual and racial deviancy. As the bodies of the Midnight Children must be rendered 'normal' to control their potential, so the women's difference comes to threaten Ruby's normalisation of its practices.[9] Indeed, Morrison's use of language strongly suggests connections between the women's pride in their sensuality and the men's fear: 'female malice' is accompanied by 'the yeast-and-butter smell of rising dough' (4), while natural practices make them 'witches' (276). When a chicken is found in grounds, the male viewer imagines it 'delivering freaks … triple yolks' (5) that act as a metaphor for the men's assumption of the deviant sexuality within the convent walls. Here they take up the stereotype of unnatural sexuality and religious bigotry – 'revolting sex' (8) – that has haunted their own women in the colonial and slave-holding past.

Such control over bodies can be seen as an extension of the spatial control that haunts the Ruby community. In her reading of the novel's spatial politics, Nicole Schröder argues that *Paradise* recounts 'how women are systematically excluded from … the construction of (national) space' (156). The town, she argues, is heavily demaracated and spatially ordered on the basis of racial and gender hierarchies. The body – and the female body in particular – thus becomes the ultimate scale on which territory is decided, itself becoming a site of spatial contestation.

In *Fury* Rushdie translates this experience to a very different context and, significantly, a very contemporary timeframe. In particular, his novel exposes the impulse to control and describe the body as a central part of postmodern society. Moving away from an explicitly postcolonial framing for the first time, Rushdie's reflections on the body point to the wider social context with which a body politics can be identified. The novel's central character, Malik Solanka, is a philosophy professor who finds fame as a doll-maker, attempting to reclaim what he sees as his disenfranchisement at the hands of unnameable 'puppet-masters'. At the centre of this world is 'Little Brain', a female doll who comes to dominate a trans-media development of Malik's ideas into an international phenomenon. Marking of the female body in this way, a body created or defined by others, is exemplified in

---

[7]   See Ashcroft, 'Constructing' 216.

[8]   The first woman to be shot is white: this is not Consolata, who attempts to save her.

[9]   See Uprety 374.

Malik's remembrances of conversations with his wife Eleanor about her doctoral thesis. Eleanor's own argument, that Othello loves Desdemona as a 'trophy wife ... not even a person ... reified ... his Oscar-Barbie Statuette. His Doll' (11) increasingly becomes Malik's own story. This process initially occurs in reverse, when Malik's doll becomes human, brought to life firstly through media explosion and secondly by the arrival into Solanka's life of Mila, who mimics the doll as she proclaims it has become 'the *basis* and *inspiration* for my whole current *personal style*' (90). Yet later, and more dangerously, it is quite literally Malik's own story, as he attempts to reclaim Little Brain, and Mila, from their freedom and to return them to simple doll status. As the body image Malik gives Little Brain also becomes Mila's, it makes her, for him, 'my doll' (41).

In this action, Malik appropriates a real body, repeating Othello's actions as he allows himself to see Mila as his creation. As Little Brain becomes mobile and Malik loses his ability to dominate, much of his masculine authority is depleted. He gradually succumbs to neurosis, hating what he once loved when he can no longer define it. While we might agree with his doubts about what Little Brain becomes, his need for control proves his ex-wife Sara's comments that 'the world in inanimate miniature is just about all you can handle. The world you can make, unmake and manipulate, filled with women who don't answer back' (30). If his actions are perverted, as Sara suggests, then her reading of his motivations are also correct: not pleasure, but dominance that mimics the act of rape in its seizure of the female body to assert power and relieve male anxiety.

Yet Mila is only the most literal doll in a culture that, for Rushdie, creates the female body in toy-like, unreal proportions: the 'squeeze-me-and-I-talk doll-woman' (53). Here bodily definition is intrinsically imbedded in modern society. What Robert Young emphasises as the passing into truth of bodily norms within colonialism makes way for this same process on a universal scale. The entire western world, in its treatment of the body, seems to have succumbed to a colonial corporeal discourse. As Malik owns his dolls, so the real women of America are equally owned in a way that indicates wider prevalence of colonial patterns of definition, becoming '*a living doll* ... born to be trophies' (72). Moreover, it is significant that not only women find themselves in such positions. Television advertisements promote an ideally beautiful America, male and female. When Malik finally acknowledges the reasons behind his own attempts to control the body, there is profound abuse to be uncovered: a desire to reclaim his own body from both sexual abuse and being raised as a female. This darkest side of bodily manipulation is also recognised in the murders underlying the main narrative, the murderer a new Othello, the victims 'Desdemonas ... property' (73), scalped to 'remain a trophy even in death ... signifier of domination' (153).

Set in the present, what a text such as *Fury* illustrates is that colonial attitudes to the body persist: it continues to be a site of great significance in power negotiations for the formerly colonised. Society has not transcended more brutal, explicit bodily violence – between April 2001 and March 2002 there were 3,728 reported cases of racially aggravated crime in the United Kingdom – but it also is still caught in the more subtle means of definition resonant with colonial treatment of the body.[10] As critics such as Steve Pile, Sanjeev Uprety and Jyoti Puri argue, contemporary racism continues to stereotype the non-white body and, in some cases, even assumes those racist values as part of its own culture, as in the case of Indira Gandhi's invasive family-planning that, for Uprety, was justified through the appropriation of western discourses. For bell hooks, non-white bodies are still demeaned. She claims that 'living in white-supremacist culture, we mostly see images of black folks that reinforce and perpetuate the accepted, desired subjugation and subordination of black bodies by white bodies' (hooks, *Art* 96). In this context, it is clear that scenarios such as Fanon's do not end with the termination of colonial rule: while prejudice may seem less explicit, it continues to exist, and permeates the postcolonial citizen's body image. It is for this reason that postcolonial novels – whether dealing with the historical or the contemporary – place the definition and control of bodies at the centre of their texts.

In Harris's *The Dark Jester*, a novel in which the narrator finds himself transported via a dream-reality to sixteenth-century Peru, those who represent colonialism also represent an ordered, whole body akin to the colonial ordering of space: the Bishop presents a 'uniform body' (49) whilst Cortez – magically transported from Mexico – is a man with 'unseeing eyes' (86) that indicate a limited, narrow colonial consciousness. The colonials are also figures who explicitly bring violence to other bodies. Cortez is associated with 'the rape of a mother', one who 'slices a wastage of limbs until it turns into dead bone and a frustrated heart' (88). Such a 'bone' is passive, and it contrasts strongly with the magical Carib bone that Harris reads as signifying a living history.[11]

An undercurrent in *Fury* is that bodily definition is part of a contemporary definition of the body for profit – the bodily ideals transmitted through advertising a part of an exploitation of our desire to meet those ideals. Equally, as with slavery, Harris's bodies also remind us of the universal, rather than particular, nature of the connection between the body and financial transaction. Pizarro sees works of art as a 'material body which he could melt all together into a monument of quick Money' (52): 'body' becomes a metaphor for a subject of economic exchange. Moreover, in the conquistador's lust for gold and profit – a precursor of the capitalist ethos pursued by later colonialism – is exploitation where it is the body that is ultimately corrupted. Here Harris's narrator speaks with uncharacteristic clarity: 'labour was an unconscious art of body bringing flesh and blood to be sacrificed and deprived of meaning save as a good, a piece of goods' (99). Such exploitation of the body for profit reaches its most extreme point in the Middle Passage, which is described as 'market places for the arts of flesh' (101). Transported to this historical scene the narrator sees one individual, one figure against the larger image, whose 'arm appeared broken' (100), awakening him to 'abused flesh and blood, my own abused

---

[10]   BBC report: 'Rise in Race Hate Crime Reports': http://news.bbc.co.uk/1/hi/uk/2731139.stm.

[11]   See Harris, 'Note' 9–10.

flesh and blood' (101). Bodies bear witness to the influence of Spanish colonial expansion in South America, while the narrator's experience encompasses both this suffering and later abuse at the hands of both Spanish and other European powers.

As 'bone and ... garments fuse' (107) Harris defers this marking of the body, displacing it on to his characters' garments so that clothes worn come to represent characters' fates and histories. Clothes act metonymically for the body itself, a transference that resonates with Merleau-Ponty's suggestion that clothes may mark an extension of the corporeal.[12] Atahualpa is 'fastidiously dressed' (25), but his royal robes are stained by food to reflect the shadow hanging over him, his flesh damaged by a 'wound or hole' (28). Such stains encapsulate not only his own suffering but – with 'his composition of skins, one flesh or garment placed against another' (27) – also signify past and future loss. King Priam appears on the robe, 'Cassandra's robe' (31), to signify a history extending as far back as Greek mythology, reflecting a catalogue of deception and also the complex interactions of colonialism:

> Atahualpa had sensed a corruption of Empires reaching far beyond his own kingdom. He sought to portray this in reverse order on his robe and in his lands and peoples. The antagonisms were there – long before Pizarro arrived – in frail sparks of food and fire that he would need to contemplate. Each spark of food brought its opposite fire into play on his robe, in his flesh. (27)

Here food is not only that which stains the body to remind of past violence, but also a representation of creative nurturing forces opposed by the destructive power of fire, the ravaging destruction of colonisation. Atahualpa also clothes the narrator, and what covers his body has equally profound significance:

> I could not, therefore, evade the signals on my dress. It had fallen to the ground but I had picked it up. And from it swarmed the crowds in the Sky of Dream signalling Atahualpa's nobles and retainers cut to pieces by bullet and sword. (37)

The body marked through clothing is also the body marked by violence, reflecting tumultuous histories. Such narrative illustrates the importance of the magical element of magical-realist narratives: not as escapism, but as a strategy to heighten the ordinary and commonplace marking of bodies which postcolonial novels often expose.

In all of these cases, the postcolonial novelist follows Foucault in seeing the body as a cultural product, at times indistinguishable from the influence of social forces. This idea of the body as a prison, culturally marked and violently appropriated, undoubtedly has its own problems. It risks repeating the Enlightenment rejection of the body, undermining the solidarity of groups that

---

[12]   See Merleau-Ponty 91.

base their allegiance on a common identity reliant on the body as indication of shared aims and oppressions, denying the power of individual agency as bodily performance. This is undoubtedly a great risk, when such 'common identity' has been central to conventional anticolonial nationalist movements. Yet as I will show, such criticism of bodily definition is for the postcolonial author a complex negotiation. It is not a rejection of the body itself, but rather of how such a body may be imperialised: denied agency in its definition by outside forces.

Final Transformation

Rather than simply accepting the colonial discourse on the body, postcolonial authors choose to re-vision this image. Not only is the marked and denigrated body reclaimed as a source of inspiration, the very foundations underlying this construction of the body are challenged to cement an only strategically solid construction. This challenges the central geometric tenets of colonial spatial ordering – questioning geometric form when to do so means 'no absolutely rigid bodies' (Kern 185). What emerges is ambiguous; solid bodies are not entirely rejected in what would deny their significance for individual identity, yet increasingly magical and metamorphic bodies are also represented.

There is one example of this spatialisation – far pre-dating Merleau-Ponty – particularly relevant, I would suggest, to postcolonial endeavours. This is the body as chora. Originating in Plato's *Timaeus*, chora is an ambiguous term that has, at times, preoccupied feminist and poststructuralist theorists. The chora has an inherent spatiality: one that has been taken up by Inger Birkeland in her study of female spatiality as offering an alternative feminist geography – a 'chorography' – with particular emphasis on how body and place are interconnected. I would like to argue through the rest of this chapter, however, that the chora, in fact, is more useful to postcolonial theory than to feminism, and that it might be of value in terms of trying to read how postcolonial authors reconfigure colonial images of the body.

Plato calls the chora that which provides 'a situation for all things that come into being' (*Timaeus* 52b, 192); it is in this sense that which exists before fixed meaning. It is widely accepted that what Plato refers to as 'receptacle' is also the chora, shifting its translation as place or space to a designation carrying connotations of the body, and explicitly the womb of the female body. This gendered aspect has been emphasised by critics including Luce Irigaray, Judith Butler, Elizabeth Grosz, and Julia Kristeva. Of these four critics, the first two largely cast the chora not only negatively, but more importantly as beyond positive restoration, while Grosz, in her earlier comments, also accepts such a position. Through Plato's representation of it as 'characterless' (*Timaeus* 51a, 186), the chora is seen to deny the status of woman (Grosz, *Volatile* 5), leaving her 'eliminated, obliterated, stopped up' (Irigaray 281), 'incomplete and uncompletable' (Irigaray 165) and 'nothing' (Irigaray 307). The choric body is 'penetrated' (Butler, *Bodies* 50) and denied form, where to be 'not a body' (Butler, *Bodies* 40) in its definition by Plato is to be seen as a negative construction without hope of being reclaimed without an impossible return to full materiality. Such readings have therefore tended to reject the chora rather than call for its appropriation; Irigaray, for example, notes that woman is 'unrealized potentiality – unrealized, at least, for/by herself' (165) but does not explore how woman might realise herself through the chora, rather than in opposition to it. It is not the case, it seems to me, that Butler is correct in allying Irigaray to Derrida's extension of the chora (*Bodies* 41); it is not that Irigaray sees the chora as more than woman, as Derrida does, but rather as less than.

Yet as John Sallis – most notable in attempting to assess what Plato meant by the chora rather than reading the term through contemporary discourses – points out, such readings often neglect Plato's original text. For Sallis, the chora's connection to 'receptacle' still suggests 'connection with the image of the nurse, a kind of surrogate mother who holds, aids, and succors the newly born child' (99) and an invisibility that is 'abysmal' (111). Yet Sallis does question feminist readings, for example the fact that Irigaray misreads the chora in Aristotelian terms as matter, rather than that which supports it, a lead which both Grosz and Butler have followed.

Moreover, Sallis illuminates how the chora may be read more generally as a body without gendered connotations. Here the chora extends to wider associations with bodies. Jacques Derrida notes this when he expresses in relation to feminist readings that the chora is 'not exhausted by these *types* of tropological or interpretive translation' ('Khōra' 95). Significantly for a postcolonial reading, it is connected to the marginal beyond the marginal-as-feminine, part of a text that disenfranchises not only women but also other marginal groups such as 'slaves, children, and animals' (Butler, *Bodies* 48), so that reinterpretation of the chora functions not only to reassert the denied female, but also Plato's 'racialized Others' (Butler, *Bodies* 48). Seen as 'harboring or sheltering something alien' (Sallis 100) it is associated with 'the other' (Derrida, 'Khōra' 89) and 'alterity' (Sallis 120). In this way, despite an element of disavowal, the chora represents an absolute difference as it 'evades all characterizations including the disconcerting logic of identity, of hierarchy, of being, the regulation of order' (Grosz, *Space* 116).

This disruption of order, I would suggest, identifies the chora as in opposition to much that is central to colonial spatial appropriation, be it of the body or of other territories. As 'a third kind ... outside the twofold' (Sallis 106), the chora is neither being nor that generated from it, 'neither this nor that, at times both this and that' (Derrida, 'Khōra' 89), but that which holds what is formed. Such a space, resonating with notions of third space, therefore must be taken as a haven from dialectical opposition: no longer 'a counting in which a third is blended from the other two nor in which the resulting three are then blended into one' but rather a third that is 'other than the other two' (Sallis 98). Derrida describes it as 'alien to the order of the "paradigm," that intelligible and immutable model ... . Beyond categories, and above all beyond categorical oppositions' ('Khōra' 90), that which 'resists any binary or dialectical determination' ('Khōra' 99), where such hermeneutic traditions are, in postcolonial terms, the foundation of western philosophy and the construction of the colonised as Other. Associated with 'chaos, chasm' (Derrida, 'Khōra' 112) the chora unravels in terms that challenge the pretence of order. It 'will limit what the artisan god can achieve' (Sallis 132), questioning authoritarian attempts to define form, and is at odds with Freud's 'totalized and mastered' (Grosz, *Space* 86) Oedipal body that is separated from others. This is even more significant when such a totalised body is also termed 'the Cartesian fantasy' (Grosz, *Space* 86), so that the chora directly conflicts with both the western idea of the body and the Euclidean space underlying all colonial spatial practice.

The choric body in this sense also resonates with a Deleuzian body. In *Anti-Oedipus* (1972) Gilles Deleuze and Felix Guattari posit a 'body without organs' that refuses both social ordering and the Freudian familial relationship, defying conventional definition, as 'neither men nor women are defined personalities, but rather vibrations, flows, schizzes, and "knots"' (*Anti-Oedipus* 362). This body moves beyond status as organism towards something 'smooth, slippery, opaque' (*Anti-Oedipus* 9). Discussing Deleuze and Guattari, Grosz emphasises how such a body might unravel the order that may be identified as colonial as well as patriarchal:

> Their notion of the body as a discontinuous, nontotalizable series of processes, organs, flows, energies, corporeal substances and incorporeal events, speeds and durations, may be of great value to feminists attempting to reconceive bodies outside the binary oppositions imposed on the body by the mind/body, nature/culture, subject/object and interior/exterior oppositions ... the body in its connections with other bodies, both human and inhuman, animate and inanimate' (*Volatile* 164–5).

We are returned explicitly to the chora's own fluid identity, a continual refusal to be hemmed in by seemingly natural boundaries of what a body can be. In the chora, the chaos that the colonial would cast as dangerous in its attempts to produce easily categorised and controllable bodies is exactly what is utilised to engender creation. Fluid and indissolubly linked to what surrounds it, 'not entirely unlike saying the flux' (Sallis 118), the displacement of the body in the spirit of the chora so that it mingles with other bodies and objects does not produce psychosis, as psychoanalysts suggest. Rather, as a result of the chaos involved in producing a body with 'space, blurred with the position of others' (Grosz, *Space* 90), what emerges is a positive event.

Such fluid bodies undermine colonial regimes because they undercut reliance on stereotypical bodies to construct relations between colonised and coloniser. The chora, it is true, is denied. It coterminously cannot be named, yet is defined by Plato's patriarchal philosophical discourse, and its form remains unfixed. Yet this disavowal illustrates why the body is the ultimate post-space, where the most extreme *is* re-visioned. Plato's text itself suggests this, when it notes that spiritual moments only arise 'when one's noetic power is fettered in sleep or distraught by disease or by divine inspiration' (Sallis 123–4). The possibility of reversal is also gestured towards by Kristeva, whose reading of the chora as a psychoanalytic model for poetic interpretation suggests an ambivalent power that she suggests we 'must restore' (*Revolution* 26). Here the chora is beyond, but also more fundamental than, the culturally defined: that which 'precedes and underlies figuration' (*Revolution* 26). It is a possibility echoed by Derrida, who suggests an excess that, unable to be claimed, hints at an unrivalled agency, where allowing itself to be named, and yet refusing to be 'determined' ('Khōra' 97), suggests in the chora a hybridity that is explicitly 'not negative' ('Khōra' 126).

In the postcolonial novel in its magical-realist form the marked body makes way for this fluid form. It is no coincidence that Kristeva locates the realisation of her 'semiotic chora' in 'certain literary texts of the avant-garde' (*Revolution* 88), the modernist works of Mallarmé and Joyce that may be seen as a defining influence on magical-realism. In Morrison's texts, flesh is not 'made word', as Vanessa Dickerson suggests (196), rather it is made space. Dickerson's own quotation from *Sula* that the dead are 'not even words' but simply 'longing' (209) indicates this, though the author seems reluctant to abandon her defining concept. Throughout Morrison's texts, such fluidity is reinforced. In *Song of Solomon* Milkman finds 'if you surrendered to the air, you could *ride* it' (336). Sula retains consciousness after death which means 'she noticed that she was not breathing' (133), continuing as a presence that can be felt as 'leaves stirred; mud shifted' (154). Beloved continues to be felt in 'the rustle of a skirt ... the knuckles brushing a cheek' (275).

This refusal of the human spirit to be confined by its body is perhaps the most common theme that can be identified in postcolonial novels: the multiple bodily transformations of Salman Rushdie's texts, the bodies of Pauline Melville which shift genders and even become multiple individuals in *Shape-shifter* (1990), the snakes imbued with human consciousness in Michael Ondaatje's *Running in the Family*, the human-monkey reincarnations and consciousness beyond death of Vikram Chandra's *Red Earth and Pouring Rain*, to name but a few examples. *Paradise*, however, is the apex of this fluidity. While the convent women are superficially united by gender, they are not united by sexuality or race. Indeed, as the well-documented ambiguity of the 'white girl' illustrates, they are not even defined in such terms. Rather they are more reflective of what Donna Haraway calls 'chimeras' (150): a hybrid fusion that challenges the absolute definitions implied by categories such as race, class, sexuality and gender. Most significant in these terms is Consolata, who discovers shapes made of ash, indicating a possibility of fluid bodies, including a Marquezesque 'girl with butterfly wings' (Morrison, *Paradise* 234). Entering 'like an apparition' (43), Consolata learns from Mary Magna how to leave her body, and to 'step in' (245) and resurrect others, discovering an essence that is not a body, but a 'pinpoint of light' (245). Such 'light' can be captured immediately after death, and willed back to fill the body and reanimate it.

It is this fluidity that allows the women to defy their own mortality at the novel's conclusion. The women have become 'No bodies' but in doing so they have defied their status within Ruby as 'nobodies'. This complicates the representation of Morrison as an author whose 'authentic' characters claim their bodies, while those who reject them are somehow divorced from their culture; for escaping the limits of the body for a time is not only to deny your own culture, but also, when that culture is marginalised, to deny the dominant images that would obliterate a marginalised body forever. Ironically, this experience is at the very heart of Ruby's own beginnings when, on the journey, Rector finds 'himself floating', the group guided by the apparition of a 'walking man' (97). It is only with increasing protectionism and the mimicking of those they were once persecuted by that such values are lost.

Within these terms, the 'occasional spilling weakness' (125) of bodies in *Fury* is in fact a positive blurring that may be extended back as far as the chora. Rushdie celebrates 'the human capacity for automorphosis' (55), dolls that become 'life-size' (97) and, in the case of Little Brain and Mila, re-enact the fable of Pinocchio and become real. Throughout the text, there is acknowledgment of the body's ability to take different forms, masks that mean Little Brain's 'body acquires remarkable new freedoms' (100), Malik imagining the merging of his own family with figures in the news, murderers dressing as Disney characters. Dolls are not unique creations, but bodies that not only reemphasise historical figures but also re-vision them, offering insights into their true form as they reveal 'a two-faced, four-armed Galileo: one face muttered the truth under its breath ... the other face, downcast and penitent' (16).

In postcolonial terms, such bodies undermine any absolute categorisation, including the racial, framed by Neela's comment that if you 'stir in all the races ... you get the most beautiful people in the world' (63). Neela is only the latest figure representing such a view through her own body, where the bodies in *Midnight's Children* indicate 'a hybrid space where the borders are being transgressed and rewritten' (Uprety 368), and the characters of *The Moor's Last Sigh* dream of being '*of no race no name no sex*' (47) to become simply 'what breathes' (53). This echoes Morrison: as Sula continues after her body has died, so Moraes stands at his own grave and reflects on its meaning, committing only to 'falling asleep' (Rushdie, *Moor* 434). Thus while Chamcha's transformation in *The Satanic Verses* may be a mark of his oppression, other figures in Rushdie's novels are involved in transformations of the body that seem to assert possibility rather than trauma, a refusal to be hemmed in by conventional boundaries or limits reflected in a flexible, choric body.

The fact that *The Dark Jester* presents not a simple and whole body, but rather a blurred image of 'partial organs' (vii), also affirms a body with connections to the chora's fluidity. It may be the latest in a series of novels that, as early as *The Palace of the Peacock*, explore 'the revolutionary potential of the un-enclosed body' (Johnson, 'Muse' 78). *The Dark Jester*'s narrator feels both 'immaterial and material' (14) as he is 'blown into gentle particles ... nebulous, miraculous body' (62). Such alteration, away from a defined corporeal entity towards a fluid construction, a body of chaotic particles in line with Harris's sympathies with chaos theory that I have already discussed, is a rejection of the primacy of the physical body. Liberation is found in adopting 'other faces' (vii), 'abstract flesh, brown and black and white and red' (28). Pizarro is 'mutilated' (103) into several forms that challenge his conquistador status. Moreover, this bodily fluidity is not limited to human hybridity, but also presents an 'animal kinship beyond tight or absolute frames' (4) so that the forms of animals merge with others, and also with humans. Such 'becoming-animal', perhaps the final stage in Harris's trickster preoccupation, is a process by which taking on animal characteristics is no longer to conform to colonial stereotype. Instead, it is a subversion of this through the assertion of a body connected to a plethora of organic and inorganic forms. In this fusion, the technological body is not an aberration or denial of nature. Instead – like Haraway's cyborg – it is a productive combination, as the dreamer possesses a 'telescopic body ... telescopic eyes' that allow him to see 'a dream-land' (20). In his introduction to *The Carnival Trilogy*, Harris outlines explicitly this theory of the body:

> *The Body's Waking Instrument.* The arousal of the body to itself as sculpture by a creator one abuses. The body wakes to itself an inimitable art, inimitable multi-faceted, living fossil extending into all organs, objects, spaces, stars, and the ripple of light. (xix)

This dynamism is perhaps the significance of the Jester in the novel's title: a carnival trickster figure transcending fixed forms in order to provide revelation. Universalised beyond the historical context of Kali, Legba or Anancy who feature in *Jonestown* to encapsulate all their qualities, the Jester is 'a voice that mingled with other conversational voices' (Harris, *Dark* 8). This is a carnivalesque body in the sense of Bakhtin's grotesque body of 'openings and orifices' rather than 'closure and finish' (Stallybrass and White 9) that, significantly, contrasts with the high status of a classical, ideal body.[13] The Jester's corporeality is evident in Margaret Harris's introductory poem – a figure leaping and dancing, running and laughing – but also in the trickster's cultural identity, Anancy a figure 'free to modify his own bodily parts' (Pelton 35) and, according to Harris, to enact limbo transformations ('History' 157). Taking on various roles – including that of a trickster Christ, the 'enemy of complacency, of the uniform body' (Harris, *Dark* 48) – the Jester signifies the power to transform the individual form.[14]

As the chora is a body with transformative power, so within *The Dark Jester* the body is central to the folding of space, the ultimate site of limbo performance:

> Lake Titicaca was a cosmos of uncertainties orchestrated by Dream, the Dream of one's changing body, one's grasp of limbs one took for granted, Dream-land-

---

13   See Stallybrass and White 23.

14   For Christ as trickster, see Jonas 54–5.

> body, Dream-air-body, Dream-sea-body … . How aware is one in Dream of the
> drift of atoms, or molecules of space, or whatever-it-is, where solidity deceives
> and appears to be constant? (63)

Here the fact that 'solidity deceives' connects explicitly to the illegitimacy
of notions of a limited body, posing a direct challenge to colonial ideology's
presentation of a natural spatial order. Morrison has her own version of such a
space in *Beloved*, for her too connected to slave-ship performance:

> It rained … They waited – each and every one of the forty-six. Not screaming,
> although some of them must have fought like the devil not to. The mud was up
> to his thighs and he held onto the bars. Then it came – another yank – from the
> left this time and less forceful than the first because of the mud it came through.
> It started like the chain-up but the difference was the power of the chain. One
> by one, from Hi Man back on down the line, they dove. Down through the
> mud under the bars, blind, groping … . Great God, they all came up. Like the
> unshriven dead, zombies on the loose, holding the chains in their hands, they
> trusted the rain and the dark, yes, but mostly Hi Man and each other. (110)

Escaping from the chain gang, Paul D. and his companions transform the
relationship between their bodies and space. It is a relationship present for Rushdie,
too, when Saleem's survival relies upon being 'in the basket, but also not in the
basket' (*Midnight's* 381), shrinking himself so that a basket is big enough for a
man, in the same way that the slave passes under the limbo bar, Paul D. under the
bars that imprison him. Making the human body small enough for any space, the
impossible is performed.

Within this transformative corporeality, as Rushdie's dolls in *Fury* are 'time-
hoppers' (17), bodies released from the order of conventional temporality in order
to give their influence greater scope, so Harris's bodies in *The Dark Jester* are also
capable of transcending time. They escape linearity in favour of the messianic
model I have already associated with Harris's cities. The narrator 'may perceive
myself … as curiously related to live fossil organs invisibly suspended and linked
across ages' (vii), he may transform into other bodies beyond his own lifetime.
Similarly, Atahualpa is possessed by 'future archaeologists' who 'stood on his
shoulders', their discoveries connected to him though they 'would fail to see his
features masking theirs' (64).

Here Harris's ending is as crucial as Morrison's own conclusion; for nowhere
is there a greater example of how the body can shift timeframes and how the
boundaries of the body may become fluid. By the novel's conclusion the narrator
has become both Cortez and Atahualpa, seeing through the former's 'infirm body'
(91) the limits of a seemingly limitless oppression, as the body unites all in its
vulnerability. Learning the lesson of this, the narrator resists reciprocating bodily
violence, refusing the opportunity to kill the conquistador. In becoming Atahualpa
he repeats the execution replayed once in the novel already. This undercuts linear

concepts not only of the body, but also of a history that would fix that body in space and time:

> I had travelled fictionally, it seemed, across centuries to approach *a form I called Atahualpa*, to know him and it, to know a living/dead form and substance that differed in its dying, in its living, from anything by which I had been conditioned in a dominant history, a dominant cultural history. (emphasis added, 102)

Like the chora, Atahualpa can only be 'called' by his name, rather than defined by it. Here such lack of definition approaches the positive reading I have suggested in my analysis. For in his execution, Atahualpa/the narrator's wound now sings, a signal of hope, representing possibility in the form of a spiritual El Dorado that emerges on the novel's last page. Indeed, Harris's bodies encapsulate the sense of re-visioning a traumatic space, as the wound that the narrator finds in his body becomes, when recognised, a powerful connection to revealing forces from which a new significance emerges. There is a 'new dress', 'soiled' and 'fallen' but also revelatory so that what results is 'half-shattered freedom' (38). The narrator proclaims 'Atahualpa was ascending not to his death but to assume the wings of a Bird and to wear the mask and colour of music on his brow' (85), a figure with the ability to 'die again to live again' (102) which extends the image first presented in *The Palace of the Peacock* and continued in *Jonestown*. Harris's choice of language is significant. For Harris's 'half-shattered freedom' may also be seen as half-shattered imprisonment, and his emphasis reflects an attempt to regenerate cultures, rather than to degenerate them. When the narrator is 'broken into pieces' (40) this is not just representative of a damaged body, but also of a hybrid, transformative power. Such a fluid body can strike at the centre of colonial mapping. Indeed, it can provide a literal alternative. In Harris's *The Whole Armour*, for example, the central character of Sharon moves into the interior. But it is no longer a conventional map that guides her, but rather love, 'the map of Cristo's skin' (308). This somatic encounter, a postcolonial map, is what will guide Sharon to a connection with her history. It is the genetic trace on the body that cannot be completely overwritten, Islam's assertion that the postcolonial traveller 'does not produce a geographical map … . If he were to do so, he would only be repeating the monotonous journeys of representation, the acts of power' (41).

Within the context of a racially prejudiced and patriarchal society, the potential of such fluidity for women can be twofold, but it is not always the case that the escape from patriarchal norms and bodily norms are valued equally. In *The Bone People*, Keri Hulme presents Kerewin as a figure surrounded by both racial definition and male violence. Kerewin relishes removing herself from patriarchal constraints: in the wake of male aggression – embodied in Joe's brutality towards Simon – she defines herself as 'neuter' (266). Like the characters in *Paradise*, Kerewin endures an experience that seems to offer an essence outside of physicality: she experiences an illness that leaves her '*decaying piece by piece*' (420). The final stage of this illness is a rejection of physical form: Kerewin finds herself 'floating upright' and acknowledges that '*There is a time, when passing through a light, that you walk in your own shadow*' (424). The mythical Maori figure that brings Kerwin back to health is 'Of indeterminate race. Of indeterminate sex' (424). With new-found strength Kerewin offers a pronoun to accompany her own reading of identity, striking at the heart of the role of language in the definition of self: 'The neuter personal pronoun; ve/ver/vis, I am not his, vis/ve/ver, nor am I for her, ver/ve/vis, a pronoun for me' (426). Yet Kerewin takes up an alternative position in relation to race. Against her longing to be free of sexual definition, she craves racial identification as a route to belonging. Defining herself as an 'Octoroon', Kerewin is located as Pākehā and alienated from the Maori culture she strongly identifies with, admitting 'whereas by blood, flesh and inheritance, I am but an eighth Maori, by heart, spirit and inclination, I feel all Maori' (62). Her lack of identifiable race, marked by her pale skin, is not something she desires. Instead, it is a mark of her isolation: described as a 'Half-and-halfer' (109) by those whose acceptance she craves. Against Harris's reading of limbo as bodily transformation, here the vacuum such limbo creates is a mark of a painful loss of meaning. Kerewin admits: '"I am in limbo, and in limbo there are no races, no prizes, no changes, no chances. There are merely degrees of endurance, and endurance never was my strong point."' (28). At the end of the novel, she returns in physical form with a 'new buoyant body' (429). Whilst her gender is open to destabilisation, her race is not.

What *The Bone People* acknowledges is the need for physical forms of identification, even where fluidity is strategically assumed. Kerewin's reclaimed body can be seen to act as a powerful counterpoint to the abuse of Maori women by colonialists, treated as commodities to be abused and exploited (Najita 102). In these terms, the chora is so productive, therefore, because it not only captures the fluidity of the postcolonial body, but also, being 'preoriginary' (Derrida, 'Khōra' 124), retains concomitantly some essence that may be used strategically to subvert political oppression. This suggests a body outside culture, resonant with a postcolonial body that escapes Foucault's structuralist argument, so that the body is never simply passive or inert, but instead is self-owned and imbued with transformative potential and agency. Michael Dash makes this point in relation to *The Wretched of the Earth,* describing it as a text in which Fanon 'equates a reanimated body with the liberatory voice of the revolutionary intellectual' (24), where the black body is celebrated for what it is, in contrast to how it is cast by colonial discourse.

Morrison exemplifies this position, an author for whom survival lies in recovering the sensual aspects of the body and presenting an alternative to western ideals of beauty. Morrison claims the body at the centre of her fiction, a factor noted generally and discussed greatly as regards *Beloved*. Small details reinforce such representation: for example the women's skating, 'holding hands, bracing each other' (174). Baby Suggs, however, is the figure that most clearly hints at such agency: her first awareness when she steps on free soil that 'these *my* hands' (141) develops into ministering at the clearing, a belief in 'flesh that needs to be loved'

(88). Such seizure reflects how the body has been central to the empowerment of black women, in particular: a strategic use of the fundamentals of black identity to claim autonomy and self-determination (Noble 135).

An alternative to the cultural construction of the body by others in *Beloved* is not simply a rejection of the body, but a desire for 'ownership of that freed self' (95). It is not simply an adoption of the chora's fluidity, but also its concomitant essence. Such distinction is seen in the quality of Sethe's bodily experiences, the difference between how her body is taken by others, and how it is given freely, placed 'in somebody else's hands' (18) that for a moment transforms a 'revolting clump of scars' (21) into something beautiful. Indeed, both Amy and Paul D. celebrate Sethe's scar, transforming it into a 'chokecherry tree' that does not deny her experience, but instead allows Sethe herself to claim it. Similarly, Sula claims her birthmark, while her celebration of her sexuality is seen as a 'refusal to be a colonized body' (Dickerson 205). Such reversal, seizing exactly what is used against one and making it the site of resistance, captures post-space, pain embraced as an act of defiance to affirm the characters' ability 'to embrace violence done to their bodies' (Ledbetter 79) as a way of claiming their Otherness.

The development from *Beloved* to *Paradise* encapsulates this process. With Paul D.'s statement that 'You your best thing' to which she answers with a question: 'Me?' (Morrison, *Beloved* 273), Sethe begins a tentative process to 'read herself … configure the history of her body's text' (Henderson 69) at the end of the novel. The women of *Paradise* may be seen actually undertaking such a task and answering Sethe's question in the affirmative. In the name of a celebrated body they claim female bodily essences – in particular blood – cast as abject by the men of Ruby in line with the stereotype of unclean female blood.[15] Choric associations with nurturing and the female are valued. In the convent, the female body is celebrated, forging a place with a 'blessed malelessness' (177). In contrast to their outside experiences of denigration, Mavis finds her hands are beautiful, Gigi sits naked, Consolata loves Mary Magda's rough hands and her 'unsmiling mouth' (224). Bodies 'unaware of any watcher' (168), at the wedding the women celebrate the autoerotic performance of their physical selves, needing nothing but 'their own rocking bodies' (157); their joy is at its height dancing in the rain. Echoing both Rushdie and also the sensual preparation of food in *Beloved*, the women revel in nourishing their bodies and in the act of providing nourishment as self-supporting bodily performance. They support the bodies of both visiting Ruby women and each other, Pallas snuggling into Seneca's breasts, Consolata raising 'up the feathery body' of Mary Magna to make death a 'birthing' (223).

This celebration of female form against its denigration in a patriarchal postcolonial discourse announces relationships indicative of Adrianne Rich's lesbian continnum in which female relationships obscured by a patriarchal system are renewed, a celebration of female community that allies *Paradise* with

---

15   See hooks, *Art* 213–14.

Nervous Conditions.[16] What Magali Cornier Michael refers to as *Paradise*'s 'bloodmothers and othermothers' (154) form a powerful construction of community that challenges territorial definitions of identity. Yet such celebration is also extended by Morrison beyond this conventional gender politics. The sensual body is represented as larger-than-life by the form of a couple hidden in the desert. Such a form is ambiguous; those who see it dispute whether the figures are male, female, or both. It represents, thus, not only gendered bodies, but a wider celebration of corporeality and its sensual possibilities. Between the physical contact of the convent and the sterility of Ruby is a stark contrast. On the one hand is the sensual, bodily action of the women: Consolata's love affair after 30 years of celibacy that means 'feathers unfold and come unstuck from the walls of a stone cold womb' (229). On the other is Reverend Pulliam's sermon, full of missionary zeal, verbose, and yet completely removed from the sensual as he argues for a love that has nothing to do with 'how your body responds to another body' (141). The spiritual is clearly connected to the former perspective: it is the convent women who are 'holy' (283).

Similarly, in *Fury*, marked bodies are a subject not for shame, but reverence. Echoing *Beloved*, Neela transcends being 'the most beautiful Indian woman' to become 'the most beautiful *woman*' (61), not through perfection, but through the way her marked body illustrates experience and pain:

> Down the upper part of the woman's right arm there was an eight-inch-long herringbone-pattern scar. When she saw him looking at it, she at once crossed her arms and put her left hand over the injury, not understanding that it made her more beautiful, that it perfected her beauty by adding an essential imperfection. (61).

Neela's beauty comes from the 'messy humanity' (74) which women with the quality of dolls lack, conforming not to western ideals, but instead representing beauty beyond the normalised. In the wake of this, the new dolls Mila demands are 'dolls that say something ... dolls that come from her neighbourhood ... . This place' (137–8), realistic carnival figures to be used for critique, no longer beautified or conventional.

As for Morrison, this means that Rushdie's celebration of transformation must not be oversimplified. There is not a loss of all bodily solidarity. Criticism of abandoning bodily identity is evident in the statement 'Jack was more or less the only black man Jack knew', confirmed when his desire to be accepted into the 'white man's club' (57–8) leads first to his suspicion of murder, secondly to his death. If fluidity is liberatory, then it can also have negative consequences. The characters in *Fury* want to own their bodies, want to claim them, and their awareness that 'their *bodies* didn't belong to them, and nobody else's bodies belonged to anyone, either' (184),

---

[16]   For a reading of female community in *Nervous Conditions* see Boehmer, *Stories* 177–83.

as they are culturally constructed is a source not of celebration, but loss, cemented in Dubdub's suicide after confessing 'your body is not … *yours*' (27). As early as *Midnight's Children* this problematic relationship to transformation is evident. Literally falling apart, Saleem's fluidity ultimately ends only in tragedy, reflecting the failure of an emerging nation divided artificially, yet also a literal warning against abandoning the boundaries of the body:

> O eternal opposition of inside and outside! Because a human being, inside himself, is anything but a whole, anything but homogenous; all kinds of everywhichthing are jumbled up inside him, and he is one person one minute and another the next. The body, on the other hand, is homogenous as anything. Indivisible, a one-piece suit, a sacred temple, if you will. It is important to preserve this wholeness … . Uncork the body, and God knows what you permit to come tumbling out. (236–7)

To celebrate such fluidity encapsulates the essence of post-space: to transform the chaotic and dangerous into a useful location. Yet, as Saleem's eventual fate suggests – 'a broken creature spilling pieces of itself into the street' (463) – such transformation is precarious. And, as Moraes notes that 'in Indian country, there was no room for a man who didn't want to belong to a tribe, who dreamed of moving beyond, of peeling off his skin' (Rushdie, *Moor* 414), it is clear that it is also not always possible.

Even as it mutates, *The Dark Jester* celebrates the biological body as 'a living work of art, living flesh, living blood, that differed from a machined being' (50). This suggests that the technological can be taken too far, a factor that is reinforced by the Bishop's wearing of a 'technologic mask' (49). Each of Harris's characters has an essence: both the Bishop and Pizarro have an 'inner face' (50) differing from how they are seen by others. For Harris, such essences transcend the colonial and offer possibility for reconciliation, uniting colonised and coloniser in a shared humanity. Here they mimic the chora as bodily essence. Moreover, Harris's bodies also celebrate the chora as femininity: female bodies empowered by 'special performance of the flesh' (76), where to be a 'symbol of motherhood' (81) is celebrated rather than denigrated. Representation of the female as 'invisible … is and is not what she appears to be' (78) resonates with the chora's ambiguity. Yet, reversing the position of the colonised women of *Jonestown*, this invisibility is no longer disempowering. Despite denial, Harris's woman is profoundly influential, another incarnation of the trickster as she becomes a 'supreme mother of Jest' (81).

The postcolonial imagination here moves beyond ideas of a culturally formed body, to conceive an essence that can be reclaimed by the individual. In this way, the postcolonial body cannot simply be equated with poststructuralist notions of deconstruction. The multiplicity of the body is not, as in the case of the latter's treatment of language, an endless process of shifting signification. This is as contentious as a rejection of the body, risking falling back into stereotypical notions that have been used not only for the purposes of civil rights unity, but also against marginalised bodies. Yet it is also necessary for the solidarity the postcolonial citizen needs to find with fellow sufferers in times of crisis, reclaiming the body not in terms of the stereotype that denigrated it, but in terms of a celebratory discourse that will celebrate.

Terminal Ambiguity

It is therefore crucial to note the ambiguous status of the body in postcolonial narratives, a full awareness of cultural construction, but also acknowledgment that, however constructed, bodies are also a physical reality that must be dealt with and somehow reclaimed, even if the idea of an essence is a strategic position acknowledging the impossibility of completing fully such endeavour. The body is neither the 'corporeal schema' nor 'body image' that Gail Weiss identifies as two extremes (2), neither Butler's rejection of 'metaphysical assumptions' nor Bordo's 'materiality of the body' (Heckman 61), but rather a third way that fits with a post-space disruption of dialectical oppositions. It is an assertion of Carol Bigwood's position that 'we need to work out a new "natural-cultural" model of the body' (103), but also Merleau-Ponty's assertion, making his argument against Descartes, that 'there is not a single impulse in a living body which is entirely fortuitous in relation to psychic intentions, not a single mental act which has not found at least its germ or its general outline in physiological tendencies' (88).

The theory that I have interwoven with the postcolonial novel is not at odds with such a position. Chaos theory has its meaning in contrast to chaos, becoming also has its 'consistency', represented in a sense of security that develops 'without occluding the infinite dissimulation into which it plunges' (Doel 179). Moreover, taking Butler's reading of Foucault, even here such elements are not necessarily incompatible. Butler argues that 'the critical power of Foucault's analysis assumes that only under certain conditions of power and discourse do bodies get signified and regulated in the ways that he describes in *Discipline and Punish* and *The History of Sexuality: Vol. I*' ('Foucault' 606). Alternatives exist, and a philosopher who argues for cultural construction is also one who 'appears to have identified in a prediscursive and prehistorical "body" a source of resistance to history and to culture' (Butler, 'Foucault' 607). [17] Agency is not denied; rather, under certain circumstances – of which colonialism would undoubtedly be one – the body is regulated to the point of control. Yet there is always potential for resistance, of uncovering a trace of individual power. The chora *is* this ambiguity. Underlying the existence of a form which 'appears by way of those things that enter it' (Sallis 109) – an entering of the female body by the male, or the colonised by the coloniser

---

[17]   Butler sees Foucault as still presenting a body 'in some sense there, pregiven' ('Foucault' 601). Interestingly, Butler herself does suggest a body beyond cultural inscription, as recent criticism has emphasised (Bordo, 'Bringing Body'), questioning instead the usefulness of trying to separate out a fixed body as 'matter has a history' (*Bodies* 29).

– is a refusal to allow such enterings to define physical form. It is a foregrounding of cultural definition as an overwriting, remaining 'very hard to apprehend' (Plato, *Timaeus* 51b, 186) and, despite these enterings, 'no*t itself* determined by any of them' (Sallis 111): thus controlling rather than controlled, an abject appearing to suggest rejection but in fact asserting itself through a remaining trace. What the chora is – a body and not a body, a body with 'no form' (Sallis 109) – offers great potential as well as risk, if it can only be claimed. For if 'forms come to be *in* it without ever being *of* it' (Sallis 109) then this openness might be read as powerlessness, but it might also be read as resistance. For it identifies an entity that exists outside definition, the agency that is suggested in the chora's designation as that which 'takes on no form' (Sallis 109): a 'taking' which suggests the ability for self-assertion. Though the chora at times resembles what enters – or in the case of the real body appropriates, marks or violates – it never becomes what such incursions affect. It is fluid, but still holds something for itself that cannot be touched, indeed, cannot even be named: both fluid and concrete, body and mind.

It is the power of this ambiguous status that the postcolonial novel uncovers. Though already evident in the carnivalised bodies I touched upon in relation to the city – transformative but at the same time always corporeal – it is in returning to where I began, to *Paradise*, that such representation is best substantiated. Morrison's narrative exemplifies reconfiguration of the body beyond both cultural and biological accounts. Her representation weaves through and between different gender positions to attack the idea of a Cartesian or constructed body. Yet it refuses endless postmodern fluidity as it hovers close to escapist desires. What is asserted instead of these two oppositions is rather the possibility of some sort of strategic essence that individuals must claim for themselves. For the convent women it is precisely such a complex body that is both their desire and achievement, a body that cannot be captured and, when it re-emerges in solid form, does so without being confined by its past, creating a sense of self no longer dependant on others. Whilst the convent itself fails to survive as a space outside Ruby's patriarchal and racist system, nevertheless the individual body continues to offer a potential space for the maintenance of alternative ideals.[18]

Near the end of *Paradise*, the two elements of the ambiguity represented by the complex body are finally fused. As Consolata's form changes at the height of her power – 'sculpted somehow' (262) – she evokes healing ritual. The women undress, lie on the floor and allow Consolata to paint around their forms. When she speaks, 'none of them understood' (263). Yet her ramblings are precisely the negotiation I have highlighted. Consolata speaks her own story. She proclaims 'my child body, hurt and soil, leaps into the arms of a woman who teach me my body is nothing my spirit everything' (263), a rejection of the physical body's importance. Yet she also pronounces that 'my bones on his the only true thing' (263), coterminously celebrating the physicality she has undermined. Without knowing it, the women echo her. Drawing their pain on the templates of their

---

18   For the convent as representative of alternative space see Schröder 178–89.

bodies so they are 'no longer haunted' (266), they create an artistic witness statement to the violence they have suffered which, as art, allows them to represent mental as well as physical damage. Refusing to write or speak their pain, instead representing it in symbol, they challenge the colonial privileging of the written word. This is a strategy equally prominent in Coetzee's *Foe* in the replaying of the Crusoe narrative: Friday speaks, but not in the words of the colonial oppressor. Rather, denied speech by the removal of his tongue, he refuses language in favour of the acknowledgment that 'there will always be a voice in him to whisper doubts, whether in words or nameless sounds or tunes or tones' (149). Here, 'bodies are their own signs' (157). Such bodies are not metaphorical: their pain stands simply for itself, a refusal to 'reify ... as symbol' (Boehmer, 'Transfiguring' 276) that means the importance of bodies, themselves, is seen in the postcolonial narrative. They may in themselves promote powerful change. In Coetzee's *Waiting for the Barbarians* (1980), for example, a colonial magistrate defies the regime he has supported by returning an indigenous girl, previously his captive, to her community. It is only his intimate personal contact with the girl, a reading of her body rather than a linguistic exchange, that facilitates this transformation of consciousness: the magistrate proclaims that 'until the marks on this girl's body are deciphered and understood I cannot let go of her' (31).

This is a claiming of the body. Yet displacing it in art as the convent women do also suggests the ability to transfer such pain and, with it, bodily violence and suffering.[19] The ending of the novel represents this process in reverse. *Paradise* confirms that the disappearance of the women's bodies is not an ambiguous suggestion of the possibility of escaping the limits of the body, created to propagate an open-ended postmodern possibility. Rather, it is an explicit suggestion of survival when Gigi, Pallas, Seneca, and Mavis all feature in vignettes in the last pages of the novel where they reconnect with their pasts. The women really can, it seems, escape the violence against them, transcending not only cultural construction but also the physical form that is its basis. Yet it also suggests that the women return, quite physically, to their bodies that survive despite death. They are restored to them, still gendered, still with a sociopolitical role, and still celebrated in their solid form. What has altered is the emergence of an awareness that while they are their bodies, they are also more than them, reclaiming them in the way that Fanon, after considering the possibility of invisibility, rejects this in favour of the assertion that 'the body is not something opposed to what you call the mind' (*Black Skin* 126–7). Such an assertion is particularly significant within the context of African identity that pervades the novel: in their ability to leave their bodies the women can be seen to have a connection to African spirituality that the Ruby men, despite (or perhaps because of) their fundamentalism, have lost: Dangarembga's Tambudzai, too, is able to leave her body and return to it (168). Such women have the ability to decide what their bodies are and, when this ability fades under

---

[19]   See also Michael 172.

the violence of others, they know they can survive it; all are confident, trauma seemingly in the past.

When the convent women return in physical form, it is without either outside impositions on their body image, or prejudiced readings of biology that might support racial and patriarchal constructions. Instead, they own a spiritual body, continually open to transformation and even transcendence, a body that may be used by the individual for themselves, where the earth is now 'Paradise'. This exemplifies a novel which 'simultaneously undercuts any notion of a stable, centred, fixed self and illustrates possibilities for constructively fashioning ... more dynamic selves' (Michael 177). Seneca has given up pain, Mavis is reunited with her daughter without fear, Pallas is independent, Gigi confronts her past and meets her father, while the last three paragraphs of the novel seem to suggest that Consolata is free to be magically reunited with Mary Magna. There are real consequences of this act as Anna, a Ruby woman, visits the convent and sees not deviancy but 'females trying to bridle, without being trampled, the monsters that slavered them' (Morrison, *Paradise* 303). There is also the hope of change for Ruby as Misner acknowledges the way the men echo the white man with their hierarchies, and Billie Delia expresses defiant belief in the women's survival. We might accept Morrison's reality as ours, might see her use of Descartes as a powerful reclamation of the colonial discourse for new, subversive purpose, taking his affirmation that 'I am not that structure of limbs which is called a human body' (18) to deny the effectiveness of violence against the corporeal. Or even seeing it as metaphor we might appreciate its worth: to throw off the weight of the body not forever, but only so that we can mentally reclaim it more solidly than before, an affirmation of Weiss's desire that we 'affirm the power of individual agency in the construction, deconstruction, and reconstruction of the very terms of our corporeality' (86).

Here it is also productive to discuss Harris's frequent return to the concept of phantom limb as a play on limbo that signifies an element both present and absent, a body that engages with corporeality but is also more than this. Harris's view resonates with Weiss's reading of Merleau-Ponty's account where the limb is viewed not only as refusal of loss but also 'simultaneously as one's active engagement in the world' that cannot be obliterated by mutilation, as 'previous body images remain accessible' (35). The phantom limb is a perfect example of the body as both culturally imagined and physically real, described by Merleau-Ponty as 'not the mere outcome of objective causality; no more is it a *cogitatio*', something that could be 'a mixture of the two only if we could find a means of linking the "psychic" and the "physiological"' (77). The limb may be seen as a 'phantom ... a possibility ready to materialize itself in any number of shapes or forms' (Weiss 35); yet it is also involved in an act that 'refuses mutilation' (Merleau-Ponty 81). What Merleau-Ponty describes as flights into 'magical acts' (86) become for Harris realisable aims: the body seems able to overcome violence as it continues to exist as a trace beyond death, caught in a 'bodiless step' (*Dark* 107) that – in this combination of two words – celebrates, as for Morrison, both physical movement and transcendence of corporeality.

Fury, too, celebrates this dual strategy. Malik chooses invisibility, 'a satisfying anonymity in the crowds, an absence of intrusion' (7), a withdrawal from difference as defined by the sight of others. Yet his story ends with a strong assertion of physical form, a body defined by the self in refusal of outside forces: Malik's final displacement of the city, jumping on the bouncy castle precisely to make himself visible and assert a claim to a bodily identity. Once again, this is not simply a new development. Rai, too, in *The Ground Beneath Her Feet* has a 'knack for invisibility' (14) that allows him to escape physical attacks as he is able to 'persuade the sniper I do not merit his bullet' (15). Yet he too ultimately abandons this, in favour of an assertion of self: to 'stand my ground, right here' (575). As early as *Midnight's Children*, this negotiation exists; Saleem's journey in the washing basket may suggest transcendence, but his death is nevertheless very real, and though this may not be a positive reclamation, it nevertheless affirms such duality. Yet it is only in his more recent novels that Rushdie has managed to affirm the positive potential of such a combination, by envisaging the physical body as capable of escaping its construction by others. What emerges is a return to the body, yet a body now owned by its inhabitant, with escape of that body only marking the individual's power of agency over it, and its separation from a body owned by others.

Here postcolonial authors seems to find the solution that escapes Morrison's characters in *Beloved*, Baby Suggs's abandonment of her celebratory project in the wake of the slave masters' continued influence. What is needed, it seems, is an identity that still owns its own body, but is less tied to that body in the knowledge that it can never fully escape cultural construction. There is an open, fluid, form that is part of a continuum of spaces to which it is connected, and which only ever marks identity strategically. The fact that the convent community in *Paradise* allows the possibility of an 'unbridled, authentic self' (177) encapsulates this realisation: 'unbridled', and therefore free, but also 'authentic', and therefore a mark of firm identity. Bodies are seized upon as the visible marker of difference, a factor that means they must be both reclaimed *and* transcended, a negotiation that counters those polemical readings that would see authors such as Morrison as explicitly either for or against the physical form. This may seem convenient, but it is the only viable solution for negotiating a space at once destructive and life giving, that cannot be as easily migrated from as the city.

In my introduction, I expressed the problematic of trying to reconcile the postcolonial need for identity politics with a rejection of colonial patterns of definition. In their simultaneously fluid and solid bodies, postcolonial authors provide a potential answer to such a concern with equal relevance to colonial, postcolonial, and postimperial societies. What the chora is in essence, ambiguous as both fixed and yet resistant of fixing in the image of others – transformative and yet facilitating transformation – is a mark of power as much as disavowal. What is required is not to reject this ambiguity, but to reconfigure it, so that the power Plato obscures in his patriarchal discourse, but never manages to deny, expands from a trace to the centre of the narrative, stereotypes not rejected as Irigaray would have, but rather used in the service of the bodies they originally limit. Foregrounding the trace in this way only reinforces the sense in which the body encapsulates post-space: pushing to the foreground the diversity and chaos the colonial space attempts to obscure. Following Merleau-Ponty, a body created in this spirit is for the individual much more that a 'geometrical outline' (108); it is the chora. As Sallis notes, it is 'not the isotropic space of post-Cartesian physics. Nor is it even empty space, the void' (115), as Derrida also confirms ('Khōra' 109), but one that both Sallis and Derrida overlook, the original third space: Morrison's transcendent bodies, Rushdie's fluid physicality, Harris's 'Atahualpan form rather than Cartesian form' (*Dark* 16). Here the idea of a postcolonial politics based on Bhabha's idea of performativity, centred upon individual assertions, finds its most concentrated form: geographical scale is reversed, the smallest becomes the most significant. Reclaiming the body, postcolonial authors suggest that regardless as to how much control is exercised by the nation-state, there is always an intimate experience that cannot be wholly influenced by outside forces. Yet by celebrating its fluidity, they refuse to succumb to any colonial discourse of bodily definition that would allow the body to become another imperialised space. This is neither essentialism nor a representation that would facilitate a stereotype of postmodernism. Rather, it is existence in a liminal space between these two extremes: the most significant post-space that might also be framed as the postcolonial chora.

Afterword

less as 'after' than as a following, going beyond.

(Shohat 134–5)

The post-space journey suggests movement without arrival or departure, a strategic nomadism that affirms a process of travelling defiant of absolutes. So to invoke at the closing of this book the idea of a conclusion – indeed, even of an 'end' – would be to counter much I have tried to assert. The book itself is a space, and it too may offer a challenge to the conventions that demarcate it as territory. For this reason, I resist the need to conclude, with the acknowledgment that, in this case, the refusal to conclude *is* the meaning. To assert a final, complete, and ultimate definition, to say, 'I have captured post-space' rather than to have attempted to represent it, is to create a book-as-space that risks mirroring the colonial absolutism, the fixing of meaning from outside, that post-space arises in order to interrogate. If process were to mirror message, then this study would have no conclusion at all, only an ellipsis that would in literary terms honour the spirit of post-space.

Bearing this in mind, my words here mark not a definitive account of what post-space is, only an attempt to encapsulate what I see as the beginnings of a far wider phenomenon. In the transition from the macro to the micro, I have had to pass by the fascinating dynamics of natural landscapes that seem to preoccupy so many accounts of the journey, and frequently provide counterpoint to urban space: seas, oceans, forests, parkland and desert, to name but a few particularly appealing examples. Moreover, the importance of the microspaces of the home, here consigned to a postscript, has raised the need for more detailed study of their power: an investigation of the points of contact between the postcolonial and the phenomenological that would trace the significance of cupboards, cellars and household containers. Indeed, in the attempt to cover a sweeping arc from the smallest to the largest – the global to the individual body – there are many in-between spaces that I have passed through: village; town; school; hospital; prison; the space of the underground; the theatres, music halls and cinemas that construct spaces of performance; the vehicles that facilitate journeys. Their place within the line I have sketched is, I hope, clear. Nevertheless, they deserve further attention.

Yet, as this afterword itself foregrounds, there is one additional space that has been present throughout the book, yet has no chapter of its own. It is the space of the book itself. For myself, the book is not the ultimate encapsulation of post-space. It is not as intimate, or as personal, as the individual body. Yet the physical text does deserve comment that would see it as more than simply another object in the domestic scene, more than the library so prominent in *Da Silva Da Silva's*

Cultivated Wilderness or Patricia Cato's 'history project' in *Paradise*. For literary post-space, it is ultimately the text itself that becomes the most suggestive space. In the cases not only of Salman Rushdie, Toni Morrison and Wilson Harris, but many of the postcolonial authors discussed here, the nonlinear nature of their narratives mean that subversion of absolutes, refusal of closure, and multiplicity of meaning is enshrined in the physical reality of the book, and in the awareness of spaces as 'texts' to be read.

This is not to reduce post-space to a literary phenomenon, and the fact that I see it as represented in the written text, rather than enclosed within it, means that the written text is more of a reflector of other spaces, than one that should be studied alongside them. To take the former approach is to risk a more introspective, possibly apolitical dialogue, where the reduction of spaces to texts means suggesting the possibility of unproblematic rewriting. Nevertheless, alternative ways of studying textuality might produce a reading at odds with this anxiety. To explore the potential of these alternative textualisations would not only mean looking at the role of books within books, such as in Gabriel Garcia Marquez's *One Hundred Years of Solitude* (1967), Iain Sinclair's *Downriver* or V.S. Naipaul's *The Enigma of Arrival*, all of which in their own ways are circular narratives recounting their own creation. It would also mean looking at books as subversive spaces in themselves, as in M.G. Vassanji's *The Book of Secrets* (1994). Moreover, it indicates how the creative space, in all its forms, is worthy of consideration, for example the dominant presence of paintings in *The Moor's Last Sigh* or Keri Hulme's *The Bone People*; the music of *The Ground Beneath Her Feet* and *Jazz*; the Masquerade of Ben Okri's *The Famished Road*; the insurgency artwork of Michael Ondaatje's *Running in the Family*, all of which demand their own attention.

The last two chapters of this study, in particular, have pointed to another prospect for further investigation. This book focuses on the postcolonial space. Yet throughout, and particularly in relation to homes and bodies, colonial space has found its parallel in the construction of a patriarchal absolute, raising possibilities of a feminist post-space. What productive reading might be developed, for example, if the bodily transformations of Virginia Woolf's *Orlando* (1928) and Jeanette Winterson's *Oranges are Not the Only Fruit* (1985), or the rewriting of both this body and also the city and spaces of performance in Sarah Waters's *Tipping the Velvet* (1998), were read through a theory of chaotic space? Similarly, though it has only fleetingly entered my own work – most noticeably in relation to Morrison, and Rushdie's *The Satanic Verses* – it seems that space may also be controlled by class interests, in a way that might mean the implementation of an absolute space by those in places of class or caste privilege, that might then be countered by subversive nonlinearity.

Such a space is gestured towards by the anti-Thatcherite psychogeography of Iain Sinclair, and, in more realist terms, in the anticapitalist critiques of Robert Newman. But its possibilities extend beyond this. Combining feminist, class-based and realist possibilities, what might be suggested by the urban spaces of texts such as Pat Barker's *Union Street* (1982) and *Blow Your House Down*

(1984) or – combining the elements of race, class and realism – Diran Adebayo's *Some Kind of Black* (1996)? As Michel Foucault's discussions in *Discipline and Punish* remind us, the prison represents an ordered space that acts against a diverse section of the population, united by neither race, nor class, nor gender.

This final example also reaffirms the fact that, throughout, I have stressed my belief that post-space is not simply the domain of the novelist. Its application might be extended to other literary genres, but also to nonfiction and, indeed, to real-world actions undertaken by both individuals and communities as a strategy of resistance. In this sense, the authors I have examined here must be seen to both reflect real-world events, and play a part in their development, by encouraging spatial transformation as a viable, valuable tactic against oppression.

Through this study, I have outlined how what I see as postcolonial authors, working with the magical-realist genre, and within the English language, have used space as a source of resistance and as a site of empowerment. Constructing fluid, open and chaotic locations, the fictions of Rushdie, Harris and Morrison offer models of space that may be seen to challenge imperial absolutes, which – as I have indicated – are also indicative of strategies taken up by an array of postcolonial authors. These writers offer up the possibility of a strategy that draws together different geographies and diverse contexts, yet does not overshadow the specifics of colonialism in different locations, and the very different legacies of this colonialism in the postcolonial world. Created through an aptly contrapuntal reading of different texts and from varying approaches, the notion of post-space defines this representation. Space is no longer determined or defined, but is instead chaotic. This chaos acts not only to capture the postcolonial experience of trauma and confusion, but also to gesture towards the possibility of a subversion of all that, in its colonial reading, order and linearity come to represent.

In their representation of negotiations of power at the levels of journey, city, home and body, postcolonial authors suggest that the nation-state can no longer be seen as the apotheosis of anti-colonial resistance. In doing so, they question the scales on which we look commonly for signs of political agency. It cannot be assumed that the citizen of an oppressive nation does not, nevertheless, make powerful statements of resistance, even if such action is not visible in challenges to national regimes, or even official forces. Thus whilst the postcolony and, likewise, the colonial legacy in the post-imperial world, may seem to hold sway on a national level, nevertheless on other scales the imperfect nature of this order is revealed. Just as for the original colonial project, what appears monolithic always shows the trace of an alternative. It therefore must not be taken for granted that, in postcolonial literature, 'resistance' is to be prefixed, as is commonly the case, with 'national'. In the wake of this awareness, it is also not to be presupposed that the postcolonial author is always writing metaphorically, that the target is always the nation-state that our preconceptions so often categorise without question. I hope I have shown that, while such figurative work does occur, it is overshadowed by representation of other spaces as very much literal, and of significance in their own right.

It is in the body that this assertion is encapsulated. Refusing a transcendental position, the postcolonial author mediates fluidity with a continued claim on the body as the postcolonial subject's most vital asset. This coterminous position – a body owned, yet only by itself and in the knowledge of transformative potential – is captured in the concept of a postcolonial chora. So often is the body in postcolonial literature read in a way that assumes it to be representative of the sufferings of an entire national population. Yet to read it only in this way is to obscure the centrality of the body, in itself and for itself, to colonial operations, and to deny the importance of intimate acts of resistance. It is individual bodies choosing to resist that become a community of resistance, which then becomes a large-scale resistance to oppressive rule. The literature discussed here suggests it would be unwise to forget this initial movement. Without the body, the process of resistance has not even begun, and it is this that makes it perhaps the most significant site of post-space.

At the conclusion of his own study of spatial ordering, J.K. Noyes proffers an unanswered question: 'how, in everyday life, does narrative function to reduce fixed postulates of unitary space into experiences of chaos? And further: how is this experience of chaos utilised in the form of a personalized yet narratable knowledge which is productive in coping with the intolerability of the regime which excludes it?' (289). In the post-space resistances of the postcolonial authors that I have charted, I think Noyes's question receives its answer. Postcolonial authors' presentation of spaces indicates a continuity of fluid, transformative power that moves from the nation to the body, and holistically interconnects each space so that the divisions I have made here give way to an overall experiential vision. Their magic in the service of resistance illustrates how fantastic subversions of space are in fact powerful challenges to prevailing order, not strategies that draw our attention away from violence, but that rather emerge only in its wake, as interrogatory and critical forces. Yet this project also illustrates the important need for hopefulness, and for a continued belief in the power of assertion. For when action against the official national discourse is not possible – as is more often than not true – personal acts of resistance are nevertheless found at alternative spatial scales. As pockets of space act as refuges where survival is facilitated, the individual is never without at least a modicum of agency. The transformative power of these authors and their attempts to present a post-space vision – to use chaos to find spaces of resistance in the wake of hopelessness – is a powerful message that is as necessary for reform as starkly realist representations of violence and oppression. For without such voices, not standing in opposition but alongside, there is no way to envisage the possibility for change. It is they who not only represent the horrors of current circumstance but, gesturing towards the future, also offer the possibility of a way to move forward.

Works Cited

Aboulela, Leila. *Minaret*. London: Bloomsbury, 2005.

Adebayo, Diran. *Some Kind of Black*. London: Virago, 1996.

Adichie, Chimamanda Ngozi. *Half of a Yellow Sun*. London: Fourth Estate, 2006.

Ahmad, Aijaz. *In Theory: Classes, Nations, Literatures*. London: Verso, 1992.

Alexandru, Maria-Sabrina. 'Towards a politics of the small things: Arundhati Roy and the decentralization of authorship.' In *Authorship in Context: From theTheoretical to the Material*. Ed. Kyriaki Hadjiafxendi and Polina Mackay. London: Palgrave, 2007. 163–84.

Anderson, Benedict. *Imagined Communities: Reflections on the Origin and Spread of Nationalism*. Rev. ed. London: Verso, 1991.

Armstrong, Frances. 'Gender and miniaturization: Games of littleness in nineteenth-century fiction.' *English Studies in Canada* 36.4 (1990): 403–16.

Armstrong, Nancy. *Desire and Domestic Fiction: A Political History of the Novel*. New York: Oxford University Press, 1987.

Ashcroft, Bill. 'Constructing the post-colonial male body.' *The Body in the Library*. Ed. Leigh Dale and Simon Ryan. Amsterdam: Rodopi, 1998. 207–24.

———. 'Forcing newness into the world: Language, place and nature.' *Ariel* 36.1–2 (2005): 93–110.

———. *On Post-Colonial Futures: Transformations of Colonial Culture*. London: Continuum, 2001.

———. *Post-Colonial Transformation*. London: Routledge, 2001.

Ashcroft, Bill, Gareth Griffiths and Helen Tiffin, eds. *The Post-Colonial Studies Reader*. London: Routledge, 1994.

Augustine. *The City of God*. Trans. John Healey. London: J.M. Dent, 1931.

Azim, Firdous. *The Colonial Rise of the Novel*. London: Routledge, 1993.

Bachelard, Gaston. *The Poetics of Space*. 1964. Trans. Maria Jolas. Boston: Beacon, 1994.

Bakhtin, Mikhail. *Problems of Dostoevsky's Poetics*. Ed. and trans. Caryl Emerson. Minneapolis: University of Minnesota Press, 1984.

Balakrishnan, Gopal. *Debating Empire*. London: Verso, 2003.

Barker, Ernest. 'Introduction.' In Augustine, *The City of God*. Trans. John Healey. London: J.M. Dent, 1931. vii–lx.

Barker, Pat. *Blow Your House Down*. London: Virago, 1984.

———. *Union Street*. London: Virago, 1982.

Barnabas, Simon G. 'Ayemenem and the Ayemenem House: A study of the setting of *The God of Small Things*.' In *Arundhati Roy. The Novelist Extraordinary*. Ed. R.K. Dhawan. New Dehli: Prestige, 1999, 296–306.

Baucom, Ian. *Out of Place: Englishness, Empire and the Locations of Identity.* Princeton: Princeton University Press, 1999.

Bell, Bernard W. 'Beloved: A womanist neo-slave narrative; or multivocal remembrances of things past.' *African American Review* 26.1 (1992): 7–15.

Bell, Currer [Charlotte Bronte]. *Jane Eyre.* 3 vols. London: Smith, Elder and Co, 1847.

Benevolo, Leonardo. *The European City.* Trans. Carl Ispen. Oxford: Blackwell, 1993.

Benítez-Rojo, Antonio. *The Repeating Island: The Caribbean and the Postmodern Perspective.* 1992. 2nd ed. Trans. James Maraniss. Durham: Duke University Press, 1996.

Benjamin, Walter. *Illuminations.* Ed. Hannah Arendt. Trans. Harry Zohn. London: Cape, 1970.

Bhabha, Homi K. 'The commitment to theory.' In *Questions of Third Cinema.* Ed. Jim Pines and Paul Willemen. London: British Film Institute, 1989, 111–32.

———. 'DissemiNation: Time, narrative and the margins of the modern nation.' In *Nation and Narration.* Ed. Homi Bhabha. London: Routledge, 1990, 291–322.

———. *The Location of Culture.* London: Routledge, 1994.

———. 'The other question: Difference, discrimination and the discourse of colonialism.' In *Literature, Politics and Theory: Papers from the Essex Conference 1976–84.* Ed. Francis Barker et al. London: Methuen, 1986, 148–72.

———. 'Narrating the nation.' Introduction. In *Nation and Narration.* Ed. Homi Bhabha. London: Routledge, 1990, 1–7.

———. 'Postcolonial authority and postmodern guilt.' In *Cultural Studies.* Ed. Lawrence Grossberg, Cary Nelson and Paula Treichler. New York: Routledge, 1992, 56–68.

Bigwood, Carol. 'Renaturalizing the body (with the help of Meleau-Ponty).' *Hypatia* 6.3 (1991): 54–63. Rpt. in *Body and Flesh: a Philosophical Reader.* Ed. Don Welton. Cambridge, Massachusetts: Blackwell, 1998, 99–114.

Bird, Jon. "Dystopia on the Thames." In J. Bird et al., *Mapping the Futures.* London: Routledge, 1993, 120–35.

Birkeland, Inger. *Making Place: Making Self: Travel, Subjectivity and Sexual Difference.* Ashgate: Aldershot, 2005.

Black, Iain. 'Imperial visions: Rebuilding the Bank of England, 1919–39.' In *Imperial Cities: Landscape, Display and Identity.* Ed. Felix Driver and David Gilbert. Manchester: Manchester University Press, 1999, 96–113.

Black, Jeremy. *Maps and Politics.* London: Reaktion, 1997.

Blunt, Alison. *Domicile and Diaspora: Anglo-Indian Women and the Spatial Politics of Home.* Malden, Massachusetts: Blackwell, 2005.

——— 'Embodying war: British women and domestic defilement in the Indian "Mutiny", 1857–8.' *Journal of Historical Geography* 26.3 (2000): 403–28.

Boehmer, Elleke. *Stories of Women: Gender and Narrative in the Postcolonial Nation.* Manchester: Manchester University Press, 2005.

————. 'Transfiguring: Colonial body into post-colonial narrative.' *Novel* 26.3 (1993): 268–77.

Bold, Christine. '"An Enclave in the Wilderness." Rev. of *Paradise*, by Toni Morrison.' *Times Literary Supplement* 22 Mar. 1998: 22.

Bonta, Marki, and John Proveti. *Deleuze and Geophilosophy: A Guide and Glossary*. Edinburgh: Edinburgh University Press, 2004.

Bookchin, Murray. 'Introduction.' *Limits of the City* (1974), 2nd rev ed Montréal: Black Rose Books, 1986, 6–10. Rpt. in *The City Cultures Reader*. Ed. Malcolm Miles, Tim Hall and Iain Borden. London: Routledge, 2000, 48–9.

Bordo, Susan. 'Bringing body to theory.' In *Body and Flesh: A Philosophical Reader.* Ed. Don Welton. Cambridge, Massachusetts: Blackwell, 1998, 84–97.

————. *Unbearable Weight: Feminism, Western Culture and the Body*. Berkley: University of California Press, 1993.

Boron, Ahlio A. *Empire and Imperialism: A Critical Reading of Michael Hardt and Antonio Negri*. London: Zed, 2005.

Brathwaite, Edward Kamau. 'Ogun.' *Islands*. London: Oxford University Press, 1969, 22.

Brennan, Timothy. *Salman Rushdie and the Third World: Myths of the Nation*. London: Macmillan, 1989.

Brownfoot, Janice N. 'Memsahibs in colonial Malaya: A study of European wives in a British colony and protectorate 1900–1940.' In *The Incorporated Wife*. Ed. Hilary Callan and Shirley Ardener. London: Croom Helm, 1984, 186–210.

Bryden, Inga and Janet Floyd. 'Introduction.' *Domestic Space: Reading the Nineteenth-Century Interior.* Ed. Bryden and Floyd. Manchester: Manchester University Press, 1999, 1–17.

Buchanan, Ian, and Gregg Lambert, ed. *Deleuze and Space*. Edinburgh: Ednburgh University Press, 2005.

Bundy, Andrew, ed. *Selected Essays of Wilson Harris: The Unfinished Genesis of the Imagination*. London: Routledge, 1999.

Burkitt, Ian. 'The time and space of everyday life'. *Cultural Studies* 18. 2/3 (2004): 211–27.

Burnett, D. Graham. *Masters of All They Surveyed: Explorations, Geography, and a British El Dorado*. Chicago: University of Chicago Press, 2000.

Burton, Antoinette. *At the Heart of Empire: Indians and the Colonial Encounter in Late-Victorian Britain*. Berkeley: University of California Press, 1998.

Butler, Judith. *Bodies That Matter: On the Discursive Limits of Sex*. New York: Routledge, 1993.

————. 'Foucault and the paradox of bodily inscriptions.' *Journal of Philosophy* 86.11 (1989): 601–7.

Byrne, David. 'Chaotic places or complex places? Cities in a post-industrial era.' In *Imagining Cities: Scripts, Signs, Memory*. Ed. Sallie Westwood and John Williams. London: Routledge, 1996. 50–70.

Carr, Robert. 'The new man in the jungle: Chaos, community and the margins of the Nation State.' *Callaloo* 18.1 (1995): 137–56.

Carter, Paul. *The Road to Botany Bay: an Essay in Spatial History*. London: Faber, 1987.

Casey, Edward S. *Getting Back Into Place: Toward a Renewed Understanding of the Place-World*. Bloomington: Indiana University Press, 1993.

Cezair-Thompson, Margaret. 'Beyond the post-colonial novel: Ben Okri's The Famished Road and its 'Abiku' Traveller.' *Journal of Commonwealth Literature* 3.2 (1996): 33–45.

Chakrabarty, Dipesh. 'Introduction'. In Chakrabarty et al., *From the Colonial to thePostcolonial: India and Pakistan in Transition*. New Dehli: Oxford University Press, 2007, 1–10.

———. 'Postcoloniality and the artifice of history: Who speaks for "Indian Pasts?' *Representations* 37 (Winter 1992): 1–26. Rpt. in, *Contemporary Postcolonial Theory: A Reader*. Ed. Padmini Mongia. New York: Arnold, 1996, 223–47.

Chanda, Tirthankar, 'Sexual/texutal strategies in *The God of Small Things*', *Commonwealth Essays and Studies*, 20.1 (1997): 38–48.

Chandler, Marilyn R. *Dwelling in the Text: Houses in American Fiction*. Berkeley: University of California Press, 1991.

Chandra, Vikram. *Red Earth and Pouring Rain*. 1995. London: Faber, 2000.

Chatterjee, Partha. *The Nation and its Fragments: Colonial and Postcolonial Histories*. Princeton: Princeton Univesity Press, 1993.

Childs, Peter, Jean Jacques Weber, and Patrick Williams. *Post-Colonial Theory and Literatures*. Trier: Wissienschaftlicher Verlag, 2006.

Chowdhury, Kaniskha. 'Interrogating "Newness": Globalization and postcolonial theory in the age of endless war.' *Cultural Critique* 62 (2006): 126–61.

Chowdhury, Purna. *Between Two Worlds: Nation, Rushdie and Postcolonial Indo-English Fiction*. New York: Edwin Mellen, 2007.

Chrisman, Laura. *Postcolonial Contraventions: Cultural Readings of Race, Imperialism and Transnationalism*. Manchester: Manchester University Press, 2003.

Clark, Steve. 'Introduction.' In *Travel Writing and Empire*. Ed. Steve Clark. London: Zed, 1999. 1–28.

Clifford, James. *Routes: Travel and Translation in the Late Twentieth Century*. Cambridge, Massachusetts: Harvard University Press, 1997.

Coetzee, J.M. *Waiting for the Barbarians*. 1980. New York: Penguin, 1982.

———. *Foe*. 1986. Harmondsworth: Penguin, 1987.

Cohn, Bernard S. 'Representing authority in Victorian India.' In Eric Hobsbawm and Terence Ranger, eds., *The Invention of Tradition*. Cambridge: Cambridge University Press, 1983, 165–210.

Conrad, Joseph. *Heart of Darkness*. 1902. Ed. D.C.R. Goonetilleke. Peterborough, Ontario: Broadview, 1995.

Crampton, Jeremy W. 'Maps, race and Foucault: Eugenics and territorialization following World War One.' In Jeremy W. Crampton and Stuart Elden, eds., *Space, Knowledge and Power: Foucault and Geography*. Aldershot: Ashgate, 2007, 223–44.

Crewdson, John M. 'Defector says Jones used 2 methods to control cult.' *New York Times* 24 Dec. 1978: A20.

Cribb, T.J. 'Writing Up the Log: The Legacy of Hakluyt.' In *Travel Writing and Empire*. Ed Steve Clark. London: Zed, 1999. 100–12.

Crush, Jonathan. 'Post-colonialism, de-colonization, and geography.' In *Geography and Empire*. Ed. Anne Godlewska and Neil Smith. Oxford: Blackwell, 1994. 333–50.

Dabydeen, David and Nana Wilson-Tagoe. *A Reader's Guide to Westindian and Black British Literature*. 2nd rev. ed. London: Hansib, 1997.

Dale, Leigh and Simon Ryan. 'The body in the library.' Introduction. In *The Body in the Library*. Ed. Leigh Dale and Simon Ryan. Amsterdam: Rodopi, 1998, 1–12.

Dalsgard, Katrine. 'The one all-black town worth the pain: (African) American exceptionalism, historical narration, and the critique of nationhood in Toni Morrison's *Paradise*.' *African American Review* 35.2 (2001): 233–48.

Daly, Vere T. *The Making of Guyana*. London: Macmillan, 1974.

Dangarembga, Tsitsi. *Nervous Conditions*. Seattle: Seal, 1988.

Darian-Smith, Kate, Liz Gunner and Sarah Nuttall. *Text, Theory, Space: Land, Literature and History in South Africa and Australia*. London: Routledge, 1996.

Dash, Michael. 'In search of the lost body: Redefining the subject in Caribbean literature.' *Kunapipi* 11.1 (1989): 17–26.

Davis, Mike. *City of Quartz: Excavating the Future in Los Angeles*. 1990. London: Pimlico, 1998.

De Man, Paul. *Blindness and Insight: Essays in the Rhetoric of Contemporary Criticism*. 2nd rev. ed. Minneapolis: University of Minnesota Press, 1983.

Defoe, Daniel. *Robinson Crusoe*. 1719. London: Penguin, 1985.

Delbaere-Garant, Jeanne. 'Psychic realism, mythic realism, grotesque realism: Variations on magic realism in contemporary literature in English.' *Magical Realism: Theory, History, Community*. Ed. Lois Parkinson Zamora and Wendy Faris. Durham: Duke University Press, 1995, 249–63.

Deleuze, Gilles and Felix Guattari. *Anti-Oedipus: Capitalism and Schizophrenia*. 1972. Trans. Robert Hurley, Mark Seem and Helen R. Lane. London: Athlone, 1984.

———. *A Thousand Plateaus*. Trans. Brian Massumi. London: Athlone, 1988.

Despres, Leo A. *Cultural Pluralism and Nationalist Politics in British Guiana*. Chicago: Rand McNally and Company, 1967.

Derrida, Jacques. 'Khōra.' *On the Name*. Ed. Thomas Dutoit. Trans. David Wood, John P. Leavey, Jr. and Ian McLeod. Stanford: Stanford University Press, 1995.,87–127.

———. 'The law of genre.' Trans. Avital Ronell. *Critical Inquiry* 7.1 (1980): 55–81.

———. *Margins of Philosophy*. Trans. Alan Bass. Brighton: Harvester, 1982.

———. *Speech and Phenomena: And Other Essays on Husserl's Theory of Signs*. Evanston: Northwestern University Press, 1973.

Descartes, René. *Meditations on First Philosophy: with Selections from the Objections and Replies*. Trans. John Collingham. Cambridge: Cambridge University Press, 1986.

Deshpande, Satish. 'Hegemonic spatial strategies: The nation-space and Hindu communalism in twentieth-century India.' In *Subaltern Studies XI: Community, Gender and Violence*. Ed. Partha Chatterjee and Pradeep Jaganathan. London: Hurst, 2001, 167–211.

Deutscher, Isaac. 'The non-Jewish Jew.' In *The Non-Jewish Jew and Other Essays*. Ed. Tamara Deutscher. London: Oxford University Press, 1968, 25–41.

Dickerson, Vanessa D. 'Summoning SomeBody: The flesh made word in Toni Morrison's fiction.' In *Recovering the Black Female Body. Self-Representations by African American Women*. Ed. Michael Bennett and Vanessa D. Dickerson. New Brunswick, New Jersey: Rutgers University Press, 2000, 195–216.

Dickey, S. 'Permeable homes: Domestic service, household space, and the vulnerability of class boundaries in urban India.' *American Ethnologist* 27.2 (2000): 462–89.

Dirlik, Arif. 'The Post-colonial aura: Third world criticism in the age of global capitalism.' *Critical Inquiry* 20 (1994): 329–56.

Doel, Marcus. *Poststructuralist Geographies: The Diabolical Art of Spatial Science*. Edinburgh: Edinburgh University Press, 1999.

Donald, James. 'This, here, now: Imagining the modern city.' In *Imagining Cities: Scripts, Signs, Memory*. Ed. Sallie Westwood and John Williams. London: Routledge, 1996, 181–201.

Donald, Moira. 'Tranquil havens? Critiquing the idea of home as the middle-class sanctuary.' In *Domestic Space: Reading the Nineteenth-Century Interior.* Ed. Inga Bryden and Janet Floyd. Manchester: Manchester University Press, 1999, 103–20.

Doob, Penelope Reed. *The Idea of the Labyrinth from Classical Antiquity through the Middle Ages*. Ithaca, New York: Cornell University Press, 1990.

Driver, Felix and David Gilbert. 'Imperial cities: Overlapping territories, intertwined histories.' In *Imperial Cities: Landscape, Display and Identity*. Ed. Felix Driver and David Gilbert. Manchester: Manchester University Press, 1999, 1–17.

During, Simon. 'Postcolonialism and globalization.' *Cultural Studies* 14.3/4 (2000): 385–404.

Durrant, Sam. *Postcolonial Narrative and the Work of Mourning: J.M. Coetzee, Wilson Harris, and Toni Morrison*. Albany: State University of New York Press, 2004.

Emerson, Rupert. *From Empire to Nation: The Rise to Self-Assertion of Asian and African Peoples*. Cambridge, Massachusetts: Harvard University Press, 1960.

Erickson, John. *Islam and the Postcolonial Narrative*. Cambridge: Cambridge University Press, 1998.

———. 'Magical realism and nomadic writing in the Maghreb.' Genre Transformations and Narrative Ideologies. School of Oriental and African Studies, University of London. 8 Nov. 2002.

Ermarth, Elizabeth. *Realism and Consensus in the English Novel*. Princeton: Princeton University Press, 1983.

Fanon, Frantz. *Black Skin, White Masks*. 1952. Trans. Charles Lam Markmann. London: Pluto, 1986.

———. *The Wretched of the Earth*. Trans. Constance Farrington. New York: Grove Press, 1963.

Faris, Wendy. 'Cities and towns: The development of a collective voice.' *Proceedings of the Xth Congress of the International Comparative Literature Association*, New York, 1982. Ed. Anna Balakian and James J. Wilhelm. New York: Garland, 1985, 3–13.

Farrier, David. 'Gesturing towards the local: Intimate histories in *Anil's Ghost*.' *Journal of Postcolonial Writing* 41.1 (2005): 83–93.

Fife, W. 'Creating the moral body.' *Ethnology* 40.3 (2001): 251–69.

Flint, Holly. 'Toni Morrison's *Paradise*: Black cultural citizenship in the American empire.' *American Literature* 78.3 (2006): 585–612.

Foucault, Michel. *Discipline and Punish*. 1977. Trans. Alan Sherridan. London: Penguin, 1979.

———. 'Of other spaces.' Trans. Jay Miskoweic. *Diacritics* 16.1 (1986): 22–7.

Fox-Strangways, Giles Stephen Holland. *Chronicles of Holland House 1820–1900*. London: John Murray, 1937.

Frank, Joseph. 'Spatial form in modern literature.' *Sewanee Review* 53 (1945): 221–40, 433–56, 643–53.

Fredrickson, George M. *Black Liberation: A Comparative History of Black Ideologies in the United States and South Africa*. New York: Oxford University Press, 1995.

Freud, Sigmund. 'The "Uncanny".' Trans. Alix Strachey. In *Collected Papers: Volume Four: Papers on Metapsychology; Papers on Applied Psycho-Analysis*. Trans. Joan Riviere. London: Hogarth; Institute of Psycho-Analysis, 1925, 368–407. Rpt. in *The Standard Edition of the CompletePsychological Works of Sigmund Freud. Volume XVII (1917–1919): AnInfantile Neurosis and Other Works*. Ed. James Strachey. London: Vintage, 2001, 217–52.

Friedland, Roger and Deirdre Boden. 'NowHere: An introduction to space, time and modernity.' Introduction. *NowHere: Space, Time, and Modernity*. Ed. Roger Friedland and Deirdre Boden. Berkeley: University of California Press,1994, 1–60.

Fulton, Hamish. *Catalogue: Walking Journey*. London: Tate Britain, 2002.

———. *Exhibition Guide: Walking Journey*. London: Tate Britain, 2002.

Galvan, Fernando. 'Travel writing in British metafiction: A proposal for Analysis.' *Restant* 21 (1993): 77–87.

García Canclini, Néstor. *Hybrid Cultures: Strategies for Entering and Leaving Modernity*. Trans. Christopher Chiappari and Silvia Lopez. Minneapolis: University of Minnesota Press, 1995.

Garvey, Marcus. 'Speech, Liberty Hall, New York City, Second International Convention of Negroes, August 1921.' In *Philosophy and Opinions of Marcus*

Garvey, Volume One. New York: Universal Publishing House, 1923, 93–7. Rpt. in *Nationalism in Asia and Africa*. Ed. Elie Kedourie. London: Weidenfield and Nicolson, 1970, 283–7.

Gates, Henry Louis, Jr. 'Between the living and the unborn.' *New York Times* 28 June 1992, Section 7: 3.

Gbadamosi, Gabriel. 'The road to Brixton Market: A post-colonial travelogue.' In *Travel Writing and Empire*. Ed. Steve Clark. London: Zed, 1999, 185–94.

Gebauer, Gunter and Christopher Wulf. *Mimesis: Culture, Art, Society*. Trans. Don Reneau. Berkeley: University of California Press, 1995.

Gellner, Ernest. 'The coming of nationalism and its interpretation: The myths of nation and class.' *Storia d'Europa* (1993): 635–89. Rpt. in *Mapping the Nation*. Ed. Gopal Balakrishnan. London: Verso, 1996, 87–145.

George, R.M. *The Politics of Home: Postcolonial Relocations and Twentieth-Century Fiction*. Cambridge: Cambridge University Press, 1996.

Giddens, Anthony. *A Contemporary Critique of Historical Materialism: Volume Two, The Nation-State and Violence*. London: Polity, 1985.

Gikandi, Simon. *Maps of Englishness: Writing Identity in the Culture of Colonialism*. New York: Columbia University Press, 1996.

Gilbert, Helen. 'Introduction to pantomime'. In *Postcolonial Plays: An Anthology*. Ed. Helen Gilbert. London: Routledge, 2001. 128–9.

Gilkes, Michael. *Wilson Harris and the Caribbean Novel*. London: Longman, 1975.

Gilroy, Paul. *After Empire: Melancholia or Convivial Culture?* Oxford: Routledge, 2004.

———. *Between Camps: Nations, Cultures and the Allure of Race*. London: Allen Lane, 2000.

———. *The Black Atlantic: Modernity and Double Consciousness*. Cambridge, Massachusetts: Harvard Unversity Press, 1993.

———. *'There Ain't No Black in the Union Jack': The Cultural Politics of Race and Nation*. London: Hutchinson, 1987.

Glassie, Henry. *Folk Housing in Middle Virginia: A Structural Analysis of Historic Artifacts*. Knoxville: University of Tennessee Press, 1975.

Glissant, Édouard. *Poetics of Relation*. Trans. Betsy Wing. Ann Arbor: University of Michigan Press, 1997.

Gorra, Michael. 'The spirit who came to stay.' *New York Times* 10 October 1993, Section 7: 24.

Gregory, Derek. *The Colonial Present*. Oxford: Blackwell, 2004.

Grossberg, Lawrence. 'Space and globalization in cultural studies.' *The Post-Colonial Question: Common Skies, Divided Horizons*. Ed. Iain Chambers and Lidia Curti. London: Routledge, 1996, 169–88.

Grosz, Elizabeth. *Volatile Bodies: Toward a Corporeal Feminism*. Bloomington: Indiana University Press, 1994.

———. *Space, Time, and Perversion: Essays on the Politics of Bodies*. New York: Routledge, 1995.

Gruesser, John Cullen. *Confluences: Postcolonialism, African American Literary Studies, and the Black Atlantic.* Athens: University of Georgia Press, 2005.

Guibernau, Montserrat. *Nations Without States: Political Communities in a Global Age.* Cambridge: Polity, 1999.

Gurnah, Abdulrazak. *Paradise.* London: Hamish Hamilton, 1994.

Gutmann, Katharina. *Celebrating the Senses: An Analysis of the Sensual in Toni Morrison's Fiction.* Tübingen: Francke Verlag, 2000.

Habermas, Jürgen. 'The European nation state: Its achievements and its limitations. On the past and future of sovereignty and citizenship.' *Ratio Juris* 9.2 (1996): 125–37.

Hallward, Peter. *Absolutely Postcolonial: Writing Between the Singular and the Specific.* Manchester: Manchester University Press, 2001.

Hansen Thomas Blom, and Finn Stepputat. 'Introduction.' In *Sovereign Bodies: Citizens, Migrants and States in the Postcolonial World.* Ed. Thomas Blom Hansen and Finn Stepputat. Princeton: Princeton University Press, 2005. 1–38.

Haraway, Donna J. *Simians, Cyborgs and Women: the Reinvention of Nature.* London: Free Association, 1991.

Hardt, Michael, and Antonio Negri. *Empire.* Cambridge, Massachusetts: Harvard University Press, 2000.

Harris, Wilson. 'The absent presence: The Caribbean, Central and South America.' In *The Radical Imagination: Lectures and Talks: Wilson Harris.* Ed. Alan Riach and Mark Williams. Liège: Liège Language and Literature, 1992. 81–92.

———. *Ascent to Omai.* London: Faber, 1970.

———. 'Author's Note.' *The Palace of the Peacock.* London and Boston: Faber, 1988, 7–11.

———. *Black Marsden: A Tabula Rasa Comedy.* London: Faber, 1972.

———. *The Carnival Trilogy.* 1985–1990. London: Faber, 1993.

———. 'The composition of reality: A talk with Wilson Harris (interview with Vera Kutzinski).' *Callaloo* 18.1 (1995): 15–32.

———. *The Dark Jester.* London: Faber, 2001.

———. *Da Silva da Silva's Cultivated Wilderness. Da Silva da Silva's Cultivated Wilderness and Genesis of the Clowns.* London: Faber, 1977, 3–77.

———. 'The enigma of values.' *New Letters* 40 (1973): 141–9.

———. 'The frontier on which *Heart of Darkness* stands.' *Research in African Literatures* 12.1 (1981): 86–93.

———. *Genesis of the Clowns. Da Silva da Silva's Cultivated Wilderness and Genesis of the Clowns.* London: Faber, 1977, 79–148.

———. *The Guyana Quartet (The Palace of the Peacock, The Far Journey of Oudin, The Whole Armour, The Secret Ladder).* 1960–1963. London: Faber, 1985.

———. *Heartland.* London: Faber, 1964.

———. 'History, fable and myth in the Caribbean and Guianas.' In *History, Fable and Myth in the Caribbean and Guianas.* Rev. ed. Ed. Selwyn R. Cudjoe. Ithaca: Calaloux, 1995, 13–50. Rpt. in Bundy 152–66.

————. 'Interior of the novel: Amerindian/European/African relations.' In *National Identity: Papers Delivered at the Commonwealth Literature Conference, University of Queensland, Brisbane, 9–15th August, 1968*. Ed. K.L. Goodwin. London: Heinemann, 1970, 138–47.

————. 'Interview with Alan Riach.' In *The Radical Imagination: Lectures and Talks: Wilson Harris*. Ed. Alan Riach and Mark Williams. Liège: Liège Language and Literature, 1992, 33–65.

———— 'Introduction. *The Carnival Trilogy*. London: Faber, 1993, vii–xix.

————. *Jonestown*. London: Faber, 1996.

————. 'Keynote address.' British Braids Conference. Brunel University, London. 19 Mar. 2001.

————. 'Literacy and the imagination.' In *The Literate Imagination: Essays on the Novels of Wilson Harris*. Ed. Michael Gilkes. London: Macmillan, 1989, 13–30.

————. 'Merlin and Parsifal: Adversarial twins.' Address. Temenos Academy. March 1997. Rpt. in Bundy 58–66.

————. 'New preface to *Palace of the Peacock*.' 'Preface.' *The Palace of the Peacock*. 1960. London: Faber, 1998, 7–12. Rpt. in Bundy 53–7.

————. 'Profiles of myth and New World.' In *Nationalism vs. Internationalism, (Inter) national Dimensions of Literatures in English*. Ed. W. Zach and K.L. Goodwin. Tübingen: Stauffenburg, 1996, 77–86. Rpt. in Bundy 201–11.

————. 'Quetzalcoatl and the smoking mirror: Reflections on originality and tradition.' Address. Temenos Academy. 7 Febrary 1994. Rpt. in Bundy 184–95.

————. 'Tradition and the West Indian Novel.' West Indian's Student Union, 1964, 7–17. Rpt. in *Tradition, the Writer and Society*. London: New Beacon, 1967, 28–47.

Harris, Wilson, and Daniel, Maximin. 'Third dialogue: The power of the word in space and place.' In *The Power of the Word: The Cambridge Colloquia*. Ed. T.J. Cribb. Amsterdam: Rodopi, 2006, 35–53.

Harvey, David. *Spaces of Hope*. Edinburgh: Edinburgh University Press, 2000.

Hattersley, Roy. 'A man in two minds.' *Guardian Unlimited* 21 Aug 1999: 5. <http://www.guardianunlimited.co.uk/Archive/Article/0,4273,3894279,00. html> (29 June 2001).

Heckman, Susan. 'Material bodies.' *Body and Flesh: A Philosophical Reader.* Ed. Don Welton. Cambridge, Massachusetts: Blackwell, 1998, 61–70.

Hedrick, Joan, ed. *The Oxford Harriet Beecher Stowe Reader*. New York: Oxford University Press, 1999.

Heller, Zoe. 'Feathered wombs.' Review of *Paradise*, by Toni Morrison. *London Review of Books* 7 May 1998: 25.

Henderson, Mae G. 'Toni Morrison's *Beloved*: Re-membering the body as historical text.' In *Comparative American Identities*. Ed. Hortense J. Spillers. London: Routledge, 1991, 62–86.

Henry, Andrea. 'More magic than realism.' *The Independent* 29 August 1998: 15.

Hix, John. *The Glass House*. London: Phaidon, 1974.

Hobsbawm, Eric. 'Inventing traditions.' In *The Invention of Tradition*. Ed. Eric Hobsbawm and Terence Ranger. Cambridge: Cambridge University Press, 1983, 1–14.

———. *Nations and Nationalism Since 1780: Programme, Myth, Reality*. 2nd ed. Cambridge: Cambridge University Press, 1992.

Home, Robert. 'Transferring British planning law to the colonies: The case of the 1938 Trinidad town and regional planning ordinance.' *Third World Planning Review* 15.4 (1993): 397–410.

hooks, bell. *Art on My Mind: Visual Politics*. New York: New Press, 1995.

———. *Killing Rage: Ending Racism*. London: Penguin, 1995.

———. *Yearning: Race, Gender and Cultural Politics*. Boston: South End, 1990.

Huggan, Graham. 'Counter-travel writing and postcoloniality.' In *Being/s in Transit: Travelling, Migration, Dislocation*. Ed. Liselotte Glage. Amsterdam: Rodopi, 2000. 37–59.

Hulme, Keri. *The Bone People*. 1985. London: Picador, 1986.

Irigaray, Luce. *Speculum of the Other Woman*. Trans. Gillian C. Gill. Ithaca: Cornell University Press, 1985.

Islam, Syed Manzurul. *The Ethics of Travel: From Marco Polo to Kafka*. Manchester: Manchester University Press, 1996.

Jacobs, Jane M. *Edge of Empire: Postcolonialism and the City*. London: Routledge, 1996.

Jakobson, Roman. 'Two aspects of language and two types of aphasic disturbances.' In *Language in Literature*. Ed. Krystyna Pomorkska and Stephen Rudy. Cambridge, Massachusetts: Belknap-Harvard University Press, 1987, 95–114.

Jamieson, Ross W. *Domestic Architecture and Power. The Historical Archaeology of Colonial Ecuador*. New York: Kluwer Academic; London: Plenum, 2000.

Jesser, Nancy. 'Violence, home and community in Toni Morrison's *Beloved*.' *African American Review* 33.2 (1999): 325–45.

Johnson, Kerry L. 'From muse to majesty: Rape, landscape and agency in the early novels of Wilson Harris.' *WLWE: World Literature Written in English* 35.2 (1996): 71–89.

———. 'Translations of gender, pain and space: Wilson Harris's *The Carnival Trilogy*.' *Modern Fiction Studies* 44.1 (1998): 123–43.

Jonas, Joyce. *Anancy in the Great House: Ways of Reading West Indian Fiction*. New York: Greenwood, 1990.

Kanaganayakam, Chelva. 'In defense of *Anil's Ghost*.' *Ariel* 37.1 (2006): 5–26.

Kant, Immanuel. *Critique of Pure Reason*. 1781. Trans. Werner S. Pluhar. Indianapolis: Hackett, 1996.

Kaplan, Caren. 'Deterritorializations: The rewriting of home and exile in Western feminist discourse.' *Cultural Critique* 6 (1987): 187–98.

———. *Questions of Travel: Postmodern Discourses of Displacement*. Durham: Duke University Press, 1996.

Kaviraj, Sudipta. 'The imaginary institution of India.' In *Subaltern Studies VII: Writings on South Asian History and Society*. Ed. Partha Chatterjee and Gyanendra Pandey. Delhi: Oxford University Press, 1993, 1–39.

Kedourie, Elie. *Nationalism*. 4th Rev. ed. Oxford: Blackwell, 1993.

———, ed. *Nationalism in Asia and Africa*. London: Weidenfield and Nicolson,1971.

Keenan, Sally. '"Four hundred years of silence": Myth, history and motherhood in Toni Morrison's *Beloved*.' In *Recasting the World: Writing After Colonialism*. Ed. Jonathan White. Baltimore: Johns Hopkins University Press, 1993, 45–81.

Keith, Michael. 'Ethnic entrepreneurs and street rebels.' In *Mapping the Subject: Geographies of Cultural Transformation*. Ed. Steve Pile and Nigel Thrift. London: Routledge, 1995, 355–70.

Keown, Michelle. *Postcolonial Pacific Writing: Representations of the Body*. London: Routledge, 2005.

Kern, Stephen. *The Culture of Time and Space: 1880–1918*. London: Weidenfeld and Nicolson, 1983.

Khilnani, Sunil. *The Idea of India*. London: Hamish Hamilton, 1997.

King, Anthony. *Global Cities: Post-Imperialism and the Internationalization of London*. London: Routledge, 1990.

King, Bruce. *The New English Literatures: Cultural Nationalism in a Changing World*. London: Macmillan, 1980.

King-Aribisala, Karen. *Kicking Tongues*. Oxford: Heinemann, 1998.

Korosec-Serfaty, Perla. 'Experience and use of the dwelling.' In *Home Environments*. Ed. Irwin Altman and Carol M. Werner. New York: Plenum, 1985, 65–86.

Krishwasnamy, Revathi. 'Mythologies of migrancy: Postcolonialism, post-modernism and the politics of (dis) location.' *Ariel* 26.1 (1995): 125–46.

Kristeva, Julia. *Powers of Horror: An Essay on Abjection*. Trans. Leon S. Roudiez. New York: Columbia University Press, 1982.

———. *Revolution in Poetic Language*. Trans. Margaret Waller. New York: Columbia University Press, 1984.

Kumar, Akshaya. 'Arundhati Roy's creative dynamics: Prettifying the small'. In *The Fictional World of Arundhati Roy*. Ed. R.S. Pathak. New Dehli: Creation, 2001, 60–69.

Lane, Richard. *The Postcolonial Novel*. London: Polity, 2006.

Ledbetter, T. Mark. 'An apocalypse of race and gender: Body violence and forming identity in Toni Morrison's *Beloved*.' In *Postmodernism, Literature and the Future of Theology*. Ed. David Jasper. Basingstoke: Macmillan, 1993, 78–90.

Lefebvre, Henri. *The Production of Space*. Trans. Donald Nicholson-Smith. Oxford: Basil Blackwell, 1991.

———. *Writings on Cities*. Trans. Eleonore Kofman and Elizabeth Lebas. Oxford: Blackwell, 1996.

Legg, Stephen. 'Beyond the European province: Foucault and postcolonialism.' In *Space, Knowledge and Power: Foucault and Geography*. Ed. Jeremy W. Crampton and Stuart Elden. Aldershot: Ashgate, 2007, 265–90.

Leonard, Philip. *Nationality Between Poststructuralism and Postcolonial Theory: A New Cosmopolitanism*. Basingstoke: Palgrave Macmillan, 2005.

Lessing, Gotthold Ephraim. *Laocoön: a Essay on the Limits of Painting and Poetry.* Trans. Edward Allen McCormick. Baltimore: John Hopkins University Press, 1984.

Lewis, Gordon K. *'Gather With the Saints at the River': The Jonestown Guyana Holocaust 1978: A Descriptive and Interpretive essay on ist Ultimate Meaning From a Caribbean Perspective.* Rio Piedras: Institute of Caribbean Studies, University of Puerto Rico, 1979.

Li, Victor. 'Towards articulation: Postcolonial theory and demotic resistance.' Rpt. in *Linked Histories: Postcolonial Studies in a Globalized World.* Ed. Pamela McCallum and Wendy Faith. Alberta: University of Calgary Press, 2005, 209–28.

Loomba, Ania, ed. *Postcolonial Studies and Beyond.* Durham: Duke University Press, 2005.

Lorenz, Edward N. *The Essence of Chaos.* London: UCL Press, 1993.

Lynch, Kevin. *The Image of the City.* Cambridge, Massachusetts: MIT; Harvard University Press, 1960.

Lyotard, Jean François. *The Postmodern Condition.* Trans. Geoff Bennington and Brian Massumi. Minneapolis: University of Minnesota Press, 1984.

McClintock, Anne. *Imperial Leather: Race, Gender and Sexuality in the Colonial Contest.* New York: Routledge, 1995.

Mackey, Nathaniel. *Discrepant Engagement: Dissonance, Cross-Culturality, and Experimental Writing.* Cambridge: Cambridge University Press, 1993.

McLaughlin, Joseph. *Writing the Urban Jungle: Reading Empire in London from Doyle to Eliot.* Charlottesville: University Press of Virginia, 2000.

McLaughlin, Eugene and John Muncie. 'Walled cities: Surveillance, regulation and segregation.' In *Unruly Cities?: Order/Disorder.* Ed. Steve Pile, Christopher Brook and Gerry Mooney. London: Routledge, 1999, 103–48.

McPherson, James. *Battle Cry of Freedom: The American Civil War.* London: Penguin, 1990.

Manley, Robert H. *Guyana Emergent: The Post-Independence Struggle for Nondependent Development.* Boston, Massachusetts: G.K. Hall, 1979.

Marc, Oliver. *Psychology of the House.* Trans. Jessie Wood. London: Thames and Hudson, 1977.

Marcus, Sharon. *Apartment Stories: City and Home in Nineteenth-Century Paris and London.* Berkeley: University of California Press, 1999.

Marcuse, Peter. 'Not chaos, but walls: Postmodernism and the partitioned city.' In *Postmodern Cities and Spaces.* Ed. Sophie Watson and Katherine Gibson. Cambridge, Massachusetts: Blackwell, 1995. 243–53.

Marechera, Dambudzo. *The House of Hunger.* Oxford: Heinemann, 1978.

Marquez, Gabriel Garcia. *One Hundred Years of Solitude*. 1967. Trans. Gregory Rabassa. London: Penguin, 1972.

Marzec, Robert P. *An Ecological and Postcolonial Study of Literature: From Daniel Defoe to Salman Rushdie*. Basingstoke: Pagrave Macmillan, 2007.

Massey, Doreen. *For Space*. London: Sage, 2005.

Massumi, Brian. 'Translator's foreword.' In Gilles Deleuze and Felix Guattari, *A Thousand Plateaus*. Trans. Brian Massumi. London: Athlone, 1988, ix–xv.

Mbembe, Achille. 'At the edge of the world: Boundaries, territoriality, and sovereignty in Africa.' *Public Culture* 12.1 (2000): 259–84.

———. 'Necropolitics.' *Public Culture* 15.1 (2003): 11–40.

———. *On the Postcolony*. Berkeley: University of California Press, 2001.

———. 'Sovereignty as a form of expenditure.' In *Sovereign Bodies: Citizens, Migrants and States in the Postcolonial World*. Ed. Thomas Blom Hansen and Finn Stepputat. Princeton: Princeton University Press, 2005. 148–68.

Meek, C.K. *Land Law and Custom in the Colonies*. 1946. 2nd ed. London: Oxford University Press, 1949.

Meiksins Wood, Ellen. *Empire of Capital*. London: Verso, 2003.

Melville, Pauline. *Shape-shifter*. London: The Women's Press, 1990.

Merivale, Patricia. 'Saleem fathered by Oskar: *Midnight's Children*, magic realism, and *The Tin Drum*.' In *Magical Realism: Theory, History, Community*. Ed. Lois Parkinson Zamora and Wendy Faris. Durham: Duke University Press, 1995. 329–46.

Merleau-Ponty, Maurice. *Phenomenology of Perception*. Trans. Colin Smith. London: Routledge, 1962.

Michael, Magali Cornier. *New Visions of Community in Contemporary American Fiction*. Iowa City: University of Iowa Press, 2006.

Miller, J. Hillis. 'Ariadne's thread: Repetition and the narrative line.' *Critical Inquiry* 2.1 (1976): 57–77.

Mills, Sara. *Gender and Colonial Space*. Manchester: Manchester University Press, 2005.

Minh-ha, Trinh T. 'Cotton and iron.' In *Out There: Marginalization and Contemporary Cultures*. Ed. Russell Ferguson et al. Cambridge, Massachusetts: MIT; New York: New Museum of Contemporary Art., 1990, 327–36.

Moore-Gilbert, Bart. *Postcolonial Theory: Contexts, Practices, Politics*. London: Verso, 1997.

More, Thomas. *Utopia*. 1516. London: Dent, 1974.

Morris, William. *News From Nowhere and Other Writings*. Ed. C. Wilmer. London: Penguin, 1993.

Morrison, Toni. *Beloved*. 1987. London: Vintage, 1997.

———. 'Black matter(s).' *Grand Street* 10 (1991): 205–25. Rpt. in *Falling Into Theory: Conflicting Views on Reading Literature*. 2nd ed. Ed. David H. Richter. Boston: Bedford/St. Martin's, 2000. 310–22.

———. *The Bluest Eye*. 1970. London: Triad-Grafton, 1981.

———. Interview (unpublished). University of East Anglia. 6 Dec. 2003.

———. 'Interview.' In Louisa Joyner, *Toni Morrison: The Essential Guide*. London: Vintage, 2003, 11–19.

———. *Jazz*. 1992. London: Picador, 1993.

———. *Love*. London: Chatto and Windus, 2003.

———. 'The opening sentences of *Beloved*.' In *Critical Essays on Toni Morrison's Beloved*. Ed. Barbara Solomon. New York: G.K. Hall and Co, 1998, 91–2.

———. *Paradise*. 1997. London: Vintage, 1999.

———. *Playing in the Dark: Whiteness and the Literary Imagination*. 1992. London: Picador, 1993.

———. *Song of Solomon*. 1977. London: Triad-Panther, 1980.

———. *Sula*. 1980. Great Britain: Triad-Granada, 1982.

———. *Tar Baby*. 1981. London: Vintage, 1997.

———. 'Unspeakable things unspoken: The Afro-American presence in American Literature.' The Tanner Lecture on Human Values. University of Michigan. 7 Oct. 1988. *Michigan Quarterly Review* 28 (1989): 1–34. Rpt. in *Within the Circle: An Anthology of African American Literary Criticism from the Harlem Renaissance to the Present*. Ed. Angelyn Mitchell. Durham: Duke University Press, 1994, 368–98.

Mumford, Lewis. *The City in History*. 1961. Harmondsworth: Penguin, 1966.

———. *The Story of Utopias: Ideal Commonwealths and Social Myths*. London: G. Harrap, 1923.

Münkler, Herfried. *Empires*. Cambridge: Polity, 2007.

Nafisi, Azar. *Reading Lolita in Tehran: A Memoir in Books*. London: I.B. Tauris, 2003.

Naipaul, V.S. *The Enigma of Arrival*. 1987. New York: Vintage, 1988.

———. *The Loss of El Dorado: A History*. 1969. Harmondsworth: Penguin, 1973.

Najita, Susan Y. *Decolonizing Cultures in the Pacific: Reading History and Trauma in Contemporary Fiction*. New York: Routledge, 2006.

Nandy, Ashis. *Creating a Nationality: The Ramjanmabhumi Movement and Fear of the Self*. 1995. Rpt. in *Exiled at Home*. Dehli: Oxford University Press, 1998.

———. *The Intimate Enemy: Loss and Recovery of the Self Under Colonialism*. 1983. Rpt. in *Exiled at Home*. Dehli: Oxford University Press, 1998.

Nederveen Pieterse, Jan and Bhikhu Parekh. 'Shifting imaginaries: Decolonization, internal decolonization, postcoloniality.' In *The Decolonization of the Imagination: Culture, Knowledge and Power*. Ed. Jan Nederveen Pieterse and Bhikhu Parekh. London: Zed, 1995. 1–19.

Needham, Anuradha Dingwaney. *Using the Master's Tools: Resistance and the Literature of the African and South-Asian Diasporas*. Basingstoke: Macmillan, 2000.

Neff, Donald, et al. 'Nightmare in Jonestown.' *Time* 4 Dec. 1978: 6–11.

Newman, Robert. *The Fountain as the Centre of the World*. London: Verso, 2003.

Nichols, Grace. 'Hurricane hits England.' *Sunris*. London: Virago, 1996, 25.

Nixon, Robert. *London Calling: V.S. Naipaul: Postcolonial Mandarin*. New York: Oxford University Press, 1992.

Noble, Denise. 'Remembering bodies, healing histories: The emotional politics of everyday freedom.' In *Making Race Matter: Bodies, Space and Identity*. Ed. Claire Alexander and Caroline Knowles. Basingstoke: Palgrave Macmillan, 2005, 132–52.

Noyes, J.K. *Colonial Space: Spatiality in the Discourse of German South West Africa 1884–1915*. Chur: Harwood, 1992.

Okri, Ben. *The Famished Road*. 1991. London: Vintage, 1992.

———. *Infinite Riches*. London: Orion, 1999.

———. *Songs of Enchantment*. London: Jonathan Cape, 1993.

Ondaatje, Michael. *Anil's Ghost*. London: Picador-Pan Macmillan, 2000.

———. *Running in the Family*. 1983. London: Picador, 1984.

Ophir, Adi. *Plato's Invisible Cities: Discourse and Power in The Republic*. London: Routledge, 1991.

Osella, Fillipo and Osella, Caroline. *Social Mobility in Kerala: Modernity and Identity in Conflict*. London: Pluto Press, 2000.

Palmer, Phyllis. *Domesticity and Dirt: Housewives and Domestic Servants in the United States, 1920–1945*. Philadelphia: Temple University Press, 1989.

Paquet-Deyris, Anne-Marie. 'Toni Morrison's Jazz and the city.' *African American Review*. 35 (2001): 219–31.

'*Paradise*: Customer reviews.' *Amazon.com*. 20 Jan 2004 <http://www.amazon.com/exec/obidos/tg/detail/-/0452280397/ref=cm_cr_dp_2_1/002-6638068-6019259?v=glance&s=books&vi=customer-reviews>.

Park, You-me, and Schwarz, Henry. 'Extending American hegemony: Beyond empire.' *Interventions* 7.2 (2005): 153–61.

Parry, Benita. *Postcolonial Studies: A Materialist Critique*. London: Routledge, 2004.

Pelton, Robert D. *The Trickster in West Africa: A Study of Mythic Irony and Sacred Delight*. Berkeley: University of California Press, 1980.

Peterson, Carla L. 'Eccentric bodies.' Foreword. In *Recovering the Black Female Body. Self-Representations by African American Women*. Ed. Michael Bennett and Vanessa D. Dickerson. New Brunswick, New Jersey: Rutgers University Press, 2001, ix–xvi.

Petras, James, and Henry Veltmeyer. *Empire With Imperialism: The Globalizing Dynamics of Neo-Liberal Capitalism*. London: Zed, 2005.

Phillips, John. 'Lagging behind: Bhabha, post-colonial theory and the future.' In *Travel Writing and Empire*. Ed. Steve Clark. London: Zed, 1999. 63–80.

Pile, Steve. 'The heterogeneity of cities.' In *Unruly Cities?: Order/Disorder*. Ed. Steve Pile, Christopher Brook and Gerry Mooney. London: Routledge, 1999, 7–52.

Pile, Steve and Nigel Thrift, ed. *Mapping the Subject: Geographies of Cultural Transformation*. London: Routledge, 1995.

Pitt-Ketley, Fiona. 'Encounters with corpses that refuse to lie down.' *Daily Telegraph.* 22 August 1998: 4.

Plato. *The Republic.* Trans. H.D.P. Lee. Harmondsworth: Penguin, 1955.

———. *The Timaeus. Plato's Cosmology: The Timaeus of Plato Translated with a Running Commentary.* Ed. Francis MacDonald Cornford. London: Kegan Paul, 1937, 9–359.

Poole, Adrian. 'Introduction.' In Charles Dickens, *Our Mutual Friend.* London: Penguin, 1997, ix–xxiv.

Pordzik, Ralph. *The Quest for Postcolonial Utopia: A Comparative Introduction to the Utopian Novel in the New English Literatures.* New York: Peter Lang, 2001.

Powell, Timothy. 'Postcolonial theory in an American context: A reading of Martin Delany's *Blake.*' In *The Pre-Occupation of Postcolonial Studies.* Ed. Fawzia Afzal-Khan, and Kalpana Seshadri-Crooks. Durham: Duke University Press, 2000. 347–65.

Poynting, Jeremy. 'Half dialectical, half metaphysical: "The Far Journey of Oudin".' In *The Literate Imagination: Essays on the Novels of Wilson Harris.* Ed. Michael Gilkes. London: Macmillan, 1989, 103–28.

Prabhu, Anjali. *Hybridity: Limits, Transformations, Prospects.* New York: State University of New York Press, 2007.

Pratt, Mary Louise. *Imperial Eyes: Travel Writing and Transculturation.* London: Routledge, 1992.

Premdas, Ralph R. *Ethnic Conflict and Development: The Case of Guyana.* Aldershot: Avebury, 1995.

Procter, James. *Dwelling Places: Postwar Black British Writing.* Manchester: Manchester University Press, 2003.

Puri, Jyoti. *Woman, Body, Desire in Post-colonial India. Narratives of Gender and Sexuality.* London: Routledge, 1999.

Rauf, Mohammed A. *Indian Village in Guyana: a Study of Cultural Change and Ethnic Identity.* Leiden: E.J. Brill, 1974.

Ray, Sangeeta. *En-Gendering India: Woman and Nation in Colonial and Postcolonial Narratives.* Durham: Duke University Press, 2000.

Read, Anthony and David Fisher. *The Proudest Day: India's Long Road to Independence.* London: Jonathan Cape, 1997.

Reicher, Stephen and Nick Hopkins. *Self and Nation: Categorization, Contestation, and Mobilization.* London: Sage, 2001.

Rhys, Jean. *Wide Sargasso Sea.* Harmondsworth: Penguin, 1966.

'Rise in race hate crime reports.' *BBC.co.uk.* 6 Feb 2003. BBC. 14 May 2003 <http://news.bbc.co.uk/1/hi/uk/2731139.stm>.

Robinson, David. 'African apocalypse.' *Sunday Telegraph.* 21 March 1993: 10.

Rodriguez, Richard. 'Complexion.' In *Out There: Marginalization and Contemporary Cultures.* Ed. Russell Ferguson et al. Cambridge, Massachusetts: MIT; New York: New Museum of Contemporary Art, 1990. 265–78.

Rooney, Eilish. 'Learning to remember and remembering to forget: *Beloved* from Belfast.' *Devolving Identities: Feminist Readings in Home and Belonging.* Ed. Lynne Pearce. Aldershot: Ashgate, 2000. 215–34.

Roy, Arundhati. 'Interview with Arundhati Roy, 15/6/97' <http://curiousgeorge. wordsworth.com/www/epresent/royint/> (01/08/2002).

———. *The God of Small Things.* 1997. Flamingo-Harper Collins, 1998.

Roy, Srirupa. *Beyond Belief: India and the Politics of Postcolonial Nationalism.* Durham: Duke University Press, 2007.

Rushdie, Salman. 'Angels and devils are becoming confused ideas.' Interview with Sali Tripathi and Dina Vakil. *Indian Post* 13 Sept.1987. Rpt. in *Conversations with Salman Rushdie.* Ed. Michael R. Reder. Jackson: University Press of Mississippi, 2000, 79–86.

———. *Fury.* London: Jonathan Cape, 2001.

———. *The Ground Beneath Her Feet.* 1999. London: Vintage, 2000.

———. 'India's fiftieth anniversary.' 1997. *Step Across This Line: Collected Non-Fiction 1992–2002.* London: Jonathan Cape, 2002. 174–9.

———. 'Interview with David Brooks.' *Helix* 19/20 (1984): 55–69. Rpt. in *Conversations with Salman Rushdie.* Ed. Michael R. Reder. Jackson: University Press of Mississippi, 2000, 57–71.

———. 'Interview with John Banville.' *The New York Review of Books* 4 Mar. 1993: 34–36. Rpt. in *Conversations with Salman Rushdie.* Ed. Michael R. Reder. Jackson: University Press of Mississippi, 2000, 152–61.

———. 'Interview with John Haffenden.' In *Novelists in Interview.* Ed. John Haffenden. London: Methuen, 1985, 231–61. Rpt. in *Conversations with Salman Rushdie.* Ed. Michael R. Reder. Jackson: University Press of Mississippi, 2000, 30–56.

———. *The Jaguar Smile: A Nicaraguan Journey.* London: Picador, 1987.

———. *Midnight's Children.* 1981. London: Picador, 1982.

———. *The Moor's Last Sigh.* London: Jonathan Cape, 1995.

———. 'The new empire within Britain.' 1982. *Imaginary Homelands.* London: Granta-Penguin, 1992, 129–38.

———. 'Notes on Writing and the Nation.' *Index on Censorship.* 1997. *Step Across This Line: Collected Non-Fiction 1992–2002.* London: Jonathan Cape, 2002, 64–8.

———. 'Pakistan.' 1999. *Step Across This Line: Collected Non-Fiction 1992–2002.* London: Jonathan Cape, 2002. 320–22.

———. *The Satanic Verses.* 1988. London: Vintage, 1998.

———. *Shalimar the Clown.* London: Jonathan Cape, 2005.

———. *Shame.* London: Picador, 1983.

Said, Edward. *Culture and Imperialism.* New York: Alfred A. Knopf, 1993.

———. *Orientalism.* 1978. London: Penguin, 2003.

Sallis, John. *Chorology: On Beginning in Plato's Timaeus.* Bloomington: Indiana University Press, 1999.

'Salman Rushdie and The Ground Beneath His Feet.' *Arena*. Dir. Kathleen Dickson. BBC Television. 22 Mar. 1999.

Salman, Sherry. 'The creative psyche: Jung's major contributions.' In *The Cambridge Companion to Jung*. Ed. Polly Young-Eisendrath and Terence Dawson. Cambridge: Cambridge University Press, 1997, 52–70.

Schmudde, Carol. 'The haunting of 124.' *African American Review* 26.3 (1992): 409–16.

Schröder, Nicole. *Spaces and Places in Motion: Spatial Concepts in Contemporary American Literature*. Tübingen: Gunter Warr Verlag. 2006.

Schwarz, Bill. 'Afterword. Postcolonial times: The visible and the invisible.' In *Imperial Cities: Landscape, Display and Identity*. Ed. Felix Driver and David Gilbert. Manchester: Manchester University Press, 1999, 268–72.

Segal, Ronald. *The Black Diaspora: Five Centuries of the Black Experience Outside Africa*. New York: Noonday, 1995.

Sennett, Richard. *The Conscience of the Eye: The Design and Social Life of Cities*. New York: Knopf, 1990.

Shohat, Ella. 'Notes on the "Post-Colonial".' In *The Pre-Occupation of Postcolonial Studies*. Ed. Fawzia Afzal-Khan, and Kalpana Seshadri-Crooks. Durham: Duke University Press, 2000, 126–39.

Simpson, J.A. and E.S.C. Weiner. *Oxford English Dictionary*. 2nd ed. Oxford: Clarendon, 1986.

Sinclair, Iain. *Downriver*. 1991. London: Granta, 2002.

———. *Lights Out for the Territory*. London: Granta, 1998.

———. *London Orbital: a Walk Around the M25*. London: Penguin, 2002.

———. 'London's orbital motorway.' George Orwell Memorial Lecture. Senate House, University of London.\, Feb. 2002.

———. *Lud Heat*. 1975. London: Vintage, 1995.

Singh, Vijay. *Whirlpool of Shadows*. London: Jonathan Cape, 1992.

Slemon, Stephen. 'Magic realism as postcolonial discourse.' In *Magical Realism: Theory, History, Community*. Ed. Lois Parkinson Zamora and Wendy Faris. Durham: Duke University Press, 1995, 407–26.

Smith, Anthony D. 'Ethnic nationalism and the plight of minorities.' *Journal of Refugee Studies* 7.2/3 (1994): 186–98.

———. *National Identity*. London: Penguin, 1991.

Smith, Neil and Anne Godlewska. 'Introduction: Critical histories of geography.' In *Geography and Empire*. Ed. Anne Godlewska and Neil Smith. Oxford: Blackwell, 1994, 1–12.

Soja, Edward. *Postmetropolis: Critical Studies of Cities and Regions*. Oxford: Blackwell, 2000.

———. *Postmodern Geographies: The Reassertion of Space in Critical Social Theory*. London: Verso, 1989.

———. *Thirdspace*. Oxford: Blackwell, 1996.

Spivak, Gayatri Chakravorty. *A Critique of Postcolonial Reason: Toward a History of the Vanishing Present*. Cambridge, Massachusetts: Harvard University Press, 1999.

Stallybrass, Peter and Allon White. *The Politics and Poetics of Transgression.* London: Methuen, 1986.

Steele, Richard, with Tony Fuller and Timothy Nater. 'Life in Jonestown.' *Newsweek* 4 Dec. 1978: 33–9.

Stevens, Quentin. *The Ludic City: Exploring the Potential of Public Spaces.* London: Routledge, 2007.

Stewart, Susan. *On Longing. Narratives of the Miniature, the Gigantic, the Souvenir, the Collection.* 1984. Durham: Duke University Press, 1993.

Stowe, Harriet Beecher. 'What is a home?' *House and Home Papers.* Boston: Tickner and Fields, 1865, 55–64. Rpt. in *The Oxford Harriet Beecher Stowe Reader.* Ed. Joan Hedrick. New York: Oxford University Press, 1999, 488–94.

Stuart, Paul. *Nations Within a Nation: Historical Statistics of American Indians.* Westport, Connecticut: Greenwood, 1987.

Synnott, Anthony and David Howes. 'From measurement to meaning: Anthropologies of the body.' *Anthropos* 87 (1992): 147–66.

Syrotinski, Michael. *Deconstruction and the Postcolonial: At the Limits of Theory.* Liverpool: Liverpool University Press, 2007.

Szeman, Imre. *Zones of Instability: Literature, Postcolonialism, and the Nation.* Baltimore: John Hopkins University Press, 2003.

Temple Wright, R. *Baker and Cook – A Domestic Manual for India.* 1896. 3rd ed. Calcutta: Thacker, Spink and Co, 1912.

Teverson, Andrew. *Salman Rushdie.* Manchester: Manchester University Press, 2007.

Traylor, Eleanor. 'The fabulous world of Toni Morrison: *Tar Baby.*' In *Critical Essays on Toni Morrison.* Ed. Nellie McKay. Boston, Massachusetts: G.K. Hall, 1988, 135–50.

Uprety, Sanjeev Kumor. 'Disability and postcoloniality in Salman Rushdie's *Midnight's Children* and third-world novels.' In *The Disabilities Studies Reader.* Ed. Lennard J. Davis. New York: Routledge, 1997, 366–81.

Vassanji, M.G. *The Book of Secrets.* 1994. Basingstoke: Macmillan, 1995.

Venn, Couze. *The Postcolonial Challenge: Towards Alternative Worlds.* London: Sage, 2006.

Verdery, Katherine. 'Whither "nation" and "nationalism".' *Daedalus* 122 (1993): 37–46.

Walcott, Derek. *Pantomime. Remembrance and Pantomime: Two Plays.* New York: Farrar, Straus and Giroux, 1980, 89–170.

Wallace, Jo-Ann. '"A Class Apart": Josephine Butler and regulated prostitution in British India, 1888–1893.' In *The Body in the Library.* Ed. Leigh Dale and Simon Ryan. Amsterdam: Rodopi, 1998, 73–86.

Washington, George. 'Circular to state governments, June 1783.' In *George Washington: Uniting a Nation.* Ed. Don Higginbotham. Lanham: Rowman and Littlefield, 2002, 115–27.

———. 'Farewell address, September 19, 1796.' In *George Washington: Uniting a Nation.* Ed. Don Higginbotham. Lanham: Rowman and Littlefield, 2002, 137–55.

Waters, Sarah. *Tipping the Velvet*. London: Virago, 1998.

Webster, Wendy. *Imagining Home: Gender, Race and National Identity, 1945–64*. London: UCL, 1998.

Weiss, Gail. *Body Images: Embodiment as Corporeality*. New York: Routledge, 1999.

Westwood, Sallie and Annie Phizacklea. *Trans-Nationalism and the Politics of Belonging*. London: Routledge, 2000.

Williams, Brackette F. *Stains on My Name, War in My Veins: Guyana and the Politics of Cultural Struggle*. Durham: Duke University Press, 1991.

Williams, Charlotte. '"I going away, I going home": Mixed-"race", movement and identity.' In *Devolving Identities: Feminist Readings in Home and Belonging*. Ed. Lynne Pearce. Aldershot: Ashgate, 2000, 179–95.

Williams, Raymond. *The Country and the City*. London: Chatto and Windus, 1973.

Wilson, L. *Space, Time and Freedom: The Quest for Nationality and the Irrepressible Conflict, 1851–1861*. Westport, Connecticut: Greenwood, 1974.

Winterson, Jeanette. *Oranges Are Not the Only Fruit*. London: Pandora, 1985.

Wolff, Cynthia Griffin. '"Margaret Garner": A Cincinnati story.' *The Massachusetts Review* 32 (1991): 417–40.

Wolff, Janet. 'On the road again: Metaphors of travel in cultural criticism.' *Cultural Studies* 7.2 (1993): 224–39.

Woolf, Virginia. *Orlando: A Biography*. New York: Harcourt Brace, 1928.

Yeldho, Joe V. and Neelakantan, G. 'Toni Morrison's depiction of the city in *Jazz*.' *Notes on Contemporary Literature* 36.1 (2006): 14–16.

Young, Crawford. 'Ethnicity and the colonial and post-colonial state in Africa.' In *Ethnic Groups and the State*. Ed. Paul Brass. London: Croom Helm, 1985, 57–93.

Young, Robert. *Colonial Desire: Hybridity in Theory, Culture and Race*. London: Routledge, 1995.

Zamora, Lois Parkinson. 'Magical romance/magical realism: Ghosts in U.S. and Latin American fiction.' In *Magical Realism: Theory, History, Community*. Ed. Lois Parkinson Zamora and Wendy Faris. Durham: Duke University Press, 1995, 497–550.

Zamora, Lois Parkinson, and Wendy Faris. 'Introduction: Daiquiri birds and Flaubertian parrot(ie)s.' In *Magical Realism: Theory, History, Community*. Ed. Lois Parkinson Zamora and Wendy Faris. Durham: Duke University Press, 1995, 15–32.

Zukin, Sharon. 'Space and symbols in an age of decline.' In *Re-Presenting the City: Ethnicity, Capital and Culture in the Twenty-First Century Metropolis*. Ed. Anthony D. King. Basingstoke: Macmillan, 1996, 43–59.

Index